LEAVING:

A Memoir

By

Frank Phelan

Anne Francis &

Frank

TITLE ID: 3794759   **ISBN-13:** 978-1470057251

Cover Photo

Sacred Heart Basilica, Notre Dame University

Photo Credit for Author's Picture: "Stuart"

Picture Credit for Frank Phelan and Anne Francis Cavanaugh (back cover): Boston Herald, June 27, 1982

"I have finally been able to give the Phelan book the attention it deserves. This is a good book. The writing is excellent and the story is everyone's story who has ever made a serious lifechange."

-- Joan Chittister

Joan Chittister is a widely-read author, known in America for her work in women's issues, she is internationally respected as well, having been invited to speak in Cairo's Tahrir Square on the situation of women in Egypt since the revolution.

"I like this book very much. It is well written as well as beautifully written. I am enjoying reading it..."

-- Paula G. Paul

Paula G. Paul is the author of 25 books, including "Symptoms of Death," and "Inherited Sins."

Anne Francis Cavanaugh

WHY YOU DO IT

"Why you do it? --*Why you <u>do</u> it?*" The Italian man looked directly at her as he asked the question. He was "Jimmy", a former New York cab driver who was now the chauffeur who drove important Nuns back and forth to meetings in the Vatican. He asked his question because, looking at one such as her, he could not comprehend.

She had just come back from an all-day session with other Mother Superiors, and had heard that there was a fine film to be shown that evening. None of the others wanted to go, but Jimmy, the chauffeur, who always heard everything and heard the disappointment in her voice, spoke back from the front seat, "--I take you, Sister! --*I take you*!"

He picked her up at the Hotel Flora and drove her out to the conference center on the Via Aurelia. He left her there.

He returned at the exact time to drive her back. On the way, he stopped at a little *trattoria* which he knew, and she says he showed her how a workingman ate; he cut mozzarella cheese and put pepper on each slice. ("--And we had a wonderful glass of red wine," she says.) After they got well started, he paused, holding a fork in his hand, with a piece of mozzarella waiting to be peppered, and looked at her with fierce Italian eyes, and asked his question: *Why you do it?*

He was an Italian man, caught in that world of convents and nuns, of monsignors and dignitaries of the Vatican, watching whatever happened, and he wondered why she let herself be trundled back and forth between its endless Sacred Congregations. He was a Communist, she thinks, privately despising what he worked for in the Holy City. But he was a man, and like a lot of other men before him, he asked her the same question, the one they all did: Why do you do it? Why do you labor so hard for those who do not care for what you are doing? Why does one like you give up everything? *For what?*

It was I think the central question of her life, and one, which she would have to ask herself; she faced it ahead of me, and she had to suffer more, earlier. But it was also the question I would have to learn to ask, too. For, you might say, I began to take Jimmy's place, sitting across from her. It took me some time, but I did learn to eat mozzarella with pepper; I liked it. And I learned to ask "Why?" I asked it of things I had never considered asking it about before. Perhaps it is the central question of all our lives: Why do we do what we do?

* * * * * *

When I first met Anne Francis she was a young nun doing her thesis, in Ireland. She was very beautiful, but since I was a priest -- and still, really, a Catholic boy-- I did not want to have much to do with her, because as any Catholic boy knew, you should not get too close to beautiful nuns. She was studying a story, a very Irish one, in which a young widow is to bury her husband, the old Weaver, who has just died. The girl does not know where to bury him, for he has the right to be buried in an ancient grave-yard called The Meadow of the Dead, but no one can remember, no one knows where to bury the Weaver. You can speculate on what the Weaver stands for; perhaps she is burying the Past. But there are also two handsome young gravediggers, waiting, as she makes up her mind. They are twins, who look exactly the same, yet one, somehow, is different. There is a custom in old Ireland, that when a person is borne down by unassailable grief, someone takes them by the arm, and steps with them across the mouth of the open grave. We are not surprised at the

7

end, after the proper place to put the Weaver has been found, that it is one of the two grave-diggers who takes her by the arm, and steps with her, across the mouth of the open grave.

I tried to help her, this beautiful young nun. We both looked at the story. We did not know it, but we might just as well have had in front of us the story of our own lives. I did not need to be told about the Meadow of the Dead. Ireland for me was The Land of Loneliness, and as for grave-diggers, you might truthfully say that, until I met her, what I was engaged in was busily digging my own grave.

And as far as that part about the twins goes, well, all men look alike, really. It is on the inside that we differ. In order to love somebody, you have to discover what is inside yourself first; you must learn to love yourself before you can love someone else. The reason that she does not appear early in this story is simply because I had to spend a long time finding myself, first, before I could have a hope of discovering her.

Yet the two of us were much alike. We were two Americans, living in a strange land; we each knew what the other knew; we had both grown up reading such books as *The Interior Castle*, and *The Dark Night of the Soul,* and had both been entranced with the idea of giving our lives to God. But that was a different world, the one in which we grew up, and it is gone now.

Today we see priests in court; we see their faces looking up as they wait to be sentenced for molesting altar boys. It is not unknown for priests to be murdered in jail by other inmates, who wait to kill them. Bishops, wearing gold crosses on purple vests, are toppled from their thrones, after years of cover-up. The people see their parish church shuttered, and closed down. It is almost impossible for anyone now to conceive of a world long ago in which bright boys studied Latin to become priests, made a gift to God of their young years, and forced themselves to look the other way when they saw pretty girls, while the girls, in that same world, often the most beautiful ones, were on the way to disappearing behind a black veil. It was a lot give up.

This is the story of my journey moving from that world of childhood; the journey from what I grew up believing to what I believe now. Perhaps life is all a journey out of childhood, for all of us, and we will be leaving childhood for as long as we live.

Yet it is her story, too. She had tried to bring the nuns of her order into the modern world, but her efforts had offended some, and she would be reported to the authorities, in Rome. The Vatican would summon her.

She was brought to Rome for a hearing in which she was ordered to do things, things, which she found she could not do. The Sacred Congregation for Religious seemed to become the Inquisition, it made me think back on the faggots used to burn martyrs. Everything quickly became a matter of life and death, for it is easy to come close to death, if your conscience forces you to; all it requires is honest conviction. Told to do one thing by authority and told to do another by her own conscience, she came close to death, in her own Dark Night of the Soul. And let no one say that it was not so, for I am witness to that time, in which she was able to look down and see a place opened in the earth for her, a pit which was waiting to be filled.

Could she manage to think of herself? Some persons have that difficulty. First she would have to understand what it was that she believed. I would have to do the same, for we could not leave our orders, simply to marry one another. No one should ever give up lightly what they have believed deeply, and we loved what we had come from. It would take thought and reflection before the moment came in which, looking into what faced us, we began to wonder, if holding on to each other, we might not together step across the mouth of the open grave.

This story is about a long journey to the stepping-off place, that one where you are told to look, before you leap. The pit in front of you is always dark, and deep. How brave are you? There is no information about the other side. Are there diggers over there, too? Yes, the story is about life itself, it is about that long ponder we all face, sooner or later, about jumping into darkness. It asks a simple question: Why do we do what we do?

I

1.

THE DROWNING OF THE SAINTS
Man is in love, and loves what vanishes.
What more is there to say?

--W. B. Yeats

It was growing dark, in the coldest time of the year. I stood before the front door of Holy Cross Seminary at Notre Dame and rang the doorbell. Inside, there was no light that I could see, and no one came; the cold was beginning to penetrate my bones, so I rang again.

The door opened, and I saw a large muscular man looking down at me with a very firm smile; in spite of the smile that was on his face, he seemed somewhat annoyed. "*You are late,*" he said, and then added, "*--We expected you much earlier...*" His name was Father Fiedler, and he was wearing a hearing aid. He told me to place my two suitcases down just inside the door, where I would recover them later, and then he held his finger up to his lips, instructing me to follow him, in silence. I walked along behind him; looking at the black cassock, black cape, and black cincture around his waist, which I recognized from "Boys Today, Priests Tomor-row" as the holy habit of the Order.

"We take down the future with a book," they tell us. We see something we like, and stand on our toes to reach it, and when we pull it down, we find that it is our future we have pulled down with it. It worked that way with me.

I had always wanted to be a priest. I had grown up reading many books. I read The Wonder Book of the World, as well as my Astronomy book, about Fra Mauro, and the Mountains of the Moon. But of all my books, my favorite was "The Drowning of the Saints", about the Spanish Armada. It was filled with things that a boy would like; it had descriptions of things lost beneath the sea. It had the names of the ships, too, they were easy to memorize because many of them were just names in Spanish for the mysteries of the Rosary, which we recited at church, like the Annunciation, or the Nativity. My favorites were one called "the towering Israfel", and another called, "the Great Gran Grin"; these galleons sailed through my life, and I got into arguments with my Protestant friends, for I said the Armada had not been defeated, that it had only been blown apart by the winds.

But you can mail away for your future, too, with box tops off of cereal. I endlessly sent away for things, usually with the tops ripped from cereal boxes, along with twenty-five cents for handling. I sent to Buck Rogers for rocket ships, and Orphan Annie for Secret Decoder Pins, and to Tom Mix for a cowboy ring made out of genuine horseshoe nails. There was a contest, too, called "How many faces can you see?" You were supposed to find all the faces in a drawing, in the clouds, in the trees, in the smoke rising from a chimney. If you got them all, you won an automobile. (A Packard).

One day, I found a form to fill out in a magazine called *The Catholic Boy*; it was for those who wanted to test their vocation to the priesthood, and I filled it out. As I waited for the postman, I knew well enough that I was not sending away for horseshoe nails, that this time it would be different. A letter came, from the Vocation Director, saying that I had been accepted, and with it a shiny book called *"Boys Today, Priests Tomorrow."*

That cold evening as I followed the priest's figure into the darkness of the seminary corridor, you would have to say that I had gotten what I had asked for, or at least mailed away for. I noticed that Father Fiedler seemed hobbled by the skirt of his cassock, for he was a big man and it forced him to take small steps; and whenever I caught a glimpse, I saw that the smile seemed permanent upon his face.

I remember him: a big man walking with hobbled steps and a hearing aid, holding his finger in warning against his lips, cautioning me to follow in silence. And sometimes, when the mind grows tired, or when I find myself thinking of the meaning of life and what I have done with it, or worrying about how much time is left, he walks on before me, with that smile that is not a smile fixed upon his face, as though, with a finger pressed against his lips, he is showing me the way to Eternity, and is leading me to meet my end.

The place smelled, it smelled strongly of varnish, and of linoleum floors heavily waxed, and of other smells I could not recognize. Father Fiedler led me through a long silent hallway and down some steps, and then through another silent hallway and up some more steps. He stopped once and pointed up toward something called The Crossed Anchors of Hope, which he said formed the Great Seal of the Order. Then I heard knives and forks being used and we came to a large dining room --Father Fiedler called it "The Refectory"-- and I saw there many tables, 8 or 10 boys to a table, all eating in silence. I hoped no one would notice me, that I would be allowed to enter quietly, but as I came in there was a great roar of laughter, and they all laughed harder as I sat down at the place,

17

which was waiting for me. I did not want to eat anything. Father Fiedler returned to his seat at the head table pulling the skirt of his cassock tight underneath him as he sat down, and I saw that a boy my own age stood on a platform behind him and was reading aloud, from a book which I thought must be the Bible, for it was huge, and the words seemed ancient. I sat in front of my empty plate and listened to the old words, while everybody ate in silence. I remember everything, the reader's voice, the sound of knives and forks, and the smell of food, the varnish from the hallway, my hands still feeling the cold of the train, the white plate in front of me, the boys laughing, and the voice of the reader reading---

And I went down among the Peoples of the Past
To the bottom of the sea; I went down into the countries that
Are underneath the earth, to the iron gates that are at the roots
of the mountains. The seaweed wrapped round my head,
The waters came in and flooded my soul: I could not cry out.

Suddenly a little bell rang and everyone was allowed to talk --they said that it was because of my arrival that they were permitted to talk. The boys at the table asked where I was from. Dessert came and I did not want it, the boy seated next to me on my right asked incredulously that if I were not going to eat it, could he have it? When I said yes the rest of the table jeered at him. Mahoney was an animal; they said to me, he acted that way all the time. And they looked at me, silently, wondering.

I asked them why, when I came in, everybody was laughing? What had they been laughing at?

The boy across from me who had introduced himself as "Billy" smiled and said, "--The reading this week is from the Book of Jonah, and when it said that Jonah had a vocation from God it sounded just like Father Gartland, our Vocation Director, and everyone laughed." He said the boys had also laughed when the whale vomited, that they always laughed at words like that, and that they laughed again because Jonah tried to run away.

In the next few days, I was appointed waiter. I remember the long tables with white cloths that I ran past on my way to the kitchen. I came running to them with huge trays of steaming food, to be sent back quickly for more, for "Seconds". I reeked of coffee and of potatoes, if you came near me I smelled of pots and pans. I was homesick. They kept me busy; I ran back and forth to the story of the Scriptures, which kept being read all week. I understood that I needed to be trained on how to use a mop, and how to stack dishes, and how to lift a loaded tray; yet it was not what I had come for.

That week was a cold week; in our dormitory, we were to keep the windows wide open to have clean thoughts; but when you reached to bless yourself with Holy Water, the font was frozen solid, so that your fingers touched ice. Each night I would try to fall asleep in the frozen sheets, waiting for the bed to warm, and I thought of them, the words I had heard, of Jonah going down, down to the iron gates that were at the bottom of the sea, where the roots of the mountains began, among the Peoples of the Past, until the waters came into his throat so that he could not breathe and had not breath to cry out to God. I fell to sleep, with seaweed in my hair.

The Drowning of the Saints, the Rapture of the Deep: It was not their fault; they could not have known how Catholic I was; I was more Catholic than they were, you see. They did not know what they had in me; how could they know about Gossoons? They knew nothing about the Great Gran Grin, nothing about the Towering Israel, nothing about Far Mauro and the Mountains of the Moon. They knew nothing about that strange love-story that happens to those who walk on the bottom of the sea, where things shine brightly that are dull in the air above. Out through our porthole we see strange things-- How many faces do you see? We tug on the safety line hoping they have not gone home up there or are not distracted. We hope that someone is minding the pumps. It takes courage to walk into the gloom.

I remained among them, like a fig tree in the desert, for thirty years. I went down among the Peoples of the Past, with seaweed in my hair. I cried out against my vocation, like Jonas, who had no breath to breathe, in the belly of the whale. I started as a little Gossoon, a boy on the deck, to become a Gallowglass. And I ended up where I began: down among the timbered galleons and galleasses, among the tippled masts, down among the Assumptions and the Ascensions and the Incarnations, somewhere between the Resurrection and the Nativity, down among the guns and plate and chalices, Aye, and the flukes of crossed anchors, the great anchors that did not hold, the skull that remembers everything. Nothing that is human escaped me: Those are pearls that were his eyes.

2

MICKEY FIEDLER DOES IT ALL FOR YOU

Holy Cross Seminary was off to one side of the Notre Dame campus, behind Saint Mary's Lake. Knute Rockne, when he was asked where the famed Spirit of Notre Dame came from, pointed across the lake, and said, "It all comes from there!"

Father Mickey Fiedler taught us Latin there. I remember Father Fiedler translating for us the story of Laocoon. Laocoon was a priest of Troy, indeed a prophet, who rightly warned that if the great horse sent by the Greeks was allowed in through the gates it would bring about the fall of the city: yet, for his pains, Heaven sent two huge-sea monsters to devour him, along with his two sons. Tommy Waldron at once protested that it was unfair. Father Fiedler smiled as he often did at Tommy, as if to say that we were there to learn Latin in preparation for the priesthood, not for other things. "-----Serpentes *squamosa*---" Father Fiedler continued, enunciating elaborately to make his point: that the word "squamous" meant "having scales". And he told how Michelangelo had hurried down to see the splendid

22

statue of The Laocoon while it was being rediscovered; how when Michelangelo saw the statue emerge, piece by piece from the earth -- the great snakes, the agonized torso of the father, the two little boys jumping in pain, he said "– Oh! --It is the statue described by Pliny! It is the great Laocoon itself!" And when Tommy protested again that it was all unfair, Father Fiedler smiled at him again and dismissed his questions: "Don't take it seriously; it is Pagan nonsense---it is all just Pagan nonsense!" And we hurried on to things we had to learn that day, to such things as "*terminus a quo*" -- the place from which you start, and "*terminus ad quem*" --the place where you end up.

The Seminary had huge lawns, sloping down to the edge of the lake, and Father Fiedler made the green grass of the lawns his special care. He watered them daily with huge sprinklers. My memory of the place is of Mickey Fiedler hopping and running around, moving his water cannon, placing them as Napoleon planted his artillery.

For that is how he used them. There was a sign he had painted himself, and nailed up on the branch of a tree over the path:

SEMINARY GROUNDS

Do not lie
or sit on the grass

It was there to keep students from the main campus and their girl friends from Saint Mary's College from necking and kissing on the front lawn of the seminary.

But some young lovers were oblivious; they did not observe the sign. In the Spring especially, when the lake warmed up and its banks became inviting, the young couples would sit down, or lie on the grass, dreamily and privately loving.

Mickey Fiedler would see them, and run out, often between Latin and Greek classes. He would haul a length of hose like a fireman to a fire -- hundreds of feet if necessary. He would place the brass nozzles into position, calibrating trajectory and range. Then he would hurry back to the House, to the hydraulic faucet. The huge water jets would spring into action seemingly of their own volition. The young lovers would be drenched, and would scurry, screaming and laughing, back to where they were from. "--They never catch on," Bill Finn would say, watching it all from our Recreation Room door.

But Father Fiedler had one great fear. From time to time he would depart from the syllabus to discourse on it. He used to warn us, "--We could *lose* this place, you know, boys! --We could lose Notre Dame! The *Laymen* would take it over in an instant! (He pronounced the world "Laymen" as if he were really saying "scoundrels") --And the Jesuits! O---the *Jesuits*! -The *Jesuits* would just *love* to have Notre Dame!"

I hated it when he talked that way; I disliked it, it always embarrassed me, for it made him sound like a fool.

I have a tableau in my mind: Father Fiedler, Tommy and I are on the lawn, on the great sloping curve of grass sweeping down from the seminary to the lake. Father Fiedler struggles with the great hoses, and I am assisting him, of course. The scene seems to be sculpted in marble, something translated from Virgil. All three of us are struggling with pythons, and Tommy is crying out, and lifting one foot, as though he has been stung: *Serpentes Squamosa.* "---It is the statue described by Pliny," I hear a voice say, "----It is the great Laocoon itself!"

The Little Seminary was eventually closed; there was fear of Typhoid in the basement. The building was used for other things, first as a Half-way House, and then as a storeroom for textbooks.

Then it became empty, and finally, it was torn down. They came and pulled it down, and demolished it; the way Father Fiedler had so often taught us had happened even to the walls of old Troy. They carted it all away, leaving at last only the site itself, the splendid site, looking like the Hill of Tara: a grassy knoll, with lush green lawns sloping down to the lake. Many years later, I found myself walking over that way, where much of me began; I walked along the old path, and looked up to see it, the one thing that was left of everything, the only thing that remained of the way things were: the little sign, still there, nailed to the branch of a tree, with its hand-painted message, up over the path to the ball-field saying:

SEMINARY GROUNDS

Do not lie
Or sit on the grass.

3

BELOW THE BELT

Which of you, if his child asked for bread,
Would give him a stone?

--- Matt. 7, 9

"You are to call one another *Mister*," Father Master said on that first day, addressing us in chapel. "It is a custom here, and custom has the force of law. If I found a Novice persistently breaking the Rule of Address, I would question seriously whether that man had a Vocation to the priesthood. There is good reason for this, as there is indeed for the Rule on Bodily Contact. Keep your hands to yourselves. Don't *paw* one another. I know that I have the reputation of being a 'bug' on this, but it is a serious matter, and you will hear more on it from me throughout your Canonical Year."

Then Father Master went on to talk of other things, and ended up the conference by quoting his favorite line from Saint John Berchmans: "I am a piece of twisted iron,

O Lord, and I entered religion to be made straight. Burn, bend, break me in this life, Dear Lord, but *spare me for an Eternity!"*

The man was famous within the Order for being the greatest Novice Master we had ever had. He had run the beautiful Romanesque Novitiate in Rolling Prairie for years. At the Little Sem I had looked forward to serving under him, and earlier when I heard that he was sick, I prayed ardently that he would be spared. He was, and I was grateful,

I wanted nothing but the best for my Novitiate year.

The farm saved everything, it was the farm that was great. The barnyard sounds and smells were all new to me, I was one of the novices from the city. Old Brother Fortunatus divided us up into Horse Men, Cow Men, Pig Men and Chicken Men, according to our tasks.

For a few glorious weeks I was allowed out with the others, pitching hay, for it was August. After that, Brother gave us buckets, and sent us out to gather stones. The fields of the Novitiate each year sent up crop after crop of stones, and we were available to harvest them. It was a job I liked, for you could wander with your battered bucket in the sunshine or the rain looking for stones in the north pasture or in the cornfields, after the corn was husked, and no one cared where you were. You filled the bucket with what you could carry, you struggled back with it, and dumped it in the wagon, and started out again. It was good to be out in the air, I counted myself happy, looking for stones.

But then I was appointed Reader. They shoved a book into my hands; they made me stand at the lectern high up behind the head table to read in the Refectory, out loud, over the heads of everybody. I was frightened, for I had not really heard the sound of my own voice before. I mispronounced names, and was corrected in public, many times each day. Worst of all, instead of working outside in the fresh air, I had to remain inside to prepare my reading; instead of pitching hay I found myself looking up words, and underlining them, and putting accent marks all over them, and separating them into syllables. The worst part was when, up at the lectern, the reading would threaten to go beyond the part that I had prepared. I would see big words coming, on the opposite page, and mispronounce them when I got there. The worst words came from the Holy Roman Martyrology, the book of saints and martyrs for every day in the year. It was full of strange, difficult names of persons and places I had never heard of, which I could not pronounce even after I had marked them. And when my voice became too quiet, when I reverted to shyness, Father Master would motion to me with his finger---Up and out! --Off the hard palate! I was to bounce my voice off the opposite wall of the refectory, so that all the priests, brothers and novices would be able to listen, above the noise of forks and spoons, to hear that at Terracina, in the Campagnia, under the Roman Emperor Gratian, there were the deaths of two thousand holy martyrs who had died in the Lord, while at Todi, in Umbria, the deaths of 42 others, who had been put to the sword under Diocletian. It was not all bad; it taught me to speak clearly, in front of people. But alone in the dark classroom where I looked up words I worried if Father Master would ever approve me for vows. I gazed out at the overcast skies of Indiana and thought of the places I read about, places like Valencia in Spain and Sigmaringen in Germany and Todi in Umbria. I spent a lot of time thinking of them, and I dreamed of becoming someone who crossed the seas, and traveled to distant countries, one who went even to such places as Terracina in the Campagnia, where, the Encyclopedia said, the sun smiled down over everything.

It was scarcely what I should be doing; to let my mind go wandering so, but the sun smiling down on these distant places helped to cheer the dark and dreary room. We were watched constantly, but there must have been many times when it looked to Father Master that I was keeping the Rule on Recollection, and readying myself to practice Contemplation, when I was only thinking of Terracina in the Campagnia.

It was hard. Especially the Rule on Silence. Novices were permitted to speak to one another only for an hour after the noon meal, and for an hour after supper. We went to bed at 9:00 and rose at 5:00. We sang office in chapel three times a day. We meditated in the black night before dawn all through the winter, and wrote down in "Recollection Books" how each meditation had gone. I had trouble writing anything in mine, and once in desperation looked into the next pew, to see what my friend Mister Teabey wrote. I could only catch one line: *"O Sanctuary Lamp!"* It said, the words heavily underscored. Mister Teabey was, I thought, highly emotional.

I went through phases. At first I had what was called "an attack of Scrupulosity," when I thought that everything was a sin. But Father Master talked me through this. Every good man had trouble with it at some time, he said; but if I remained faithful, God would take that cross away. He was right. My scrupulosities disappeared.

But my standards remained high. I worried about the Novices who caused Father Master to call attention so often to the "unseemly behavior" he had mentioned on that very first day. Why did they misbehave? Why was it necessary for the Novice Master to lecture them? What was going on? Who were they, anyway? I had never seen anything. I had problems, but mine seemed nothing compared to the positively sensational ones that others, apparently, were having. And I wondered about it, in the long periods of silence.

Only one of the Novices failed to treat the mention of Father Master's name with utmost respect. Mister Dolan was a bit older than the rest of us, partly because he was a holdover from the previous year: Father Master had not thought him ready to take vows. Mister Dolan talked very openly about this; he did not like Father Master, and called him quite a few names, some of which were extremely vulgar and certainly broke the Rule on Modesty in Speech. Mister Dolan would sometimes try to win the rest of us over to his side, but to a man we sensed temptation, and walked off.

We were giddy, too, sometimes, because of all that Silence. Once Mister Mironski knelt down on the Chapter Room floor, in the weekly Chapter of Accusations, and accused himself of an outlandish number of failures, ".... and I accuse myself of having broken the Rule of Silence," he said, rapidly checking his Fault Book,".....267 times, and Custody of the Eyes..... 301 times." Someone giggled at Mister Mironski, but then Mister Zimmerman got down, the undeniable leader of us all at this sort of thing. He had managed to break the two rules an amazing 417 and 554 times respectively, in one week, and the roar of laughter that greeted his achievement sounded to my ears like an ovation.

Spring came, and even though I saw it mainly through the glass windows of the classroom, it somehow made more bearable the rules that were so hard to keep in the stuffy house. I had never seen Spring on a farm before. We were happy and enthusiastic; we had survived the winter, and were even then looking forward to our departure in late August.

One day before the morning conference, Mister Dolan came into the pantry where a crew of us was drying the breakfast dishes. "He's going to do it!", he whispered gleefully, hopping around on one leg and carrying on. "I saw him in the garden picking tulips! -- Today's the day!" he shouted, raising an imaginary horn to his lips and going "Haroop! Haroop! Haroop! Then he ran on with his message to the people setting tables. "The day for what?" I whispered to Mister Teabey, who I always felt I could trust.

"The Birds and the Bees," answered Mister Teabey. "Mister Dolan thinks Father Master is going to talk to us on Sex." He grinned idiotically back.

Mister Dolan was right; he had remembered accurately from the previous year. At the lecture, Father Master strode into the room with two tulips in his hand, one red and one yellow. He began by saying that, of course, if a man's problem was "below the belt," that man had no business being among us; yet, all the same, the time had come to talk about Sex. Men were reasonable beings, and the taking of the Vow of Chastity presumed an intelligent choice. He would not have us leaving his tutelage ignorant of the true nature of the difference between the sexes.

In other words, it was time to talk about stamens and pistils.

There was much creaking of benches, much coughing, and much restricted breathing. But the tension passed after a while, as the conference more or less evolved into a series of statements common to every conference by Father Master, and which we had all heard many times. I remember looking out dreamily at the massive Novitiate tower, its gold cross shining in the morning sun, the swallows sweeping freely in and out of it, around the bells. I was longing for work period to begin.

Quietly, however, my mind was pulled back to the conference room by a new tone in the speaker's voice: he had begun to talk once more about Particular Friendships. Once again there was creaking of benches, my own as well as those of others. "The Dutch Theologian Vermeersch," Father Master said, enunciating the name with elaborate clarity and precision, "has a great deal to tell us about this subject. He says that we are wrong, in friendships between man and man, to think that the matter is completely innocent and free from sin merely because there are no outward, visible manifestations of a perverse attraction. No, the theologian Vermeersch goes on to say: even without gestures, words, actions and without thoughts, even, which would plainly reveal the presence of an unhealthy *pondus* in that direction, there can and does exist in some religious men a certain hidden, secret gravitation of the sort to which Vermeersch wisely gives the Latin name, *Luxuria Larvata.*" The two words came out of a mouth contorted with the effort to pronounce them correctly, just as the learned theologian's name had come. Father Master was rightly proud of his knowledge of words, and of his enunciation.

He would speak more, at the next conference, of the theologian Vermeersch, and more about *Luxuria Larvata.* In the meantime, we should study our notes on it.

I never did make it outside that day. After I had prepared my reading, old Brother Fortunatus caught me in the hallway, and put me to work cleaning windows in the refectory.

This I found very depressing. In what was left of the morning, I looked out upon the bursting springtime through a lattice of small square windowpanes. The subject of the conference preyed upon my mind. I had been wrong, then, in thinking that it was only certain Novices. We were all suspect. No matter who you were, no matter how virtuous, you could be prey to a thing like that. *Luxuria Larvata.* What a revolting name. It made you feel that there were a lot of little insects, or maybe maggots, attacking the vital inwards of your Spirit, that you were filled with vermin somehow without knowing it, that you carried everywhere within you something that would make you a gigantic pupa, as of a fly. Even the name, Vermeersch, sounded a little that way.

I wondered, in the name of God, did I have anything like that? It had never seemed possible before. My evil dreams were all of girls, and women of every description, which populated the long meditations, and the hours of Holy Office, the battle against which constituted the major effort of my Spiritual Life.

Was it possible that I was deceiving myself? Was it perhaps all along that I was one of the Novices Father Master was cryptically correcting? Was I the one who was causing him this grief?

In the name of Christ and His Blessed Mother, I thought, as I polished the panes. Was it too late to be checked? Could I still be salvaged? Was there a way that the Dutch theologian Vermeersch told you that would infallibly eradicate the thing he had named? Perhaps we would hear at the next conference.

But who? Sweet Jesus, Redeemer of the Human Race, with what other Novice was I guilty of this thing? Mister Mironski? Mister Zimmerman? Or was it even Mister Dolan? The very thought made me laugh, for the first time that day.

Then the bell for the end of work rang from the tower, mournfully, as though it were a passing-bell. I hurried to finish the windows. After I had removed the last specks of soap from the now very clear glass I looked out through a window to see the fields, and as I did so, saw through it, perfectly framed, the small, weary figure of my friend Mister Teabey, bringing himself home from work.

Of course.

How could I have been so stupid? He was the most emotional person around. He was the kind of individual Father Master had described in detail, conference after conference. "O Sanctuary Lamp," I thought. It was like a revelation direct from Heaven. The thing had been eating away at my soul, probably from the opening day of my Novitiate. In the Divine Providence of God, I had been let stumble along, all unknowing, through the entire year, only to be brought up short in this shattering moment.

I thought for a while, and decided that I would cooperate with Grace. If Heaven had been so fair with me as to inform me of my precarious condition, I determined to be no less fair with Heaven.

I knelt down at once on the pantry floor: "Burn, bend, break me in this life, Dear Lord, but spare me for an Eternity!" I cried, as I had heard Father Master do so many times.

I instituted a Program of Reform. First I went to Father Master, to check to see whether I had the real thing. Of course I did, he said, or I would not have been able to tell him so much about it. I must be severe with myself. *Luxuria Larvata* had a way of destroying a man. This kind of devil was not driven out except by prayer and fasting. He recommended cold showers and the Way of the Cross.

And he said that of course I must break with the other individual involved. He would mention no names, but he had noticed that I was friendlier with some of the men than with others. Whoever it was must be dealt with decisively, even harshly. And if I found myself approached in any way, I was to report it.

I mentally decided to break with Mister Teabey that very evening. He had gotten a box of candy from home for his birthday, and as he opened it, offer-ed it around. As I came into the Recreation Room he held out some candy to me.

Naturally, I thought to myself, what else, and walked on by, without speaking, and brushing his arm so that he practically dropped the box from home. He had been harshly dealt with.

I could scarcely wait until the bell sounded the end of that recreation period. It had been one of the most uncomfortable hours of my life. But I was to have ones that were even more uncomfortable. I went to chapel, to my room, to work, and thought of the intractable nature of the problem. Perhaps there were other Novices who caused *Luxuria Larvata* in me, too? Maybe I should deal harshly with them, too, whoever they were. Perhaps I should cut off contact with all of them.

I began to wish I had the Scruples again, instead of this. Anything was preferable to such mind-wracking worry. Perhaps I should leave. The prospect of being free and having drinks and money and girls and a home of my own seemed attractive. But no, I had dedicated myself to work for God and Souls on the foreign missions in Bengal, and would not weaken. I would see the thing through. The Scruples had gone, doubts against the Faith had gone. This would, too. "All things pass away," I said, "God never changes."

But by this time Mister Teabey knew that he was being harshly dealt with. I had a feeling he was being harshly dealt with by more than one of us. What suffering this caused him I did not know, but I could well imagine that he was talking to the Sanctuary Lamp again. He tried to talk to me again and again, but each time my gaze passed right through him.

At last one afternoon I had enough of it.

Now no longer Reader, I had been assigned to work outside, with the others. It was getting on to summer. I had just been engaged in taking the remains of a hog out and burying them, being helped by a Mister Hedlovak. We had wandered this way and that, and settled on a place where there were pine trees, planted in rows. After we were finished, Mr. Hedlovak sauntered back to the slaughter-house to replace the tub. I walked into the pine trees, which I had seen so often from the refectory.

The ground was strewn with brown needles which crackled as I walked. It was dark, yet the sky appeared between the tops of the trees. The wind, which I had not noticed before, made a sighing sound around the needles still on the branches, and the cones.

The world was so beautiful. How far away was the peace of the pine grove from the hateful problems of the Novitiate building only a few hundred yards below. How could anyone be so foolish as to destroy it all? And I decided by myself, walking along the rows of pines, that Father Master was wrong.

I went to Mister Teabey that night in the recreation room. I did not apologize in the way that I should have, I was lucky to be able to say what I did. I cleared my throat. And said to him, "--Mister Teabey, I accidentally read something in your Recollection book once..." He looked at me horrified. "Don't worry, old man," I hurried on, "-- it just said something about Sanctuary Lamps." I smiled broadly. "Sorry, I am really sorry. I should have kept my eyes under better control."

He relaxed and laughed when he heard what it was. "We're all going nuts around here," he said. "Everybody's crazy. The Boss is down on me. I'm beginning to think I'll never make it to August."

I protested, generously, and assured him that the worst was over, and that we would all be out of there in a few months and attending the University. We would laugh at what we had gone through.

But Mister Teabey left the Order on August second, a week before we were to take Vows. He did it in the manner dictated by custom: no good-byes. We checked the trunk-room; that was the one sure way of knowing. Poor old Teabey's boxes were gone. He had given up.

In the conference following Mister Teabey's departure Father Master gave the greatest performance of the entire year. He pulled out all the old warnings and his voice became more shrill as most of us sighed, and creaked in our benches, and looked out the windows. He went on to new assertions. The previous evening, he said, the first Novices out on the cloister walk after supper had been shouting things up to the men who had not come down from their rooms yet. They had been *flirting* with them, and he stressed the word "flirting".

I wished he would stop talking. I wished we would have no more conferences. I longed to be out walking through the pine rows. I wondered what chance there was that Brother Fortunatus would give me a job outside, in the fields, for they were cutting alfalfa that week.

Suddenly Father Master's voice stopped in mid-sentence. I looked up, to see him sliding off the chair behind the speaking desk, and, unbelievably, impossibly, falling to the floor in front of Mister Gorch, who had jumped up, clutching his notebook and fountain pen.

The Assistant Master of Novices told us as we were going out to work that it had been a serious seizure; that Father Master had worked himself out on our behalf, and that Father Provincial was arranging for someone else to replace him.

I got my job mowing hay. And all that day rode high upon an old horse-drawn wagon, taking the fork-fulls of it that Mister Zimmerman and the others tossed up to me. It was terribly laborious work, placing each mass of hay properly on the wagon in the best spot to form a kind of floor of it: floor above floor of hay, upon which I walked and struggled to keep my balance. I got hay down my neck, I itched and sweated, but I was happy, Vows were only a week away, I would take them, and go on to the University, and the priesthood.

I thought as I worked. People, even older people, did not always speak what they appeared to speak with their tongues and lips. There was far more to things than I had been thinking. I was free. I was as whole as the next person. There was nothing with an awful name eating away at me. My instincts all along had been trying to tell me this, but I had chosen to listen to words. I promised myself, and God, that I would never again let any man tell me who I was, or what I was, or what I was to be. I liked women. I loved their bodies. I would want to have one share her life with me. But I loved God more. I would stay true to the thing I had begun.

Between wagonloads we rested, and were given water. At three o'clock the tower bell gave out four or five clangs, and we all paused to say, "My Jesus, Mercy." As I stopped to do this, I saw the figure of Mister Dolan, over near the edge of my pine trees, waving frantically for me to come over. His bucket was sitting on the ground, with no stones in it; he could not have been working very hard.

"Look!" he said out loud as I came up. "They're sending him to the *nut*-house!"

Down below, its departure carefully planned for the middle of the work-period, a white ambulance was quietly winding out and down the front drive from the building toward the main road. Mister Dolan assured me that the ambulance belonged to a mental hospital in another part of the state; he had carefully checked it on his way up.

I looked for a moment, very hard, and thought I saw in the rear of the vehicle the outline of a body wrapped in blankets and not moving. I turned to go back, before I should be missed. As I did so I saw out of the corner of my eye the lean, lithe figure of Mister Dolan on the brow of the hill. He did a little pagan dance of delight. Then he shouted out, loud and with no care of anyone hearing, a most loathsome obscenity after the departing ambulance. And he headed toward the sub-kitchen, where, I felt, he surely had a supply of Cola stashed away.

II

4

THE LAUGHING LESSON

I thought that I was learning how to live,
but found that I was learning how to die.

-Leonardo da Vinci

I was free. Free of them all. At last.

Standing on the top deck of the Italian Line's *Leonardo da Vinci,* I looked down at the ship's First Officer, who was looking at his wristwatch, waiting for High Noon; he held up a little silver whistle and blew on it, and the longshoremen who had been waiting in twos along Pier 84 lifted the loops of the hawsers up off their bollards and tossed them out and away, into the Hudson River, where they splashed in the water. Suddenly the ship's horn gave off an enormous blast of noise from the funnel immediately behind me; the roar caught me with one foot raised in mid-step, and the sound was so loud that it made the leather on my shoe vibrate and tingle against my foot until I placed it back down. The roar was only a navigational signal, but to me it sounded like the voice of God at the beginning of the world, breathing out over the surface of the deep; the sound first echoed off the buildings of Manhattan, then it went rolling over to the cliffs of New Jersey, and finally came back to us, still strong enough to fill the chest, and satisfy something deep inside the soul. The pier seemed to be moving backwards, all the people on it dressed in bright colors, happy for us and waving us goodbye. We were the last of the old passenger liners, we were leaving, we were going for good; and whether anyone knew it or not, we were taking a world with us which would not return. It was what I had been waiting for; at that moment, we had been disconnected from the mainland, the ship had become an island complete of itself; it was like tearing a page out of a book: we were no longer connected to the United States of America, or to anything else.

"They will never get me now-- " I said, when I saw the last cable splash. I said it out loud, and I repeated it with feeling, "---*They will never get me now!*" Two German tourists with huge Zeiss binoculars turned and looked at me: they were standing next to a gangster.

I sounded like a criminal. I sounded like Cain, running; and yet I had done nothing wrong. I was only referring to my Religious Superiors. They had been with me since I was a boy. They had told me which bed to sleep in, which tables to wait on, what dishes to wash, and how I should wash them; later they had told me to edit a magazine, to chair an English Department. But it was the year 1963, I was thirty-seven years old; and I was tired of them. They called themselves Competent Authority; and referred to themselves in the plural: It has been brought to Our attention, they said; We are shocked and saddened, they said; We are refusing permission, they said. They said "We" a lot, they said We so often that I used to wonder where it came from, what it referred to; it took me years until I finally concluded --for I am a slow learner-- that it only meant themselves, and God. And they changed their minds; that was what you had to watch, for they could take away what they had granted, they could rescind permissions, they could order you off the boat, and send you back --back to where you had come from, back to what you were before, back, all the way back, until it seemed at times that they could send you back to childhood.

I did not like it; I did not like any of it; you might say that I was raised to it, that I had even felt called to it; but I never liked it. Besides, of course, it was not just Superiors; it was all of them, the whole crowd of them, there were just too many of them. They were there all the time; they made it difficult to breathe.

But something else happened, too; it was back a few years, between classes at the University: Hank Hughes taught me to paint.

He went out and found me canvas, and taught me to stretch it, and how to prepare it. Then with the smells of turpentine and thinner and linseed oil and the smell of fresh unrolled canvas surrounding us, he would teach me about brushes--bristle brushes and sable brushes and brushes made of camels hair; he showed me the painter's palette, and the pigments on it with their names: names like Cerulean Blue and Ultramarine Blue Deep, Naples Yellow, and Burnt Siena and Umbrian Red Earth. And finally there was Caput Mortuis, which he explained meant Death's Head, which the splendid Italians --who must have known well enough what that looked like-- had named for the color of death itself. Yet I loved it all; for each time Hank Hughes rolled out more canvas, it seemed to be life itself that he was rolling out for me. It is not really so surprising that things turned out the way they did.

My Sister saw me off in New York; she came down to West 44th Street in a yellow dress, to see me off, to Ireland. But as we talked she began to grow suspicious. She finally asked, "Where is this boat going?" And when I said "Naples" she became upset and responded heatedly, almost angrily, "--You know very well that if Mother and Dad were still alive, you wouldn't be stepping onto this boat! ---You wouldn't be going *anywhere*!"

She was right about that, of course, she was right about our parents. You see, what the ship's horn had been announcing, all that morning, was nothing less than a new heaven and a new earth: When my Sister asked me where the ship was going, I should have come right out and said that it was going to Terracina in the Campagnia, and to Todi in Umbria, that was where it was going. It would first cross over the Ultramarine Blue Deep, to the Cerulean skies of Italy, that world of the painters palette that had so far been kept from me. After which I would arrive in Ireland; the rest would be self- evident.

But instead of bothering to explain, I only nodded agreement with her, admitting that she was certainly right about our parents, and said my Good-byes.

You see, when my Superiors ordered me to go to Ireland by the cheapest way possible, I listened very carefully. I took them at their word, and did extensive investigation. After much diligence, I was not really surprised to find that in fact, the cheapest way to go to Ireland from the United States turned out to be on the Italian Lines, by way of Naples, Italy. I was delighted that this was actually true; and moreover, I knew that I was not obliged to tell them, if no one thought to ask me. Besides, I really wanted to do a good thesis, and I knew myself; I honestly did not think I could spend three years in Dublin wondering about Paris and what you could see in Europe.

And so I never spoke of how I was going, but kept it "*in pectore*" as the Pope says -- hidden in the breast. Only, to a few close friends, I spoke fondly of what I called my Slow Boat to Naples.

It was not what I expected, however. I was disappointed with the sea. I stood at the ship's rail surprised at how cold and clammy everything was. The salt air clung to the fingers and to the wood of the rail itself. I stood at the rail, and was lonely. Looking at each slate-gray wave flowing upon each slate-gray wave, watching for tankers and feeling sad for them, I began to realize that it was in fact the first time in my life that I had ever been alone, truly alone. It did not seem to matter at all that there were 2000 passengers behind me, and another 1500 crew; and I began to feel very lonely. I wondered where I was going, at the age of thirty-seven.

I looked for ships. We were fast; we caught up on tankers and freighters. One tanker I remember, it appeared on our left (port) bow in the morning, hull-down (as they say), and we gradually caught up to it -- or rather, to *her,* we caught up to *her.*

She stood alongside of us on the horizon for hours; it took hours to pass her. I became acquainted with her, I talked to her, and I was not lonely while she was there. I told her everything. What kind of man is it that talks to a passing oil tanker? What does he say? *Hi, there, --I really like your running lights. What's a beautiful girl like you doing in the middle of the ocean? Nobody can wallow in a trough like you can, Baby.* Oh, I don't remember what I said. But when, finally, late in the evening, she disappeared slowly over the curve of the earth behind us and was gone in its gloom, I turned and looked at all the people, there were thousands of them, and I felt lonely again.

Later on, after my ship was gone, I found out from the Bursar what her name was; she was the *Rose Revived*, he said, she was called the *Rose Revived*, and she was bound for Milford Haven.

But I should honestly explain something, right off. You see, I had hoped to step on the ship as an ordinary person. Much of my suitcase was taken up by the habit of the Holy Cross order: black cape and black cassock and heavy linen cincture, with a bronze crucifix. I was carrying my Roman Collar and all the priestly things that went with it, but it was not my plan to wear them except when they were clearly called for. It was not that I was trying to pull anything, it was just that I wanted to see the world as the world was, I wanted to study it, objectively; and you cannot do that if people see you all dressed in black, and wearing your collar backwards.

But the Italian Lines knew better. They sat me at a table full of priests. There were twelve of them, and they were high-ranking, purple stuck out from under their collars. They were called "The *Periti*"---they were experts--- and they were going to the Second Vatican Council. I asked what they did. They might have said that they changed life for persons like me, that they had my future in their hands. But instead they said that they all worked for the "Sacred Congregation". When I had to ask them which one they meant, they looked at me, and said "---The Sacred Congregation for *Religious*", in a tone of annoyance, as though I should have known. After they looked at me that way I began to understand; they worked for the Papal body under whose jurisdiction people like me fell; and they were on their way to Rome to review the Rules that pertained to persons on my level, to change how we did everything, and how everything was done to us.

I remained rather silent among them; they sometimes spoke Latin among themselves, whereas I could not even speak Italian; I found myself ordering *risotto in brodo* simply because I liked the way the words sounded, not because it was what I wanted. I never knew what anything was that I had ordered until it came. I listened, while they spoke to the waiter of "*Primi Patti*", of "*Risi e bisi*" and "*Pancetta*", of "*Secondo*", "*Dolce*" and "*Vini*". I told them what I wanted and then let them order; they taught me how it was done, for there, on the eve of Europe, I really knew nothing about anything.

They called me "*Francis*" as though I were a little boy; they teased me; they asked me what I was doing, and when they heard that I was going to Dublin to bury my head in books for three years, they said "*Francis, You are going back to the Middle Ages!*" And they laughed at the Irish church, for its backwardness, all around the table. They wondered what I was going there for, and why I chose to study literature. They said upsetting things; they warned me, " We are going to change *everything* for people like you! We will be changing your life for you!   We guarantee that you will not be able to recognize anything on your return!" They were what was called "Romans", and I knew what that meant; it meant what it had always meant, that of all gifts given to men, their gift was to *rule*.

The *Periti* were nice enough--- they helped me order in Italian, and stopped me from saying "risotto in *brodo*"-- so that I didn't always get rice all the time-- but as I looked at them I could not help wondering just what it was that they had in mind for me, just what was it that they were going to arrange for me? And what might everything be like, what would I be like, when, after finishing my studies, I raised my head back up and began again to look around me? What was it that I would see? But I should add that there were also two young men with us, slated to make vows at a Novitiate in Murcia, Spain; sometimes they seemed a bit "herded", to me, though they seemed eager enough for the future.

It got so I did not like to go to table; I did not care to hear any more about Cardinal "Settimio" and Cardinal "Aegidio"; it felt like eating with the twelve apostles; it felt like being in that painting of the Last Supper, it was like a Passion Play, with all of them dressed in purple, and everyone heading for Rome. It was like traveling with a table full of superiors, lined up just for you, which you could not get rid of, even in a boat on the ocean. You wished you could paint them, with the wrong emulsifier, so that they would gradually deteriorate and just vanish forever; but that would not be generous. It would in fact be rebellious.

And so I would leave the table and go out to the rail, to look down at the dolphins. We are told that the real journey is the one we make inside ourselves. I stood at the rail, my back turned to those dignitaries at table who had been appointed to plot my future for me. In those moments, I surely thought that I was simply going to Italy, or that I was going to Ireland. It did not at all occur to me that I might be going on another kind of journey entirely, and to a land where I had never been, a place where I would think new thoughts, thoughts I had not dared to think before.

I wondered about the men back at the table; it bothered me that they had such control over my life. The *Periti*--- they were called The Skilled Ones, they were "the ones who knew"--- and they had been appointed by Rome; if I had a problem with them it was also a problem with Rome. Poor old Ahab, he thought his whale was a stand-in for God. ("He *heaps* me! He *tasks* me!" he complained) but I was no Ahab, with a great white whale; I was just another tourist, I had to settle for dolphins. Yet such matters were starting to trouble me, as they had never done before.

I cannot claim that I had any deep new thought, standing at the rail looking down at my dolphins. But it was in such moments that I was starting to ponder a lot more about the claims of others to rule over me, without concern for anything I thought. I had always struggled with that, but I had handled the problem. I do not know if being out on the open seas had anything to do with it, but whether I knew it or not, it is clear now that I was not just going to Italy; I was embarking upon a different voyage as well, and it was one which would last the rest of life. Yet my own Order was sending me, and paying for things; I should not forget that perhaps
the argument was with myself.

I explored the canting decks, learning to walk at sea. I got lost a lot, and I kept running into the likeness of Leonardo da Vinci, which was positioned at the top of the grand staircase; every journey I went on always ended up with him, and when I found him, I knew where I was. It was a self-portrait, he had drawn himself; and it showed him very fierce, as an old man, with wild, streeling hair, and I wondered why he had done it, this man who knew everything, who did everything, who took our bodies apart, who examined our cadavers, to see how we are put together. I had to look at him a lot, for you could not tell really, from the portrait, whether he was scowling or laughing.

I looked him up, in the Ship's Library. One of the books quoted him telling about how the smile was different from the frown, that different muscles were used for each. I went back to check on it, and looked at his portrait again; I looked closely to see which muscles he was using, so that I could tell whether he was frowning or really only laughing. But no matter how much I looked at him, he seemed at one time to be smiling, and another to be glaring fiercely.

I slept in the lowest cabin, just above the water level, six portholes down, under the letter "d" in "da Vinci" on the ship's hull. Down there like Jonah, in the belly of the vessel, I could hear the water rushing past my head, and knew that I was in the middle of the deep blue sea. I would think of Leonardo, as he appeared in his portrait, his eyes looking out at me from under that wild hair;

"*Onesto Rigore*" he kept saying "--*Onesto Rigore!*" as though he did not want me to be a liar, and was appealing for more honesty, and, with the water rushing by my head, I felt sorry for him, for I knew he was one who thought his life had all been a mistake, as though he had done nothing but make mistakes, and had never finished anything. On my trips through the vessel I would stop and look at him. I found a quotation from him; it must have been late in life, about the time of the portrait, he had said: "I thought that I was learning how to live, but found that I was learning how to die." Why had he said that? He had invented everything, he knew everything, and he was the world's greatest human. What was it that had made him come to such a conclusion? What-ever the answer, I consoled myself that it did not apply to me, that my own life was just beginning.

There is always a warm spot on a ship, if you can find it; it is usually astern, beyond the lifeboats, on the side opposite to where the wind is coming from. I got good at finding it, and would go to where it was and think of what was going on. I thought of Leonardo, and his doctrine on smiling, and whenever I thought of that, sooner or later it always made me think of my friend Peter.

I once knew a fellow named Peter, who had the strangest laugh, like a horse neighing; he was from one of the richest families on earth, from Boston, and he said his father had tried to make him laugh "the way a gent ought to", when he was little, making him take a lesson, after the Sunday meal, in how to laugh properly. I thought it odd, the strangest thing I ever heard, that anyone had to take laughing lessons. Yet if Leonardo was right, I supposed we all had to teach ourselves, somewhere, how to use the muscles for laughing, and how to use the ones for crying.

On the Eve of Europe, just off Gibralter, the two young men from my table, the ones I felt concerned for, came to me in the night at the ship's rail and said, "--Empty bottle, what'll we do?" One of them had it on his finger, swinging it, and I think all they had in mind was hurling it clear of the ship.

"--- It's not Amontillado, is it?" I said, though I could see plainly from the label it was not. "No? -- Well, anyway you could put a note in it. From here, it might end up anywhere--Greenland, Buenos Aires, Cape Town. You need a cork." One of them ran back to the dining room and got a cork, while the other found a pencil and tore a little piece off the ship's menu.

"--Now, what will we write?" they wanted to know.

I remember it. I spoke as though giving them instructions, but I was talking beyond them, to the sea and to the sky, to anything that would listen. I said, -- Write, We are at Latitude this, and Longitude that --if anyone knows those figures. Then say, whoever reads this note: It is the Fourth Day of September, in the Year of Our Lord 1963. We cannot see, for we are writing in the dark, on the night before Gibralter. Say, we are a man and two boys on a boat; there is nothing more to tell you. Then throw it out far, so as not to hurt anybody and let it land among the dolphins.

But first, let us find someone who knows these things; let us see if we can find someone, who can tell us exactly where we are.

5

HOUSE OF BONES

We all know where Dreams come from, Virgil told us. They come up from the Under-world, through one of two Gates. He said that false dreams rise up to us through the Gate of Ivory, while true dreams come up though what is called the Gate of Horn. And yet my teachers taught me that it was through the Ivory Gate that Aeneas came back up from Hades; they drummed it into me that it was through the gate of false dreams that Aeneas returned to earth, leaving me to conclude that this voice of Civilization was telling us something: it was reminding us to be very careful of where our dreams come from.

I was the first one off the boat in Naples; all I possessed was one black suitcase, with little other than my holy habit inside; I ran down the gangplank, I went running into Europe with it, over my head; I had my Roman collar visible on me, I was a priest, Customs and Immigration waved me on through. I kept on running; I ran all the way to the little Hotel Florence recommended in *Europe on Five Dollars a Day.*

I was already out at Pompei, among the excavations, in the Street of the Bachelors, or The House of the Tragic Poet, or The Villa of the Mysteries maybe, when I heard the familiar hoot of the old *Leonardo* in the harbor, its last hoot, leaving me there among the ruins. I paused, at the sound of its voice. "--Same job--" the Italian guide was saying to a group of male tourists, as he displayed a vivid wall painting of the sexual activity, which had taken place on the site.

"--Same job as today." he repeated. I decided it was better not to travel as a priest, and took off my Roman collar. I learned to handle the Italian lira, and learned how to ask "*Dov e*?" as in "Where is the Men's Room?"

I was doing well. I thought I knew what I was looking for. I did not have to put it into words, I knew that I was looking for something, which, once known, would make me a man, a cultured person who knew the world, someone very different from a boy in a darkened classroom, say. But as evening came on, the train rolled up through the Roman Campagnia, I began to be not so sure of myself, or where I was; I watched the broken arches of an ancient Aqueduct -

-the Claudian? --Rise and fall, rise and fall, on our way to Rome. I was startled by a sign marked "Terracina", but we rushed past without stopping. I consulted the guidebooks; it seemed situated in the center of plague and pestilence. We passed a restaurant called "Aeneas's Landing" so we must have been near the shore. The best I could do was crane my head and look back at things in darkness.

It was not my intention at all to bother them at our house in Rome, which was the Generalate of the Order. If there was anything that I was sure of, it was that I wanted to pass through Rome without alerting those at the center of things to my presence in that part of the world. I would pay for a cheap hotel near the Stazione Termini, and visit the Holy City without any advice from them In the name of God, had I come this far, only to hurry back and be among them? But to be honest-- to have a little *onesto rigore*-- I was also very much afraid, I was terrified of seeing them, or rather, of letting them see me. For to tell the truth, though I was satisfied in my own conscience that I had sufficient permission to travel that way --to go to Ireland by way of Italy-- I knew that they might well be very surprised to see me. They would want to know what I was doing in Rome. They might not exactly want me to conjugate my Latin verbs for them, but they would ask questions, and if they were not satisfied, it would be well within their power to make a few inquiries, and quite easily send me back, all the way back to where I had come from. And so when I arrived late in the evening in front of the modern electronic Hotel Accommodations board at the Stazione, it was the new me standing there, determined to go by *Europe on Five Dollars A Day*, trying to be mature and get by without anyone's help. But as I looked up to see what was available, all I saw were the last green lights going out, and everything turning to red. By the time I finished looking, all the hotels had a big red mark for "No Vacancy," there was no room in Rome for me. My new courage left me; I worried and talked to myself, and in the end, capitulated rather quickly: I put my collar back on, and I decided to try the Generalate. It was a frightening decision to make; the only alternative was to stay up all night in the train station; and yet knocking on that door of theirs struck me as a foolish and dangerous thing to do.

It meant meeting all of them, and explaining what I was doing in Europe. It meant meeting "The Chest"-- Father Ed Heston, our man in Rome, who would be standing at the door with his arms folded like Mussolini and his chin stuck out. He would not know me, he would have difficulty placing me, but he would find out quickly: (What is this man doing in Rome? he would be asking, Why were we not told of his coming?)

I explained to him, that the cheapest way to Ireland had been on the Italian Lines to Naples, even including the surface to Dublin. His eyes rolled, I think, a bit. I talked of "getting Europe out of the way" and not being distracted there in Dublin, as I wrote my thesis. I could imagine him sending word back to the States: Does this man have permission to be in Europe? Is he attached to any *House?* He passed through here in September. Should he not be sent back? It frightened me; I forced my mind to think of something peaceful, like my dolphins leaping from wave to wave. They must have prayed to Poseidon, for he astonished me by accepting my reasoning, agreeing that it was the way he would have done it, himself. I said I would stay only three days to see the Sacred Shrines, the tomb of Saint Peter, the Basilica of John Lateran, the Cemetery of Saint Callista, and then be gone, to do my thesis. But as I headed out the door the first day, to see Rome, they stopped me --something heavy black and round came down over my head, to my very eyebrows-- they had given me my Roman Hat.

"--Here-- You will need one of these!" one of them said, planting on my head a large round Roman Hat from off the rack. I protested, for I did not want to wear it. I tried it, turning it this way and that. It did not fit, but they laughed and said it fit better than most of them did, they never fit anybody. With its huge brim it made me feel like Don Quixote wearing the washbasin on his head, but when I tried to take it off they all shook their fingers at me, and I knew that I had better wear it.

I raced around in it, trying to see Rome in three days. I got caught in the heat of the sun on the Appian Way. I walked along the ruts and stones of its pavement, holding a Guidebook in one hand, wearing that enormous Roman hat upon my head, all the way in the heat from the Pyramid of Cestius, stopping in my black cassock to stand and read whatever Lord Byron said in front of the Tomb of Cecilia Metella. I was obviously an American as I stood under one of the Pines of Rome to get out of the heat of the sun with that round hat on; the real Romans were all eating, but I was standing in front of two big grassy green mounds and looking at my guide book and finding that they were the Tomb of the Curatii and the Tomb of the Horatii-- you know, Horatio at the Bridge. And at that moment a Roman prostitute with her customer whizzed past me up the flagstones of the Appian Way, she swerved over to park and do her business, and as she turned off the motor, she saw me there, standing on the Appian Way, in my cape and cord, and wearing my Roman Hat, and she called out in a loud cheerful voice "*Aie, Padre*! And waved gaily at me, and she laughed and laughed.

I got out of Rome; I hung my Roman hat on the peg with them and left, knowing that the train was the safest place. If they wanted to order me back, I knew I would have to obey, but first they would have to find me, and it would be almost impossible to reach me, on the train.

Once I was away from them, I was happy in Italy. I liked the color of things. I took off my clothes and swam with Dante in the River Arno above Vallumbrosa, there was nobody else around. Everything was cheap, even fine restaurants were cheap; I remember gleaming white table-clothes spread in front of me, and great salvers with serving fork and serving spoon lifting morsels for me, most lovingly, onto my plate. And when, out of nowhere, from behind me a splendid waiter would arrive, pouring out an ivory cascade of hot milk and another one of black-ivory coffee into my cup, my cup being filled up for me, which met and churned, white and black mixing in the bottom, foaming up to meet me, filling my cup to the brim, until it was almost overfilled, almost running over, --but not quite, not ever quite. I would look out at Spello, or Spoleto, or Perugia and wonder at this feast of life, and tried to think of some reasonable way to prolong it. In the galleries I could smell the varnish and pigments, and at times almost thought I could smell the canvas under-neath. I thought of Hank Hughes and what he had done for me, and felt that I had at last become a man, I had become an adult, though it had taken thirty-seven years. There was nobody around to share this victory with, of course; no one could look at me, and see that I had made it, that there, surrounded by fountains, I had made it after all, and accomplished something, as though I had at last joined Fra Mauro in the Mountains of the Moon.

Of course I knew that it was all only tomfoolery, I knew that I could only look down into ivory black coffee or drink red wine for so long. I knew that I was postponing Dublin. I could not make that world last, and it could never turn into the real one. The real one -- whatever that was-- was waiting for me; and I think even then I understood, in some way, that it would not be painted in my colors, at all.

When I was little, my Mother in the kitchen used to play for me "The Battle of Aughrim", the musical version of an old catastrophe of Irish history. Our side lost, and at the end of the piece, which is what I waited for, she would pick up two sets of spoons and use them as castanets, and make a great rattling sound, which went on and on, and then faded away. That was the sound of the bones, rattling, after the battle was over. This sound, set alongside the sound of numerous other sad old ballads, formed my impression of what

Ireland must be; based on what I had forever heard of it, I feared that it would be a land of bones.

It was on the beach at Rapallo that the future began for me, really --the journey into what would turn out to be my life. The Italians had all left, they were back at work; it was, after all late September. The striped little circus-tents of their beach-houses were all empty, and flapping in the rising wind; it looked like a scene out of Death in Venice, the film-maker saying to you, " This is not Real, This will not last." It began to rain, a mean cold rain began to fall, and I knew it was the end of summer, which -- *Onesto Rigore*-- even in Italy, meant the summer was ending.

I left the tents flapping on the beach at Rapallo, and worked my way to the international train heading for Geneva, and to Paris and, ultimately, to Ireland. The warm light of Italy was gone and the evening became increasingly dark as we swung and bounced toward the North. And in the coming on of night, as the last local passengers left me, at Domodossala, and as the train moved into the Alps, I found that I had been right, that what had been a cold rain on the beach was really the early beginnings of what would gradually turn into the European winter; indeed it would turn into three years of upset and wrenching change, something I was not ready for.

70

What was the name of that process Leonardo had used on the Last Supper? One of his failures: was it not *sfumato?* It certainly sounded like something that would not last, something evanescent, it sounded like smoke, blowing, something you would put up upon a wall and you would ask the Italians where it had gone and they would say *"Sfumato*---Partito!" as they did when you had missed a train. Whatever it was, you had to ask yourself whether or not you might be painting your own life in sfumato, throwing up pigments on the wall that would not last, so that people would ask What ever became of him? Where is he now? *"--Sfumato,"* the Italians would reply, " --He is gone. He said he was going to Ireland, and he just disappeared!"

I looked out the train window but could see nothing. Customs and Immigration came through, and I tried to sleep. After feeling once again for my passport, my wallet, and my ticket, I grasped my suitcase by the handles and pulled it up between my legs. I curled up and went into the Simplon in this embryo position: now to rob me they would have to wake me up, or worse. Suddenly I began to miss people and to become very lonely. I was doing what I had wanted to for my entire life, yet at every turn I had somehow managed to remove all contact with my fellow man. I wondered how long this would be so.

I tried to think what the name "Domodossola" meant, going into the tunnel, going into mother earth. House of Bones? House of oil? Home of dust? I decided that it was House of Bones, probably.

I pushed myself to hurry through Paris and London, and made myself catch the night boat for Dublin. It was time, certainly; it was far beyond any reasonable post-pavement. I sat up on the boat all night, surrounded by families sleeping on benches.

It was in the blackness well before dawn that I came into Ireland. I did not like it. A sign said "Irish Horn Rosaries for sale --- genuine Horn". After the warm light of Siena and Certaldo and Poggibonsi, and the bright lights of London, everything seemed silent and dark. I remembered my Father's voice singing on about the flowers in May, that surely, Ireland would "steal your heart away" -- that endless, lilting dream of his. But it was late September and not the time for flowers. Instead everything seemed to possess an air I was not sure I wanted to breathe. But I breathed it in anyway, I had to, and I knew what it was: it was the dead Odor of Sanctity; it was the smell of childhood, the dank smell of Irish history. I began to be afraid.

It is the land of death and sorrow, I said to myself. *--A person could die here.*

72

6

HE WAS A FRIEND OF MINE

I bumbled into Wynn's Hotel, off O'Connell Street. Except for a table with two nuns, I found the place filled with priests, all reading the morning newspapers. I read the names: *The Cork Examiner, the Kilkenny People, The Times of Limerick*. Later I found that it was a hotel that especially catered to priests up from the country; it was near the train station. In my blue navy tanker-jacket I would appear strange. They would know, of course; they would be reading their newspapers, but each of them would know, it was one of their skills. They would have the knack of appearing to read their papers through horned-rimmed glasses, while actually reading me. I had been in their country two hours, yet I knew this, I knew about them, I knew it in each of my bones. They would dismiss the tanker-jacket, and the lack of Roman collar, and see the creases in my right shoe from genuflections, they would see the priestly gawk, and they

73

would know everything. Or else the Holy Ghost would come and tell them, sitting on their shoulders, the Paraclete. You have made a mistake choosing this gray damp land, I told myself again, satisfied that I had been right the first time.

The Church in Ireland did not welcome me. I was told at once that there was no room for me. They told me that there was no room; they said, "We have our own housing shortage, Father". It was the beginning of my education -- this was part of the unrolling canvas, too-- for I believed them, and everything they said. But there were informers on the inside who could not keep a secret; they told me later privately that there was of course plenty of room all along, they said that there were whole wings of buildings quite empty, it was simply that the Irish Church did not want outsiders, and would not want me.

But there was a thing more ominous. At least it should have been, if I had had wits. I was informed that Dublin was the Episcopal See of Archbishop John C. McQuaid, and that "clerics were to wear proper covering". I had to ask what "Proper Covering" was, and was told that "Proper Covering" meant a hat; it meant that hats were to be worn outside, at all times, in public and that no cleric in the Dublin Archdiocese was "to venture forth" without "Proper Covering". Everyone referred to him as "John C." I had heard that the Archbishop's favorite pastime was to have his chauffeur ride him around in his big black limousine looking for clerics without proper covering. When he saw one of those, John C would have his chauffeur call that fellow over to the car window; and he would send him back down to the country, wherever he had come from; that would be the end of Dublin for him, the end of life, certainly the end of such things as Wynn's Hotel near the train station, for it was in the nature of an execution. So I determined that if I ever heard a voice call to me from a limousine that I would just not hear it, I would hurry on and disappear. My vow of obedience was not for obeying chauffeurs. I did not want to be sent back to the country, for my country was America; it was far away, and I simply could not afford to be sent back. (Decades later, reading about the scandals of the Irish priesthood of this period, I think of Bishop John C. McQuaid, worrying about hats.)

"Gentlemen's Luxury Bachelor Flatlet" it said in the *Irish Independent* as I read it under the Westland Row Railroad Viaduct. I had been in Ireland long enough to wonder what "luxury" might refer to, but thought I knew what "Batchelor" might imply. It was at Number 80 Pembroke Road. It had three original oil paintings, the one above the bed was a rich one of a redheaded girl signed by the artist, saying "To Sheila--In memory of a beautiful weekend." I took the flat; the man from Concordia Investments said that it was heated.

I could not believe that I was so fortunate as to have my own place after all these years. I was happy again, happy the way I had been with my triumphs in Italy; I remember thinking that it was what I had been moving toward through my entire life. It was not a luxury, it was cheap, I explained to Father Brown, the one who sent me money. The girl over the bed--Sheila-- worried me; though she came with the apartment. What would visitors think? Maybe I could take her down and hide her. But I didn't. I never got around to removing Sheila; all through my time in Dublin she smiled down on things. I still wonder if Sheila over the bed had anything to do with what happened to me there.

I was delighted, and could not wait to be left to myself. But I found that though it was quiet, it was not very warm; it was not heated, in fact it was cold. Moreover, it was explained to me at the

76

University that for Doctoral students there were no classes to take, and no grades be given; what you had to do was find your professor, get a research topic approved, then go to the library and work for three or four years until you came up with something that no one anywhere, in the British Commonwealth of Nations or in Europe or in North America, had yet come up with. You were to have it typed up and sent out to external readers at places like Oxford University, or Exeter, or Hull, or Edinborough, and in the end, if they pronounced it "viable" or "publishable" --that is to say, if you had done what no one else anywhere had ever yet done--you got your degree. There would be no foolish little things like courses and grades, they explained, the way you had in America. These were world standards, and they wanted you to be aware of that, and to look into yourself and see if you had the resources to work on your own and produce something "publishable". What they said was effective; I began to worry about it, to wonder if I could measure up, and if I could last, whether I could finish a thesis over three years in such a place.

I hurried over to the University regularly to find my professor. He was "on holly-day" they told me. Every week I would go over and ask for him, only to be told that he was still on holly-day, and that they did not know when he would return. It was into

October. I began getting angry; in a fury I demanded to know when had he gone on holly-day, and when he would be back? The girl at the desk in Earlsfort Terrace did not even shrug; she simply said "In May, or April, I should think..." I began to understand. Things were going to go on Irish Time. If your Soul could stand it, if it could support such sky-blue trades without going insane, why then you might succeed. You had to do it the way they did it. You had to creep up on them and watch how they did things; then you had to do it that way -- only, since you were a foreigner-- better. The real test was to see if you would be destroyed.

Finally I badgered them into approving my topic. I was to pour through periodicals from the turn of the century, exploring Ireland "as a ground for a national literature." It would be most tedious, but it was a safe subject, old papers and magazines, I did not think any one else would ever do it.

It made me aware of something called The Stage Irishman. You see, every ethnic group has a stage version of themselves which stalks them; and no matter who we are it is very easy to fall into the role waiting for each of us, and to become what others expect you to be. If you are black, you become Step n' Fetchit, if you are an Indian you say "How!", if you are Italian you talk like the Mafia, if you are an Englishman you fawn like a Butler; and as The Stage American, you are loud and coarse while you compare the plumbing to what you have back home.

It did not take long to realize that such a life was very lonely, and that my flat especially was very lonely, and that it would be prudent for me to get away from it from time to time. I went on long bus-rides out to Enniskerry so that I could walk down the banks of the River Dargle to Bray, and come home alone to my dark flat, to start in work once more. I longed for the sun of Italy and its ivory-black coffee.

Since I was a priest, people were kind, and respectful. Waitresses were kind, the girls who sold you cinema tickets or newspapers smiled out at you from their booths and kiosks; people tipped their hats to you. One crazy old woman, whenever she saw me in Pembroke Road, would come up to me and grab me by the sleeve. "---You're a _Yank_, aren't you?--" she would say, looking up at me, and tugging at my sleeve, "--You're a _Yank_ priest?" I would nod that I was; she looked like Old Lady Ireland, weighing me with her gaze. She would pause, still holding onto my sleeve, as if to wonder how much she could trust me with, then she would say, in a stage whisper so loud that all of Pembroke Road could hear, " ---_I know who shot Michael Collins!_" (He is one of the Fathers of Irish freedom who was betrayed and shot, almost within my lifetime.) She would give my sleeve one final pull, then she would let go of me and hurry off, leaving me always to wonder. I later found out that she actually had been in the Easter Week Rising, she had carried ammunition for the rebels as a young girl; and that she quite possibly *did* know who shot Michael Collins. I began to worry if she was not some kind of Seer, the kind they are famous for, over there, one of those old crones who could, possibly, fore-tell the future, or other secret things. I did not want my future told for me, and I began to not want her tugging at my sleeve. I came to think of her as Lady Ireland, when I would start out in the morning I would say to myself "I wonder if I will see Lady Ireland today", for she was, practically speaking, the only person who regularly spoke to me.

My first visitor to The Gentleman's Luxury Bachelor Flatlet turned out to be Warren Leamon, an American from the Deep South. I had been in Ireland long enough to recognize an American accent in the university cafeteria one day. I went over and introduced myself. We were an odd couple: He was my first Southern Baptist, and I was the first Catholic priest he had ever spoken to. It was during his first visit to my place that he asked what my church's view was on "ho-mo-sex-you-allah-tuh." I had raised my hands into the air comically and quoted Scripture "--<u>Let its name be not so much as mentioned among you!</u>" Warren had thrown his head back and laughed and laughed--- "--Ah thought so--" he was saying, "---Ah *thought* so!" Neither of us had at first been able to find our professor, to have our topic approved, and now we needed to talk and laugh. We entertained each other with stories, about the South and the North; Warren told about Atlanta Georgia, and then I began telling him about my friend Peter, and as I imitated "how a gent laughs" for him, Warren laughed and laughed.

Warren was always disabusing me about Ireland. He went around with the young Irish, and knew more than I did. He said, "--You know that old song about 'The Holy Ground Once More?'" I did know it; it was a lovely lilting old Irish ballad; I had been raised to think it was about sailors returning to Ireland; they were far away, and you wondered whether they would make it, if they would ever return to walk its sacred soil once again. It would be like Warren's view of his own American South, his sacred view of the Confederacy. "---Well, everybody thinks it's about *Ireland*, of course, you know," he said "---- and about how the sailors are longing to return to it. But Liddy tells me--*and he knows*--that 'The Holy Ground' was really the name of a house of prostitution in Cork, and *that's* what the sailors were all singing about!"

As we both laughed some more, I heard the voice of old Mrs. Murphy who lived in the apartment downstairs, calling up to me. She shouted something up to me in such an Irish accent that I had to ask her to repeat several times; finally I got what she was saying: "The President has been shot!" she was saying "--They have shot your President!" I went down one step to hear her say it, "--*Your president has been shot, they have shot the President*!" I called in to tell Warren, and he asked me to find out where it happened, and when I reported back "Dallas," Warren said angrily, "Damn! *Damn! --*Now they'll blame the *South* again!"

I remember smiling at his response -- the news at first did not seem to matter much to me. I was shocked a bit, but I was not a Kennedy person; I had voted for him; I had been relieved when my country showed it could elect a Catholic, it seemed to write some kind of an end to prejudice, it certainly seemed a good moment to be stepping into Ireland; but by the time I had left America, I thought I had enough of the Kennedys, I was more or less tired of it all, I did not think that the news would affect me, much.

The Irish however took it very hard; everything closed down, and the people came out into the streets, milling aimlessly. All that week, if someone heard your voice and recognized you for an American, they looked right at you and said with deep feeling,

"--Sorry for your trouble" --that is what the Irish say at wakes and deaths, and they said it to you "---Sorry for your trouble" --as if you had lost someone in your family, and it made me uncomfortable, but after a while it started to make me feel about him the way others said it did, that he had been a friend of mine. More than one person said it made them want to steal away and cry, although I never admitted that myself.

At first I was only interested casually, but as I paid attention a feeling came over me that I was wrong to think that I was not involved. I found myself standing outside of pubs, that long weekend, watching television sets that had been placed in their windows for passers-by like me, shifting from one foot to another on the wet pavement. Standing outside of McDaid's Bar in Leeson Street and outside the Waterloo Pub in Upper Baggot Street and Crawfords in Ballsbridge, I worried that it would indeed seem strange to see a priest in black standing on the sidewalk outside a pub, looking in, but I had no TV of my own and it was the only way I could see anything.

I watched it all, standing in front of one pub or another, the whole thing. To do this entailed some risk, for that week might be of course also full of John C. McQuaid, with me standing in front of various bars looking in their windows, not wearing proper covering, and sensing over my shoulder the presence of such a one as could put a stop to me, to all my efforts and everything I was about. And do not say I imagined things; I am certain that he was there, that time, for I saw the black Episcopal limousine slow to a stop behind me. But he must have said to his chauffeur: Let it not be now, while he is at his prayers. It always makes me think of those last lines from ee cummings:

> and what i want to know is how do you like your
> blueeyed boy
>
> Mister Death

I thought of my Mother in the kitchen with the spoons, playing for me "The Battle of Aughrim." What I was watching now seemed only one more part of that; it was the long rattle once again at the end of the song, with everything fading away.

I stood there outside McDaid's bar, watching it with passers-by like I on the little black and white television set in the window which flickered. I saw the gun carriage down Pennsylvania Avenue and the riderless horse with the boots turned backwards, and the little boy saluting. I saw his mother push him forward and watched him raise his hand in a little salute as the coffin passed. A voice was reciting "When Lilacs Last by the Dooryard Bloomed." It was like an old black and white movie, some old film played over and over. And the gun carriage looked like the exact same one I had buried the young naval officer with, my first summer s a priest, in Arlington Cemetery.

It was growing late; I could feel the damp cold of the Dublin sidewalk seeping up into me. The box in the window showed a drawing, of where the bullet entered, a scalp of hair thrown back, the catastrophic damage to the brain, repeated over and over, in its flickering, purple light: We have had too much death in Ireland, I heard someone say. The long northern light of evening began to cover everything, turning Leeson Street into a purple color; it was the soft light that you often saw in Ireland, coloring everything. I wondered if there was a name for it, that particular tint, and then I recalled that of course there was, it was the one called Caput Mortuis, the Head of Death. I had come a long way to see it. A choir in Westminster Abbey was singing " In the Beauty of the Lilies."

The bell from Haddington Road church began to ring. The others must have heard it that was why they left. I was alone now, everyone else was gone, and it was calling me. The TV set was still

85

flickering its purple light, and a voice was going on. I decided that I had had enough, and turned away. I started toward my flat and thought how long this journey of mine was getting to be, and how lonely. At first it had been filled with the smell of fresh unrolling canvas, for was I not a student of life? I had watched as portions of it were lifted lovingly from the salver onto my plate, and seen many steaming cups poured for me, to their very tops, just short of overflowing; had I not been learning how to live? I looked behind me one more time, for the figure of John C. McQuaid. I could not account for my feelings. The dead man had never known me, and yet he was a friend of mine, I felt that I had lost a friend. The bell was still ringing and I hurried towards it: home, I thought, home to Sheila, over the bed. I moved briskly, for I did not want to meet that poor old woman, with her Sorry for Your Trouble, and all the rest, Old Lady Ireland, who would only start tugging at my sleeve, whispering things I did not want to hear.

7

IN THE MEADOW OF THE DEAD

I roll up my life like a weaver,

he cuts me off from the thread.

--Canticle of Isaiah

It was the Sixties and a cultural revolution was going on, but I did not know it. The Beatles had passed through Dublin the previous year on their way to America, screaming. They screamed "I Want to Hold Your Hand" and "Love Me Do," and they made everyone want to dance; during the day I kept my head down doing what I was supposed to be doing, reading old newspapers before they turned to dust at the National Library of Ireland in Kildare Street; each evening I returned numbly to my flat, a regular Bartleby---Bartleby the Scrivener, covered in brown newspaper dust. The only human voice I regularly heard was the weather announcer on the BBC, with his daily warning that "a succession of foul-weather troughs will cover Ireland," or the standard English forecast: "There will be bright periods."

I talked to myself: " A succession of troughs will cover Ireland," I said, "--But there will be bright periods --There will be bright periods."

In the lonely nights I listened to the Voice of the BBC; and on the airwaves in the night, I heard lovely, distant things, that came and went, from all over Europe: classical music from Radio Nederland, music from "L'Orcheste de la Suisse-Romande" and Mozart, from the "FestSpielhaus" in Salzburg --a feminine voice there seeming to say the words "neunzehn hundert drei und sechzig". She was telling the year of course, that it was nineteen hundred sixty-three; but to my ears she was saying that it was "dry and sexy", that everything was "dry and sexy" and that we were going to hear Mozart. I would turn the light off, and the little room would be full of Koncert-Gebows and Camaratas, full of Cellos and Cimbulos. Then finally at Mid-night, there would be the rolling national anthems, one after another, congratulating themselves, "Deutschland, Deutschland," and the Marseillaise, and the Internationale, and finally God Save Everything -- all Europe closing down and leaving me to myself again. Except, of course, for the Beatles, who were singing "Yeah, Yeah, Yeah!"

It was at that time a young American nun named Anne Francis Cavanaugh came to do a thesis in Dublin. We met at the Registration line for Michaelmas Term. She had gone through that whole business of finding her professor, as I had done the previous year, and was a confused by it as I had been. I had taken her to Bewley's in Grafton Street, for that was where you took new Americans, where the fresh roasting coffee beans sent up an aroma through the sidewalk grating which called out and called out, to us, to everyone. *" Comfort ye*," it said, *"—Comfort ye! Come in and be warmed! Life is all a bitter mystery-- Have some Round Brown rolls! Oh, have some Sultana Buns*!" I did have to admit that I owed something, surely, to her--an introduction to how things worked, for example--- but that was all that could ever be expected of me.

My job, I felt, was to tell her clearly that what she was trying to do was impossible. She seemed bright, but I did not believe that anyone, no matter how bright they were, could possibly pull it off from a convent. Dublin was a swamp of strange ways, you had to live in the swamp, and I thought honestly that there was really no hope for her. I considered that out there, where she was, no matter what her qualities, her situation would be hopeless.

Yet she had, all the same, come up with something already-- a remarkable story, apparently, something called "The Weaver's Grave."

I had never heard of it, nor of Seumas O'Kelly, its author. She outlined the story for me, and I leaned forward to hear better, the way we all do, when we are being fair.

In the story, the old Weaver has just died, he had married four times, and now his Young Widow has to go looking for his grave in the old cemetery, in 'Cloon na Morav'-- the Meadow of the Dead. But the Weaver is very old, so old that he is the last one with rights to be buried there, the last one who will ever be buried in the Meadow of the Dead. After him it will be closed, they are opening up a new cemetery in the suburbs. But before the young widow is finished with him, before she can get on and live her own life, the young girl must find the proper place for him-- and no one remembers where that might be, no one knows at all where to bury the Weaver.

And that is mostly what there was to the story-- a young widow, searching for an old man's grave. (Though of course there were the two young gravediggers, as well.) She handed me over the book she had discovered, to read of Cloon na Morav, the Meadow of the Dead: a burial ground so ancient, so full of tumbled crosses and fallen tombstones and cracked slabs with hidden people under them-- so full of lichens and mosses and moisture, so full of crowded graves from the ancient past that no one could remember who belonged anywhere. I read of old men meandering through a grave- yard with the young girl, trying to remember who should be buried where.

"--My God," I said smiling into the book, "My *God!*-- He's just describing Ireland, that's all. -- It sounds like *Dublin*. It sounds like *this* place." I looked at her, wondering just who she might be; she had a kind of race-horse quality about her, that thing the Greeks called *arête;* they gave it to horses racing with chariots on their friezes, and to tell the truth, though she was very much a nun, she did look like she could fling her head back and win in spite of things, even from a convent out in Clonskeigh; and I wondered if in the end she might not succeed in Dublin, after all. (I later found that it was a Hostel for Nuns attending University, and it was in Donnybrook, not Clonskeigh. I was wrong about some things)

Then, however, that morning in Bewley's, to the clack of heels outside in Grafton Street and the sound of the double-decker buses swinging top-heavy on their way out to Blackrock, I doubted if I could remain for the end of her story. That morning I was sure of two things: one, that bright and beautiful as she was, the odds were against her, as they were for all of us; and two, that whatever else happened in this world, I could certainly have nothing to do with her. She was a nun and I was a priest. It was sad, but that was the way it was. There was nothing I could do about it. And I was impatient, waiting to be gone.

Suddenly I saw Warren Leamon come into the restaurant, one more American looking for his coffee, that handsome young Baptist from the deep South, who had now survived one full year. I called him over, he knew how things worked, and I needed him to help welcome this nun to Ireland.

It was of course unfair to him, he was Protestant, a son of the Confederacy and of the Bible Belt, he was from the red clay country of Georgia, and I knew he would be uncomfortable with a Roman Catholic Nun. But he was my friend, the only other American I knew, and I introduced him anyway; I needed his help.

Warren behaved the perfect gentleman, he asked "the Sistuh" about her work, and they got talking literature; they were both literary---Warren was the most literary person I have ever met.

Warren was consumed with the poetry of Yeats. When he recited the Wild Swans of Coole I heard the bell-beat of wings above my head, and it was Yeats himself calling out "*Bring me my Mask of burning gold!*" Or saying "*O heart! -If she'd but turn her head*" or "*Come away, O human child, come away!*" And sometimes it would be that passionate cry of Yeats, "*--Too long a sacrifice can make a stone of the heart, O when may it suffice?*" That was Warren's favorite line for me, he directed it towards me over and over, that too long a sacrifice can make a stone of the heart, spoken so compellingly that I didn't know whether it was Warren or Yeats himself telling it to me. But I always laughed. I did not take Warren seriously.

And of course, I was not listening, really, that morning; I was thinking.

"--Commend all Women to God," I was thinking "--And as for Women, they are to be consigned to their Maker." That was the Rule, the Holy Rule itself. "—"Keep the Rule," I was used to saying, "--and the Rule will keep you." Do your business and get out.

And so Nun and Protestant talked on without me; I heard snatches; I heard Yeats again. "*Gaiety, transfiguring all that dread*" he was saying. Yeats, speaking for all of us, in that damp lonely place. The line kept repeating itself, like a wave washing up upon a shore; there in Bewley's above the Round Brown Rolls and the Sultana Buns, which were of course waiting to be counted up by the waitress for the bill at the end. And in the drowsy warmth, with the invigorating coffee, the sweet steamy life of Dublin began to reassert itself once more, strongly, just as it had so often, just as it did always, turning into something lively and lovely and full of goodness if you let it, just when you had given it up for good and forever. What did those words mean, 'Transfiguring all that dread." All *which* dread? Some of all the dread that was in the world? It could be all just nonsense, my mind said, for I was tired of thinking.

Pay your bill and be counted, I heard a voice say; Stand up like a man! It was the Rule again, the old Rule: *And be not sleeping but awake!* I awoke, with some difficulty; I extricated myself from my thoughts. There were too many voices saying too many things; I was tired of listening to Warren, saying them, things like "*-He speaks to his heart, bidding it have no fear,*" or "*Friendship is the only house I have.*"

And so, while Warren talked poetry, I finished reading the story, I wanted to find out about the two handsome young gravediggers, who turned out to be twins. Both were impatiently waiting to be told where to bury the Weaver, but one seemed to be different, somehow; he looked just the same as the other, yet to the young widow he was different. And in the end, after the Old Weaver had been buried in the right place for him, after the grave had been dug sufficiently deep and the old man placed into it, you were delighted how one of the two gravediggers, the one who made a difference, reached over and took the Young Widow by the hand, and holding her tightly, stepped with her across the open mouth of the weaver's grave, as they do in Irish country places. For it is their custom to help the grieving person actually step over the open grave of the departed to show them that it is over, so that they understand, and to help them get over their sorrow, help them step over their past and bury it with everything else that is buried, which in the Young Widow's case had included that unfair union which had been thrust upon her, and you almost felt yourself stepping across with him, the young gravedigger, and you could feel yourself holding her hand, to help her back into life. I wondered if the story was not a small masterpiece. I pretty much decided that it was. To find the right place, the exact right place, to bury the Past. To step across the open grave, and live life, while you had it, in spite of the gaping earth, the open hole that awaits all.

Would it not be quite fine if I could say that I held out my hand to her that morning and that together we stepped across the chasm which both surely faced? But I knew of course that I could not; for in those days you see there were certain things you might think you wanted to do, but understood abundantly well and beyond all question that you could not do, in any case, or under any circumstances. And so I thought, The story is all well enough, it is perfect, but it will not be enough to save her.

I heard Warren say "Transfiguring all that Dread" one more time, and suddenly I did not want any of it, I did not want to hear any more. I stood up. I broke into the conversation; someone had to bring us back to what we had come for.

"---*You will die,*" I said. "Sister, you will *die*! -- You can't *do* it from a Convent," I said, "You can't do it *from a Convent out in Clons-keigh.*" I spoke in my firmest voice, "--It all happens down here, you will only die out there, you will *die* " I said, "---Isn't that so, Warren?"

Warren was surprised at my interruption. Yet he nodded, in perfect agreement with what I said; he had to -- he had almost died himself.

I looked at Warren; I wondered what he was thinking; he had been no help at all. We all sat, drinking our coffee. She was doomed. I shook my head; time to start commending her to God.

I gave a few more words of advice on things like how to find one's professor. And then, after a human interval had passed, I stood up. I do not remember exactly, but possibly I paid for her cup of coffee, possibly I left a shilling tip. Then, I excused myself, explaining that it was already late and that, whatever anyone else was going to do, I had to get back to my thesis. I said good-bye to both of them, left the restaurant, and hurried back to Number 80 Pembroke Road --back to that same old place, back to my dear beloved thesis, back to my empty room, back to dear dreary nothing-- leaving Nun and Southern Baptist to do as they saw fit. I had done what was expected of me.

Oh, I know that it was all foolish. It is painful to think of it. I sounded like one of those madmen in Russian literature. But it is all true enough: I come out from under Gogol's overcoat.

But you see, that was the sort of thing I did in those days. I had a name for it--"Ditching," I called it. I went around ditching people.

I was good at ditching people. I was always telling them when it might be good for them to move on, or explaining that I would have to be going myself, shortly. "The Ditched" became quite numerous over the years; there were a lot of them.

And I--- who was getting rid of all these people--, was I, then, an attractive person, myself?

No, I was quite unattractive; indeed, I was the most ordinary and lonely of men, suffering because of my loneliness. Yet I went around Dublin "ditching" people --especially, if they were beautiful women.

Oh, I was out of a Russian novel all right, someone who sends notes up from the Underground, saying: I live alone and am lonely, come and save me, come and talk! Someone who if he keeps it up will go crazy will go quite mad. Someone like good old Raskolnikov.

I was hardly back ten minutes, had hardly got my thesis out, hardly got to the typewriter, when Warren was there, knocking at my door, pounding on it, pounding like the police after some criminal. Angry at being left with a nun, angry about being involved in such foolishness.

"--Now," he demanded as I opened up "-- What was *that* all about?"

I put the teakettle on, probably out of nervousness, for we had just had coffee. It would be a struggle even to begin.

What was I going to tell him? Where would I start?

This Southern boy from the red clay country of Georgia, what did he know? About anything --about the Councils of the Church, say, or even, say, someone like Theodore of Mopsuestia?

Oh, I do not remember precisely what I told him. It was a speech I gave whenever people asked me about my life, a sermon really-- it could start as far back as the Council of Nicea --if people were patient-- or with Tertullian, 160 A.D.; it mentioned the Virgin of Chartres, it could roll on, all the way from Bernard of Clairvaux to the monastery of Cluny, and the Cluniac Reform; but it always concluded with the life of purity, the life of chastity, as it had to, that bright shining jewel of the Clergy, ending with the words of the eloquent preacher Lacordaire, with the line that had filled Cathedrals, bellowing out, through nave and transept, that fighting spirit of Counter-Reformation which I had been raised upon, was imbued with: " --And it is *yours!,* It is *yours,* O priest of Jesus Christ!"

Warren waited until I got done--Warren had, certainly, heard most of it before, it had all been said numerous times, had all been uttered more than once, in that little apartment.

But when I had finished, Warren just looked at me, and said simply, "---It's about this nun, isn't it?"

He had tramped all the way out from Bewley's to say this. It was simple, and decisive. It had the effect of finishing my catechism lesson for me.

Perhaps a few more words were said, we probably had the tea, I don't remember. Shortly after, he got up to go back out; he left, and I closed the door behind him. After he was gone out into Pembroke Road I knew that Warren was right.

It was not about Theodore of Mopsuestia. He was right about some things, and I could stop talking.

8

THE HORSESHOE

I knew about nuns. I had been raised by them. Two of my older sisters had gone off to the convent when I was very young, and the nuns who taught me at my school belonged to the very same order. For the eight years of grade school, any nun who taught me would be in regular contact with one or other of my two sisters.

My memory of childhood is of the Sunday afternoon trip up to the Pennsylvania mining towns by train in winter, counting coal cars and locomotives, being allowed to visit, once a month, on the polished floors of the convent visiting room, and then returning in the fading light to my unfinished homework, waiting for me on the dining room table. If I did not hand it in next day, Monday, the nun at school would tell my sisters; it always happened.

As a Catholic boy, you were to keep your distance; you were to answer Yes Sister and No Sister. Someone like Ray Stockhausen might try to catch the tip of Sister's veil after she went past us, down the aisles between the desks, but that was very bold, you knew that people who did things like that ended up in jail. Still you had questions, about all that black serge, and how deep their pockets were. You could always hear them coming by the rattle of the beads on the huge rosaries they wore. It is not possible to tell the great awe with which my family regarded that world of black serge and wimples and coifs and rosary beads and polished convent floors. It was a side of things I was not fond of; it became to me a world of endless dreary Sunday afternoons in winter; I was not supposed to say so, but truly, I had had quite enough of nuns.

And so when Sister Anne Francis appeared, and everyone remarked on her obvious attractiveness, I was steeped in what I had come from and refused to think about such things

Yet in spite of all this, you would not have been able to find any two persons living in Dublin at that time with more in common than the two of us; we were already a pair before we were introduced to one another. Each of us had vows, and belonged to a religious order; we were both studying the same literature in Kildare Street; and we were Americans, dropped down into that place in history together. We had different temperaments, but each of us knew from the first that we instinctively understood everything about the other and that there would never be need for explanations. We had been deposited there, in that unusual place, by whatever it is that controls such things, which some say is Divinity and others say is Fate. To me it sounds more like a nursery tale: "Once upon a time, two people awoke to find themselves together in a place called Cloon na Morav- - The Meadow of the Dead...." And that is accurate enough for I often felt that I was looking for tombstones. But we were there, that was clear, and there together. What we had to do was to keep our wits about us. No one was going to do anything wrong.

It was a mystery to me how everyone knew that she was beautiful. She was almost totally concealed under her holy habit; all you could see was her face and hands; yet everyone in Dublin called her "that striking American nun." Whenever I found myself starting to wonder about her, I would catch myself, and caution myself, that she was "hidden with Christ in God" as the *Imitation* would say. "She is hidden with Christ in God", I repeated, and reminded myself to finish my thesis. Furthermore, Sister Anne Francis lived up in the Nun's Hostelry at Muckross Park, which kept her quite distant from me, not so much in miles only, but in layers and layers of culture and meaning.

Time passed, the rest of my second year, and my life seemed lonely beyond all loneliness. Warren and I continued on. We were all students, we ate where it was cheap. Boiled potatoes, of course, boiled cabbage, Irish turnips, carrots and celery, all boiled. Everything tasted of dishwater. There was a restaurant at the end of Waterloo Road called The Horseshoe; it was cheap, and it was full of boiled Irish food.

Once, I invited Warren over near my place, to the Horseshoe, in among the paper napkins and the tea-water and the steam rising to cover the windows, with everyone sitting in their rain-coats or folding them behind on the backs of their chairs. At another table sat a lone, black, African priest. He was young, and I figured him out, at once; he would be from one of the numerous Irish missions in Africa, of course, had grown up among Irish priests who would have baptized him away from his original unpronounceable name and christened him something decent like Patrick or Kevin or Timothy; he would have entered the mission seminary, gotten good grades, and been rewarded by being sent to Ireland, to Maynooth College or Clonskiegh, with all the Irish lads. Now he would of course be alone in Ireland; and it would be a lonely life, surely, eating their strange food in Baggot Street, listening to them with their strange accents. I felt sorry for him. He was so black in such a white culture.

I told Warren to look over at him, to see how sad he looked. Warren glanced at him, only an instant, before turning back again fiercely to his plate. "--_Ah_ don't feel sorrah for him," he said, "Ah don't feel sorrah at all." And then looking directly at me, as though he was talking about me, Warren added "---He couldn't *hep* being born *black* ---but he didn't *have* to be a *priest*!"

I looked at him, and shook my head; Warren was clearly hopeless, he could never be expected to understand anything. I thought him a fool.

Months later, when Warren would be gone, returned to the States, after I had learned to suffer Ireland without him, I would sometimes find myself thinking again of things we used to talk about-- God, and religion and what a person should do. I would think about him especially in front of the fire-- the fire of Irish peat that he had always had so much trouble igniting-- thinking of some of the things he had said, that awful thing about the "stone of the heart".

I would find myself again in his company, and it would be Warren all over again, who when he spoke would be always looking me straight in the eye, as though I were black, somehow a very black man --though I am clearly white-- and he would be saying to me over and over, in that fierce righteous voice of his, what it was he had to tell me, and which summed up everything: that he did not feel sorry for me, that he did not feel sorry at all, for though I could not help being born black, I did not have to be a priest.

9

IT'S THE RUNTS THAT BREED

I was not at all interested in meeting Mary Lavin, the famous short-story writer, when I first went to study in Dublin. I knew enough about her from her stories in the *New Yorker Magazine*; they were full of nuns and priests, and were, I thought, quite mean.

One story I would not forget. It was about a little girl standing in the garden with her young widowed mother. The little girl watched and listened while the parish priest talked to her mother, scolding. While he talked, he fingered the cabbages; the little girl watched him feel along the row for the best head of cabbage; then when he had found it --still talking, still lecturing the mother on the need for getting married or something-- the priest pulled out a little pocket knife, neatly cut the head off, wiped and folded the blade, returned it to his pocket, and then walked off to the Rectory, with the best head of cabbage under his arm.

When I read that, I knew that Mary Lavin was anti-clerical; and when I came to Dublin, with a Roman Collar around my own neck, I thought that it might be well to give such a one a wide berth. Oh, I did not think it at all likely that I would ever be introduced to her; but still, Dublin might prove to be a small place, and I did not want to give anybody anything bad to say about priests; and I certainly did not want to recognize myself among the cabbage-pickers, in the *New Yorker*.

But Warren already knew her; his old professor back at Vanderbilt had arranged an introduction. And one day walking in Molesworth Street, Warren suddenly said, "--There's May-ruh-- HELLO MAY- RUH!-- That's May-ruh Lavin, the writer! --I'll introduce you to her!" She smiled, and called back across Molesworth Street, "Hello, War-ren!" She spoke his name clearly, in two syllables, from the front of Buswell's Hotel. She threw up both arms in greeting, and bounded across Molesworth Street to us full of life and smiles. Warren introduced me to her and she smiled some more. Look at all the smiles, I said to myself, she's even smiling at me. But I thought, I wonder when the smiles stop, and she brings out the knives?

The smiles never stopped, and the only knives I saw were the ones she brought out for carving roasts to feed us with. She showed herself to be a generous host, inviting me with Warren over to the Mews in Ladd Lane, and later, even to her lovely farm at Bective, out in County Meath.

And after the first year of knowing Mary, I must have begun to mention fairly often in conversation the name of Sister Anne Francis-- that nun she saw working in the library every day, my good friend. One day Mary came over to Anne Francis working at a desk in the Kildare Street Library and said, "Sister, I believe we have a friend in common--"

The two of them became close. Mary was able to talk with her in a way she never talked with me; it was quite a friendship. Anne Francis tells a story that sums it up; the story says a lot, about Mary and the rest of us, as well as something about the Dublin of that time. " --Mary and I were walking up Leeson Street one day," she says, "-- and one of those long double columns of Seminarians from Clonliffe College cycled past us, all in their black suits, on the way to the university. You know what a handsome lot they were--- every manly face with that fleck of red in the cheek, smiling and saying good day. But as they cycled off, Mary stopped right in the middle of the sidewalk and said, passionately, "--Now would you look at that!' she said, '--Now would you look at that! --Would you look at *that,* Sister--' "

I waited, for Mary to tell what it was that was bothering her. Then finally she explained, -- "You see, Sister --There's none left for the breeding! *There's none left for the breeding!* " In Ireland, Holy Mother Church gets the best of the litter, and the runts are left to breed! It's the *runts* that *breed!*"

When Sister Anne Francis first told me the story of Mary and the Runts, I laughed loudly, but I scarcely knew what I was laughing at. There was much more to Mary than I knew; Anne Francis always knew her better than I did.

But I caught some things. I understood from the beginning how Mary thought the world of her, whether Anne Francis knew it or not. Mary came to me, and told me. I remember what she told me, privately, about Sister Anne Francis, after she had come to know her well.

"--You know," she said to me, "--There must be *something* good about the Religious Life! There has to be *something* good about it, to have a being like *that* in it!"

The two walked together all over Dublin. And at the library, Mary would ask her over to the Tea Time Express. When she had finished some-thing, and had something to read to her, she would want Anne Francis to listen to her latest story. One story was called "Happiness", and it was Mary's favorite among her stories, for it is the story of her own life; she took Anne Francis over to the Tea Time Express, and read it to her. It is really the story of her own death, and that was the first time anyone ever heard it.

She adopted us, she adopted the whole group of us; she turned Dublin of the Sixties into our Paris. Often, coming home to the lonely flat in a soul-chilled despair, the phone would ring; it would be Mary, telling me that someone famous was coming to her place, and would I like to fill out the table? I would hurry to Smyths of the Green, get a bottle of red wine, and then try to find the little stone archway in Baggot Street that led to Ladd Lane. We all filled out the table more than once; we ate with the likes of Elizabeth Bowen, and V.S. Pritchett, and Padraic Colum, with the Belgian Ambassador, and often, with Frank O'Connor.

It was a great continuing Feast for us, around Mary Lavin's table, a ring of bright faces under the green rim of the lampshade at the Mews in Ladd Lane off the Grand Canal, and --for a few of us at least-- in her country house as well, the Abbey Farm in Bective, out in County Meath. Beautiful Bective, its fields sloping down to the River Boyne, with the ruins of the old Cistercian Abbey of Bective on the property, the Hill of Tara itself only a few miles away, and the prehistoric burial mounds of Newgrange as well. I remember Bective.

That was where you saw people, at Bective. To me it was a bright gleaming mead-hall to which I was attracted; for I lived by myself where everything was all cold and dark, and there was no one to talk to. But being with the people, with Mary, and Padraic and Warren and Anne Francis and the Belgian Ambassador sent to Mary by the Tourist Board, and Frank O'Connor and all the writers and poets and artists she assembled-- it was as though I had flown into a bright mead-hall full of light and feast, and did not know what to make of it.

There is that very famous story of the bird. The early Christian missionaries are talking their strange talk to an early English king in his mead-hall with his thanes. He does not know what to make of this new talk, of Saving Grace, of Heaven and of

Hell, and asks his men what they think. One old adviser gets up and says, "O King: It seems to me that life is like a bird, flying in the night. The bird comes to your mead-hall, attracted by the bright light and warmth, and flies in the window. For a brief moment it sees the fire and feels the warmth and hears the joy and laughter of you and your men, and then, startled, flies out again the other window, going back into the black night from which it came. O Highness, it seems to me that each of us is like that bird, for no one of us knows anything of the great darkness from which we came, and no one knows any-thing of that black night into which we go; so if these men have any truth of it, if they have word to tell us, it seems to me that we should hear them, and all listen to what they have to say."

And so it seemed to me that I was very like that bird; it seemed I came in out of the darkness through one window, delighted and surprised by what I saw, but startled and frightened, only to fly out another, and looking back, looking behind at Bective, and thinking on it, and wondering what to make of it, as my soul flew on into the night. And the only time I saw Ciaran Ryan was there, when he entertained us all with his brilliance and his wit, that one time, at the Abbey Farm, in Bective.

The Irish have something they call "*Craic*", though they seem to be saying "Crack". Do you know what "Great Crack" is? It is how

113

they describe such a scene of gifted conversation, good food and drink, with plenty of music and performance. It is good times, far away from any bad times that may be coming. And it was Great Crack we had that evening, there was wonderful talk out of Mary, and Ciaran, and Anne Francis, and Frank O'Connor, and the rest, the cows out under the stars looking in and listening. There was the French red wine that Mary favored, and her own quick but excellent cooking. There was singing.

My memory has it that maybe one of these who sang was Ciaran. At least that is how I always remember him, with his handsome face lifted in song. Yet I am told that he never sang, and did not sing that night. Perhaps I should remember him for what he was, the country's premier Physicist, working at the nuclear laboratories in CERN, Switzerland. He was certainly a commanding presence.

That was the only time I ever saw him. I never really got to know him. But he was a friend of Anne Francis; and people started to warn me, as though he was my rival, of sorts, they lectured me, as though I needed waking up. I was annoyed with this. If I had let them, they would have tied us both together in some kind of mortal struggle, making us an altogether fanciful pair like Holmes and Professor Moriarity, falling down into the Reichenbach Falls. But I never felt like that, I refused to think that way, and I doubt if they much bothered to ask Anne Francis.

Ciaran Ryan left, rather early that evening; it would in fact be the last I saw him. I began thinking of heading back, on the long damp road to Dublin. Though of course I suppose I was thinking about a lot more than that. I would have been thinking, in some way, as I always did, of what I always refused to think about: that vague, distant, and impossible thought of ever actually "leaving". Of coming right down to it and leaving the priesthood, and the order; and, of course, wondering also how Anne Francis thought about such things, and what would happen to her. It was pleasing to be there with her, with someone of her sensibilities. She was as bright as any of them, --and they were all very bright. It would be satisfying if there were some way in which I could remain with her always, in such a setting, surrounded by the warmth and brightness of life. I thought of various possible ways in which that might happen, kept on thinking a while, and then did what I always did; I stopped thinking in that way, and did the next thing to hand, the thing nearest to me, which that evening pretty much reduced itself to getting on my little motorcycle, and cranking it, and hoping that it would start, and take me back to Pembroke Road. I always did that, fled from the general worry about what was going to happen to such persons as the two of us, and found myself settling for something easy, like starting up a motorcycle. Such thoughts upset me, especially when Mary began to talk about priests and nuns.

On the long way back, I certainly had time to think, I always did, for it was dark, and slippery, and hard to tell your way. I believe that it is not wrong to be afraid of the dark, only a fool does not fear it, for we really do not know much about what it hides, we know little about the darkness into which we are going.

That night I was afraid, leaving Bective so late, for it would be pitch black heading back into town on the motorcycle. "--That's a good little sound that you hear, when it starts up like that" Mary said, out in the cold field and the quiet darkness, with the cows out there somewhere, looking. I left her reminding me to close the wire gate behind me, and all I had was the little headlight, powered by the little engine, as I bobbled along between the car ruts out to find the Navan Road, to turn left on it and follow it as it ran through damp, soft, County Meath. I would stop at crossroads and twist the front wheel and handlebars in such a way that the little headlight would point up at the road signs which would send me to Dunsany and Drumshauglin and on toward the lights of Dublin. I began to be able see clearly only at the gate of Phoenix Park past numerous warm and well-lit pubs, when I was by now shivering so badly that my body's

116

shiver made the little motorcycle shiver too, and I wondered how close I was to "Empty".

That night there was a moment I still remember, the moment when the heat of the city made the temperature jump suddenly, I was in out of the damp countryside, and I found myself no longer cold. I hurried on, looking for Cabra Road or Phibsboro Road or the top of O'Connell Street, and some Butt Bridge or other so that I could get across the Liffey to Pembroke Road and into my bed.

But that time when I entered into the flat, something was waiting for me there. It was a surprise. As I opened my closet door to prepare for retiring, I saw something very strange. I saw something inside, big and dark, it was looking out at me as though it was ready to pounce on me, it looked like someone who had hanged himself, it looked like a hanged man. I stepped back, startled; I tried to instruct myself there in the darkness that it would be nothing, I ordered myself to stop quaking and to figure it out at once, that it was only something I had forgotten, I should be able to figure it out if I remained quiet. Then I saw: it was just my old religious habit, the old Holy Habit-- black cassock, black cape, and the black rope cincture, dangling from a hanger. But on the coat-hanger in the blackness it managed to look like a human figure, it looked like someone who

117

had become a ghost, it was frightening, for it was a hanged man, and it looked just like me.

10

THE MEWS IN LADD LANE

I applied for summer work as a chaplain with the US Army in Germany, serving troops strung out in "*Kaserns*" defending the West from possible Soviet invasion. My first summer was at Grafenwhoehr, the home of the 7th Army Training Command, where field artillery thumped away all night and all day with live ammunition, and tanks did the same thing. You heard the shells being fired, and one time in history there was the famous "long round", when one unit overshot its target and the shell landed in Tent City, killing a number of men from another unit. You had to watch out when driving across the dusty tank trails, for a collision might well be with a tank hurrying toward its next target. Another summer I went to Bamberg, where our motto was "Supporting the Line," we supported the line facing the forces of the Soviet Union. There were helicopter trips to Hof, and a night out with the other chaplains at a place called "Tantsplatz". In the war it had been a recuperation spot for Wehrmacht officers, and was still run by a very tough woman who had been through both war and Occupation; she was a kind of "Pauli Girl" grown older now, who shoved beer steins at US Army chaplains the same way she had to Wehrmacht Officers when she was a young girl.

I picked up some salary, and I supposed that I was helping out, but I don't think they needed me. It was not exactly like being under fire. Yet it was a distant world from Dublin, and I was beginning to forget the pain of that; the big green tanks rumbling in their cloud of dust gave a kind of peace to deal with what was going on inside me.

When I got back, Ireland was filling up with old veterans from the 1916 Easter Week Rising, preparing for the fiftieth anniversary of the heroic stand which helped free the country, and they all wore their medals out and about, and some had returned from the States. They sat around on park benches or wherever there was sun. When I walked with Anne Francis any distance back from the library, I would notice, I saw the way they looked at her. With her bright brown eyes looking out from that magnificent old Mercy habit, they noticed her, they were old heroes, always pausing and tipping their hats to her, and offering to help and opening doors for her, as if they remembered her from somewhere long ago, as if she were a heroine right out of Irish legend. When she walked abroad, with the fresh air of Ireland on her face, she was one of Yeat's great ladies, walking through the land of Irish Myth.

And one of them, a rather well-known hero, positioned himself, and would wait for her to come, each day, at the corner of Leeson Street, where he knew the beautiful Sister would have to cross when she walked to or from the Library. "--I was perfectly capable of crossing Leeson Street myself--" she said, "--but he was always there, with a tip of the hat, saying '--Let me help you across, Sister!' "

One week she disappeared; she went to London, to the British Museum, to read up on her subject, Seumas O'Kelly. When she came back, and reached the corner of Leeson Street, the same old gentleman was still there. He jumped up, and he was annoyed with her. "--Where _wair_ Ye, Sister?" he complained, "-- I've been waiting for Ye all _week!_"

But there was another individual who had had nothing to do with 1916. He was a very strange fellow in the library, was doing arcane research; he was doing Astrology; he was back there with Joachim of Flora, all that about the circling Gyres of Being; I had noticed him myself, he wore exotic symbols draped from his watch chain across his front, the huge boar's tooth is what I remember. He

121

kept his eye on her, on the beautiful American nun at desk 76. And one lunch break, he waited for her out at the top of the stairs, beside the marble memorial tablet to David Lyster, where James Joyce himself used to wait and meet people.

He explained to her that he was actually capable of foretelling a person's future, and would gladly do so for her, if she would only supply him with her exact longitude and latitude, that is, of the place of her birth. But Anne Francis was used to strange men coming up to her. She smiled and said "--*I don't give anybody my longitude and latitude!*" and went on down the stairs.

With Anne Francis come among us, it began to seem that Winter was over, there was some warmth to the sun, and I would begin to think that maybe Ireland was not what I thought it was, all damp and cold with water running down its walls. Without her, life had resembled one of those old classic black and white films about Welsh coal miners, where the dreadful siren at the top of the mine continually announces another mine disaster, and the whole town comes running, to see who the survivors are, coming up the mine shaft, with their faces covered with black, and to find out who was lost. Except that when I came up to the surface from my diggings I was caked over with the brown dust of old newspapers.

Aside from Anne Francis, there was no one to tell of certain success I had, flailing away against the face of the mine, where I followed a rich vein, for I had found and identified many pen-names, behind which famous people had been hiding. These identities were a key to their times, so that once you knew who they were, you knew what others did not. I would go down in the bucket they lowered me in, walk with my lunch pail to the spot I had been digging the previous day, and pick up my hammer again. If I was lucky, I would signal, and they would raise me to the surface. No one ever asked what I had in the bucket, or how it went. But I fervently hoped that what I was doing was pounding out my future, the only future I would ever have, isolating a vein of discovery which would establish me a discoverer of such competence that they would have to accept me, and have to give me place among my peers, and let me live my own life without fear of what others would think, or fear of what anyone could do to me.

And so we both pounded away, concentrating, ignoring much else that was happening. Whoever finished first for the day waited for the other, at the head of the mine-shaft. I would tell her about my pen names, and she told of Seumas and of her latest adventures with a certain Alphonsus Sweeney.

Mister Alphonsus Sweeney, who lived in Dun Laoghaire. He was the literary executor of Seumas O'Kelly's estate, a distant relative, I think, who had been left everything, which he kept in a large footlocker at the bottom of his bed. He went through life hauling this thing, the papers and remains of Seumas O'Kelly, it was one of the claims he had on life. He opened the lid a crack to publishers or to anyone doing research; and he would promise to open the whole thing up, under proper conditions; he seemed to promise everything to everybody, he had a grand time entirely, for he knew that it was the one last thing in life that anyone needed him for, and he was in no hurry to dispose of the contents. Alphonsus Sweeney seemed to have stepped right out of Irish Literature, he seemed to have stepped out of the pages of O'Kelly's stories, he seemed to have stepped right out from *The Weavers Grave.*

She scurried from Dublin out to the graveyard at Loughrea and over to the British Museum and to the Manchester Guardian, to track down what she had to learn about her subject as well as his tombstone in Cloon na Morav, the Meadow of the Dead. Though in the end it sometimes seemed that what she was doing was tracking down Mister Alphonsus Sweeney in Cloon na Morav, who acted as though he had read the story himself, and that it was there that he had learned so perfectly how old men are to act.

At the end of each day we told one another of our efforts, no one else cared to listen; and so each of us came to know a lot about the other's work. That is how we came to know each other, in those conversations at the end of work, explaining to one another what we were up against, what the obstacles were and what successes we had had. I would not have admitted it, but I began to live for those moments; it was those moments, which kept me alive, walking out of the library with her, up Kildare Street, past the gray eighteenth century houses. I would be lying to claim that my mind never spent much time thinking of what life would be, if the two of us were somehow ever allowed to be together. Our friendship was based on work and respect for each other. If you asked me then about the two of us, and whether we were putting our vows to the test, I would have been annoyed, that others saw a problem where there was none.

Mary Lavin thought I was at times, almost, a fool. She liked me, but considered me hopeless. When I was certain that I was not bothering her, I would go to see Mary. I would go over to The Mews, I would walk over along the Grand Canal, and knock on the outside door at Ladd Lane, and see if she was in, and willing to be disturbed--only in the afternoon, of course, or evening, not when she was writing. I would bring a bottle of red wine, which she liked, and we would talk.

When Warren was there, he would talk to her about her writing. But alone, I asked her other questions: I asked once if she believed in God. She replied, "--Oh, I don't know if there is anybody up there. But if there is, He certainly isn't worried much about _someone likes me_!" I asked her about the future of the church, and the priesthood. She said, with a wave of her hand "--Oh, there will always be a need for _you boys_, for someone like you, if that's what you're asking --just to help people _die,_ if for nothing else!"

She told of an accident, out in Meath; the local harriers had been riding by on their bikes; there was an accident, one of the boys had broken his neck. The lads came running to her: "Mary! Mary!" They shouted. There being no priest available, Mary went out into the middle of the road and cradled the boy's head in her arms, reciting the rosary for him as he died. "There will always be a need for someone like you, if only to help people die," she repeated.

One evening after returning from my summer in Bamberg, I was greeted by an invitation from Mary for supper at Ladd Lane. After the others had gone, and the two of us, slightly warmed by the red wine that we had consumed, talked about mighty things, looking at each other across the table under the bright warm glow of the Tiffany lamp shade. She held up her hand against it. Then she said, _a propos_ of nothing --although what Mary said was never really without connection to something--"Do you know that the name 'Lavin' means 'Small Hand' in Irish? It may be small, but that's a strong hand!" She made a grasping motion with it, as though she were reaching out to throttle something, which I took to be Fate or Life or the parade of events coming at her, and I understood. "---*Sometimes I think it is only the ones who reach out and grasp life and throttle it by the throat and make it do what they want who will ever succeed!*" I thought she almost was talking to herself, hardly thinking of me. But then she suddenly addressed me. She suddenly called me by the name that Warren called me and that everyone had taken up ---"Old Phelan---" she said, "--'Old Phelan', <u>*Look at that hand*</u>---" she said, making a fierce choke-hold movement with it in the air in front of us, as though grabbing something by the neck "---You know, -- *'Old Phelan'*-- those are small hands, but if there was to be a fight between the two of us, <u>you wouldn't last five minutes!</u>" I took another drink, and nodded agreement, for I knew that she was right.

She knew well enough that she herself had reached out often, and grasped her monster by the throat, and choked it, every time it popped out at her--in Molesworth Street, or in New York, or in Cannes, or in Trastevere, and she was proud of the way she had conquered. But I knew she did not think I would ever have that in

127

me. She thought I was "well spoken for" by being lodged within the priesthood, where I would be safe and would be looked after, along with the rest of the cabbage-snippers.

What I actually did do, was, in the end, enough for me. It took some time; it took I think twelve more years altogether, but in the end, in another time entirely and in my own country as well, I did follow her advice, I did finally confront the monster. I reached out and dealt with what I had to, surprised at the strength in my own two hands, and was able to walk calmly on.

But it was strange enough. It never occurred to me that I was changing, myself.

It seemed to me that Mary was softening her stand on Clerics, she had slowly changed, from someone who might be a critic of all I was to being a Mentor. I see now that it was she always who stayed the same, and that it was I who changed.

II

11

OFFICIAL VISIT

Word came to me: I was to enjoy an Official Visit. Father

Howard Kenna, the Provincial, and Father Chester Soleta were on

their way to Rome, and it would be convenient for them to stop off in

Dublin, so that I would have my Official Visit. You were supposed

to be visited every year or so, officially, it was part of the Holy Rule;

it was a check-up, to see how you were doing.

Father Soleta arrived first. It is hard to describe the

enthusiasm with which I awaited his arrival. He would be the first

member of my Order to see me in several years---I was beside

myself, that I was actually to be visited by one of my brethren; that I

would be visited right there in Dublin where I had worked for years

without any of them. I looked forward to it, rather foolishly: he

would bring it all with him, bring it all back to me, it would be the

solution to all my problems. I was eager to show my Order how I

worked, hard and faithfully, and without any Superior having to urge

me on, to rise up in the morning and to go to the library and do research, each day. I was proud that I had become so responsible. And I wanted to make sure that my visitors would see how well I striven to live the religious life, without any bells ringing for me, or any common chapel to go to.

I absolutely fell upon Father Soleta at the airport, embracing him the way a French General does, cheek to cheek. This must have struck him a little strange, for he was a person I would scarcely have spoken to at all, if we were back in the bosom of the community. The fact was that Father Soleta had always been exceedingly distant from me. He clearly regarded himself as a true academic, and regarded whatever I did as something-- well, as something he would really not be very interested in. He had the misfortune to possess some facial resemblance, I always thought, to those images of Frankenstein we see, with dark circles under the eyes, and fierce black hair falling down over an excessively large forehead. He was a good man, of course, and when he was asked to be my Official Visitor, I suppose he obeyed like a good religious. It was just that I never had much of anything to do with him, and would not have chosen to be visited by him. But the extended isolation I had endured in Dublin had the effect of transforming him completely, so that in the days before his arrival, he began to resemble the dearest friend I had.

Yet in spite of my best efforts, a pall insisted in casting itself over everything in the visit. I had deliberately put up the two of them at the Shelbourne Hotel, because of its innumerable literary connections. Every great writer in the British Isles had been connected with the place, attracted by its shabby gentility, and I thought this would not be lost on them. But Father Chester Soleta was shocked at it, he kept remarking on how old and worn the place was, comparing it most unfavorably to an "American Hotel."

When Father Kenna arrived, I was even glad to see *him*. Father Kenna was used to being Provincial, he had poor vision and thick glasses, and he plainly expected to be chauffeured around. I had arranged for a taxi at the airport; he was surprised I did not have a car. He called me "Francis". "Don't you have a *car*, Francis?" he asked. I told him No, I did not, that I went everywhere on a small motorcycle, often in the rain. His comment annoyed me very much; actually it infuriated me, for like Sister Anne Francis and Warren and all of us, I lived on next to nothing. It worried me, that he should be so far off in his assessments.

He rather quickly fell asleep, at table, tired from his transatlantic flight. I worried about how the Official Visit was going. While he kept nodding, I talked with Soleta. I gushed forth information out of my thesis, telling the latest about the year 1902,

Arthur Griffith and the Irish National Theatre Company and the various pen-names I had discovered; for a while he seemed interested. I also gushed forth about Mary Lavin, apparently a little too much. Father Kenna woke up. He asked, "---Who is this Mary Lavin you keep mentioning?" His tone startled me, for it was the tone of that old Retreat Master who used to warn us again and again, that there were only two things a priest had to look out for, "Punch and Judy." Punch of course was liquor, and Judy was "Woman." I firmly explained that Mary Lavin was a famous writer, perhaps the most famous in Ireland, and I quickly added that she was a woman well into her sixties.

"---Oh--" Father Kenna replied, "---Oh---" He closed his eyes behind his heavy glasses and went back to sleep.

I saw that I had to be very careful not to mention a name like Julia, even in passing, was in "I was talking with Warren and Julia the other day..." They might not want to know much about Warren, but they would certainly ask who Julia was. And of course I would not mention Sister Anne Francis at all, for they might see even greater danger there. I did not see that it was part of an Official Visit. Instead, we spoke about other things. Father Soleta seemed to know a lot about the composer, Darius Milhaud, and talked about him. I kept quiet, and learned something.

At the end of the Visit, Father Soleta said "--Well --We will tell them that you are working hard, and that you are very, very enthusiastic about your thesis," he laughed. "--And that you expect to finish...."

I left them at the airport; it was a relief to wave them off to Rome. They could not have failed to notice that my work was everything for me; they would give a good report. But in every other way, in the matter of renewing a warm and satisfying connection with the Order, the Official Visit had been a flop ---a rather miserable affair, really--- and it did not leave me happy.

That same evening ---after they had gone, and the two of them had begun to fade away and be absorbed back into the ranks of my Absent Brethren once again--- I decided resolutely to return to my ordinary life. But I wanted to talk with somebody, first. There was still a chance that if I hurried I might see Sister Anne Francis; the last rays of the evening sun were disappearing over Kildare Street as I skipped up the library steps. Sister Anne Francis was still there, at desk 76, trying to make use of the last light coming down out of the huge dome. I whispered that I would wait for her, outside the reading room, at the stone tablet to T. W. Lyster. She came out. My thoughts had been full of my two Official Visitors, whose heads seemed like two floating cabbages moving around on top of two black suits as they trailed me around Dublin. Now I was with her. She wanted to know at once about how the Visit had gone, for she was concerned about my priesthood. I described the Visit, and heard myself honestly telling her something of what I had just been through. But my two Official Visitors were gone now, the pair of them, with the somber gloom they brought with them; I was in her presence. I quickly asked her about her own life; and as we talked about that, I could hear in the sound of my voice that I was happy once again.

12

SALLY GAP

One day I went out by myself to Lough Dan in the Wicklow Mountains, up past Sally Gap near Mount Kippure. It was astonishingly warm, it was the kind of Spring-Summer day the Irish call "a pet", they have so few of them. I left the little motorcycle at the road and worked myself out among outcroppings of rock, out among the pines, to a spot looking down a thousand feet more to the tarn, its blue water reflecting the Irish sky. I lay myself down there among the grasses; and in the quiet, I could actually hear the waterfall across the valley, plunging from the high peat slopes under Mount Kippure. There was a thick smell like turpentine or creosote -- the pine sap and the various saps of all the heather and bracken, you could smell things growing, the air was sweet with the fluids of life. It was getting late in my time in Ireland; I was lonely, and I was sick of being lonely, I had had two years of it.

Behind me someplace, back where I could not see it, lay Dublin; I was sick unto death of it; I was tired of hearing that it was Joyce's Dublin, Yeats' Dublin; it was a hated, loved place where everything was perverted, twisted upon itself, entwined in an endless inward growth. In front of me the valley was like a bowl, huge granite cliffs cupping in the sun's lazy heat. And I heard behind me for the first time in my life, the beautiful song of the Cuckoo Bird; there was no mistaking it, even though I had heard it only on cuckoo-clocks and in Beethoven's Pastoral Symphony it was astonishing in its own reality; I heard it, and heard what the poet had heard, what man has heard going back to when bird and man differentiated themselves from the grasses, from the schist and mica of the cliffs, from one another: man and bird. I loved it, even with all the jokes about it in Joyce, about poor old Bloom. I was only beginning to know Joyce.

Then, a second cuckoo answered it, across the valley --there were two of them now, one would first call to the other, the other would answer, and it was impossible to keep the flutes and oboes of Beethoven's Pastoral Symphony out of it--the valley of the Lough filled with The Village Wedding, the Dancing of the Peasants, the Coming of the Storm. I alone was there in the valley to hear it, thinking of what men have made it mean, the beautiful song: that someone has been betrayed.

I smiled at myself; I had no one to be unfaithful to me. Each lovely one who had come along I had steeled me against, so as to be only Con-fessor to them. I preached to myself: What did you expect? This is what you wanted, isn't it? And I quoted Scripture to myself: "Unless the grain of wheat falling into the ground die, itself remaineth alone; but if it dies, it bringeth forth much fruit." It was by life itself that I was cuckolded. I had brought it on myself, had no one to blame but me. Who cared that I was lying in the grass there in the warm afternoon sun, above Sally Gap, and the cuckoos calling? I would have been better off as one of the birds of the air.

"Sally" means "reed" in Irish, and the wind in the reeds is supposed to say things that need saying, the reeds are always whispering to us.

I do not recall any reeds at Sally Gap; but if there were any, I know what they would have been telling me. They would have been telling me what Julia already knew, what Warren knew, what everyone knew, very likely what Anne Francis herself knew, and which only I among them appeared not to know. And yet, all the same, I knew it too,

I knew it as well.

They would have been saying what was not allowed to be said, the thought which I never permitted myself to think: it was the thought that, in the end, I no longer was able to believe that magnificent body of faith in which I had once believed.

I would, therefore, somehow have to gather up the courage to "leave", and if Sister Anne Francis could shake herself free as well, why, the two of us might then be able to spend our lives together. Though I am certain that I did not think it in precisely those terms;

I more thought it in the sound the reeds make, when the wind rustles its secrets through them, for those who have ears to hear.

The moment changed; the sun could be perceived to have moved on a little angle; my moment was going, I could not hold it, it was gone. I got back on my little motorcycle, cranked it gently and got it rolling quietly down around the shoulder of Tibradden, and Table Rock, stopped briefly to look out over it all: out over the little town of Stepaside ("Step" I heard them call it, "--Step is our Local") and the little town of Golden Ball. Rathfarnham, of course, below there, then Ranelagh, leading on to Leeson Street, Stephen's Green, on out to Dublin Bay, the Ben of Howth, everything that I would soon be leaving. I hated my life. It was all down there someplace, and I hated it.

I coasted in gear down into Rathfarnham, stopped at the Yellow House for a Guinness. Then I returned in a kind of resignation back to bloody Upper Baggot Street.

We remember moments, times when Reality seems to gather itself together for us; I remember that moment, after Warren was gone ---warmth of the grass, song of Beethoven, the cuckoos calling, one to another, across the valley.

But the sun still had some time to run before I would decide about such matters. Up there, on the gray screes above Lough Dan, the cold dampness started to return, and whatever the wind said to me, it whispered in vain. With all the cuckoos in the world calling out to me, I heard nothing.

13

FUGITIVE FROM JUSTICE

(Anne Francis invited me and another priest, Father Tom Jordan from Chicago, to Muckross for a cup of tea. Another nun getting ready for the visit asked Sister Anne Francis how she would tell the two of us apart? Anne Francis thought for a moment. And then replied, "---Well---Father Jordan looks like a Chicago policeman, and Father Phelan looks like a fugitive from justice!")

But I have been putting off Ciaran Ryan, handsome and athletic; a fuller account must be given of him. Perhaps he had more to do with the way I felt up there in Sally Gap than I was aware of. Father Ciaran Ryan did research at the CERN nuclear laboratories in Switzerland, and was Ireland's greatest physicist. He worked at their huge atomic collider, under the ground, perhaps with the Big Bang theory, perhaps with how everything began ---I do not know much about it. But he was Mary Lavin's idea of what a man should be, I knew that --you know what your friend's think-- for Mary made it clear that she thought he would make a good match for Sister Anne Francis, just in case the two of them ever left the religious life. She was not pushing it, mind you, but you know, just in case they did. He was my idea of a man, too, it would take a Muse of Fire to describe him, and he reminded me of those handsome Irish heroes of my childhood, Errol Flynn playing the pirate and Tyrone Power the gunman in the movies I went to on Saturday afternoons. And he was brilliant too, and he liked Sister Anne Francis, we all knew that; I knew it. He even followed her to Oxford once, when she was taking a group of students on a tour of England. He simply showed up, at their hotel entrance, and took her out to the best restaurant she had ever been in, The Elizabeth in Oxford, with its candles and elegant old wood, and with the finest Sherries and quiet, intelligent talk.

I minded what I thought was my own business, and went soaring in the clouds. I knew that I was a deep and loyal friend; I considered that I was not in competition with anybody, any idea of rivalry would have been shocking and repulsive to me. And Sister Anne Francis, I knew well enough, was not con-templating romance. She accepted his hospitality graciously, and she never forgot The Elizabeth, but then she returned to her American students, who were all up waiting for her, so that they could ask her "Who was that *handsome fellow*, Sister-- the one who came to see you?" I refused to let myself entertain certain thoughts. Whatever else happened, I felt supremely confident of Anne Francis's friendship.

I doubt if much of that way of life will ever be present in the world, again. We were keeping our vows. I felt that I held my head down, concentrating on my work. But the two older women who ran the Baggot Bridge Book Shop saw everything; they saw everyone come and go; every famous writer passed through, and would sign their book for them. They saw Anne Francis, and they saw me. Miss Flannery said once, almost as if scolding me, "---Do you not know that she is the most beautiful woman in Dublin?" But there was also some advice for me. Miss Flannery had seen on television, gliders, out at Baldonnell near Tallaght. She told me she thought it might be good for me to get away from my thesis, and go sailing in the clouds.

I thought about that; I needed to get away. I took her advice, I went out there, and joined The Dublin Gliding Club. I was never much good at it. You were supposed to watch the seagulls, they knew how to do it. But our planes seemed to always keep coming down or were always reported missing near ancient Tallaght; Tallaght is where the Tuatha are buried, the First Peopling of Ireland, the old heroes, who historians said "fought three battles, during their time above the ground." Then they went under the ground, and became Gods.

Those two names, Tuatha and Tallaght, still make my teeth chatter, I think of the moist hedgerows and a worry that someone is

143

down, and maybe hurt, on a cold Sunday afternoon. And it may have been there among the clouds that I began to change. Up there with the seagulls, I was coming to know that my problem was not always what I thought it was. It was with what I believed, and what the Church taught. Each Sunday, after I finished flying, I would look back up there, where I had been, among the clouds, and think of how I preferred that to my life on earth. And I would go back to my empty room in Ballsbridge.

But I should tell you. Some years later, as Anne Francis and I were moving closer, Father Ciaran Ryan died, in a skiing accident, in Switzerland. He had gone to help a friend. He fell into a crevasse; his body was discovered in the Spring. His death all alone at the bottom of a glacier deeply affected Anne Francis. People had always tried to tell me that we were rivals, that Ciaran and I had thoughts for Anne Francis. I refused to honor such comments.

Instead, we were all walking, above the ground, together. That's what we were doing. We were like the Tuatha, in their time above the ground.

That is what life is, isn't it---a time we all spend above the ground? We spend time, in various places, on very different grounds. Some of them can have strange, Romantic names, like the ones they go skiing on, around Geneva: like Courmayeur and Courcheval and Les Arcs, but which can also be dangerous. It is no secret, that none of it is forever, though we do not think about that a lot. And some of my time, I spent, back then, over Clondalkin and Saggart, a time when I went flying in the clouds above Tallaght, unhappy with my life on earth, and on my way, really, to Anne Francis, without ever knowing it.

Fugitive From Justice? Not really; maybe from too many Superiors. I have not done much wrong, but I have often felt like someone out of the Bible, like God's Jonah, told to convert the Pagan City of Ninevah, which was too big for me. And I do think of him, the missing Ciaran, though not as much as I should. We were never in competition, I think, and he was no rival of mine. He was a great man, and I do sometimes find myself thinking of him: of poor gifted Ciaran Ryan, lying in his icy crevasse, dying all alone.

14

THE SHEETED DEAD

In the most high and palmy state of Rome
--A little ere the mightiest Julius fell--
The graves stood tenantless, and the sheeted dead
Did squeak and gibber in the Roman streets.

--Hamlet, speaking of Ghosts

When Warren left, the young American girls felt bereft---
Julia, Trish and the rest. A priest, you were supposed to listen to
their problems, without noticing how beautiful they were, without
getting yourself involved. I succeeded in doing this, at great effort.
But one day I overheard one English girl advising another, to go talk
to a priest. "-*That's what those boys are for!*" she was saying.

I thought to myself; there were times when I wondered what
we boys were for. As time went on, I wondered some more. I tried to
assist people, but I am afraid I was not much help.

We were all lonely. Others, too, had returned to America--there simply was not enough left to sustain life. Dublin began to be over-whelming with its gray skies. It became a city of empty streets with old newspapers swirling in corners; I thought of the Russian poet Achmatova in her loneliness:

> *I went to your place in the wintry time of the year;*
>
> *but it was empty; and you were not there.*

I knew I should speak with Sister Anne Francis; I had always known that I should be speaking with her. But how could I ever speak with her, and say what I had to say.

("--- You do understand that I move with the students half my age because I cannot be with you?") I wondered if somehow what Warren had said might not be right.

I dropped off George Moore's endless *Memoirs* back at the main desk and started walking. It would be a long walk, from the Library all the way out to the Hostelry at Muckross. My intention was to go to see Sister Anne Francis, and have a talk with her there. I thought that I would go up to the door and ring the doorbell, and,

147

with my Roman collar much in evidence, have them go tell the American nun, Sister Anne Francis Cavanaugh, that she had a visitor who wanted to speak with her about something. But the more into the walk I got, the less sure I was of myself. Her hostelry, though it was not called a "convent", was a most imposing place, with a wall around it, and you were not---even a priest was not--- expected to just drop in.

I was not even certain of the right way to her convent. I went up Kildare Street and along the Green, and out Leeson Street until it became Morehampton. I supposed I was on the right track. My thoughts were not new, they were the same old ones. Young Julia had been a worry. It had not been too surprising that a man living alone would smile at a young girl, and enjoy the smiles he received back; nothing would come of that. Sister Anne Francis, however, was a very different matter. We were in similar states of life. What would happen-- in the name of God, and my two nun sisters, and my holy mother-- if everything started all over again, with someone like *that?* There was nothing either of us could do about our lives. We were entitled to a good friendship, but that was all. And if I did speak to her, what would I speak about?

I came to within sight of the corner of her convent wall. Ireland is filled with walls; they have to have somewhere to put the stones. All the big Estates have walls around them, as high as twenty feet, which can run for miles. My people built them, for a shilling a day, walling off their own countryside from themselves for the sake of the lordly English.. There is always green on the other side of the wall, and you seldom see the Manor House, it is so far away. But you do not know what a wall can be until you have met an Irish Convent wall. It is of the mind, and of the faith, as much as it is of stone

I stood there, on the damp Irish sidewalk. Knocking on the door did not seem such a good idea. Perhaps the wall was mostly in my own mind. I know now that she would have welcomed me, I would have been well received. She was ahead of me in what she thought. When she had surprised me by saying, "*The religious life is under attack, Father!*" It startled me, to hear anyone talk that way. She would have been the best person on earth for me to talk with at that moment.

Instead, I turned, and headed home; I walked back down Marlborough Road, past Herbert Park and the children playing in the lengthening shadows, to the Clyde Road and along Raglan Road, to where I lived, as much alone as ever, and no closer to a solution.

After that, I spent a lot of time walking, I don't know how long. I thought about what those fellows on the boat had told me, that everything was going to be changed during my absence. They had laughed at my going to Ireland, and had said that I was going back to " the Middle Ages". I wondered what changes they were making now. But they had been right, I was walking around Dublin in my own Middle Ages, carrying them with me, thinking of Abelard, and Duns Scotus, and the School of Paris, and William of Sens, with his flying buttresses. I turned myself inward and outward, turned myself upwards and turned myself downwards, for my spirit was back there tumbling in the clouds over Tallaght. I wondered if maybe I had been cast up on one of those Ultimate Islands that George Moore spoke about, in his *Dead Life*. It is not surprising that I had started "to show symptoms." I knew I must be careful; I began to think of checking myself in to Baggot Street Hospital, for a check-up.

Old songs sang themselves at me, whether I liked them or not: *"It's a long, long time from May to September"* kept repeating itself, though I asked it to go away. I found myself scoffing at what I called my "life". Frank O'Connor, at Mary's place, had insisted to me, over and over, that I acquaint myself with a great story called *The Overcoat* by the Russian writer Nikolai Gogol: "--*We all came out from under Gogol's Overcoat!*" he would say, in that great booming voice of his. I grew afraid when I would hear him saying that, for he knew a lot about me, and when I finally read it, I saw the story of a pitiful creature who had his coat stolen, the story of a man who had lost his only possession, who had lost the thing he was living for, and who had to roam the boulevards of the city in the Russian nights searching for it, talking to himself, saying to himself over and over, "There now --That is how it is, *That is just how it is!*" And even though I knew that it was a great story, and his favorite, I was astonished and frightened that Frank O'Connor would think that anything in it should apply to me.

I was now in Dublin alone, that was clear, and Dublin was becoming a haunted city, filled with contagious fogs. The American Tom O'Keefe stood at every corner waving his endless thesis on Irish Humor, his yellow tablets full of interminable fools-cap, the sheets of yellow fools-cap waving in the winds of Duke Street, or the winds of Great Ship Street, or in the winds of Molesworth Street, O'Keefe asking each passer-by if it was funny, was his thesis on Irish humor now sufficiently funny, or should it be made more so?

And so I hurried through Dublin's streets. I hurried now to keep warm, to keep living.

You found yourself wondering how others were doing. "--What became of So-and-so?" you would ask fearfully, "--What ever happened to them?" You dreaded to hear the answer. And when you heard that they were gone, or had died (and several did in fact die) you gritted your teeth, or whatever it is that you do-- people do different things. Some people pull themselves together. You can see them when they hear the bad news about somebody else: you can see them reach for the edges of their jacket or their coat to pull them closer, they tighten their belts a notch, they look down and dust them-selves off, from an invisible snow, they take a deep breath, and head up the next street. They walk up that Next Street with their tightened belt now too tight, with their teeth on edge, with their sleeves cleared of all imaginary flecks, a deep breath held within their lungs which they are afraid to exhale, afraid even to let it out, from between their teeth.

As winter came on, the darkness of evening would start to begin in mid- afternoon around 3 o'clock and you realized how far north you were. You were surprised really, how the sun disappeared, it simply went elsewhere, south with the cranes for the winter. It left everyone to the wind rolling in off the Atlantic, damp, coming up each street, which was what turned Dublin into a city of ghosts. One by one we were all turning into ghosts.

I must have attended Laurence Olivier's *Hamlet* at this time, or maybe Richard Burton's, or that of John Gielgud. And I felt I was coming close to my end, when I began to hear the voice of one of them--sometimes Olivier, sometimes Burton, some-times Gielgud reciting the same lines from Hamlet, -- the voice of his conscience, Horatio. I began to hear those eloquent voices speak certain words over and over, those lines about "the sheeted dead" --of what happened at the death of Julius Caesar:

In the most high and palmy state of Rome

-- A little ere the mightiest Julius fell

--The graves stood tenantless, and the sheeted dead

Did squeak and gibber in the Roman streets.

I passed the Huguenot Cemetery in Baggot Street; it had always seemed calm enough, I had never seen any movement there; and yet as time went by I began to wonder. The compelling voices kept saying the same line, repeating "squeak and gibber" and "the sheeted dead" as if trying to get my attention, until I thought I felt a hand pulling at my shoulder, and wanted to hurry on, to avoid the contagious fogs.

The Sheeted Dead. The departed spirits, they say, at certain times, do rise and haunt the earth. They meet the Souls of the Just and frighten them. They are given speech, a kind of gibber and squeak, in which they pose fragments of remembered things to the

153

Faithful-- half-doctrines, Moral Cautions, pieces of old Prayers, antique Dogmas, forgotten Resolu-tions: "Quickly return to your Father's House," they say, "--lest you perish of wretchedness and hunger!" At times it may be a line from an old hymn,

"--*Pray for the Wanderer, pray for me!"* While at others it can sound like Mister Death himself, saying fiercely, "*Thou Fool,* this day thy Soul is required of thee!"

* * * * *

"DOCTOR SYNGE WILL SEE YOU NOW!" the nurse said. She was speaking to me from the slit between sheets she had arranged to hang down around my bed as curtains for privacy, because I was a priest. I had gotten sick, you know; I was in Baggot Street Hospital. The nurses were all Catholic, the Doctors all Protestant. I had gotten sick working on a thesis which included among other things the plays of John Millington Synge. His relative, a Doctor, still alive and in his eighties, was resident physician there, and he would see me, to cure me. It was confusing: maybe he was really nothing but a foot-note. Now, looking down with his white hair, he did seem something out of the Irish Dramatic Movement. One more ghost arising. These ghosts kept coming back out of my thesis; I was no longer sure of things: he must surely belong to the

154

sheeted dead. And I myself, then-- was I the tenant of some grave? Was I now one of those to Gibber and to Squeak?

Doctor Synge did not squeak. He was kind. He tested me, in many ways, and said in the end that there was nothing wrong with me. That the only thing wrong was my thesis and that when I finished that, I would be all right. All the Med students went through something like that. Could I not go somewhere for a rest? Did my Order (he was Protestant, I supposed, but Irish enough to know about Orders; he expected me to have an Order, or at least a Diocese; he knew how these things worked.) Was there not some place I could go to, in the sun, where I could go, and recuperate, before coming back to finish up?

"--Rome--" I said. "--We have a house in Rome. Near the Vatican, it is on one of the Roman Roads, on the Via Aurelia Antica. If I go there they will have to take me in."

O for a beaker, full of the warm South.

Doctor Synge's eyes roved absently above my head at the mention of the old Roman Road, he was thinking. He surprised me; he said, "--I followed the Via Latina once, all the way to Terracina, and to the ruins of Paestum, when I was studying Medicine..." He paused and added wistfully, "-and on to Capua--old Capua-- Santa

Maria Capua Vetere...." He stood there holding his stethoscope, thinking of ancient things. He said that I would be alright, then he went off, returning to the land of my thesis, I supposed, back to the year 1902, back with Arthur Griffith, and Molly Allgood and *Riders to the Sea*, to the time of the Boer War. Perhaps he went back to being a foot-note again. Or perhaps it was I who went off, sailing away, the owls of sleep at each corner of the bed, dreaming me across the seas, past the Brecon Beacons of Wales, over chop of Channel to Cherbourg, through French cathedral towers up where the gargoyles are, past Viarregio and Sestri Levante, over Rapallo, toward Rome.

I woke up. The nurse's smiling voice was saying "He's behind those sheets, Sister." The sheets parted, and Sister Anne Francis stuck her head in; it was Anne Francis, she had come to find me.

She laughed. "---I couldn't find you because of these sheets around your bed!

--- *You're* the only one with *sheets*, Father! --They have you curtained off from the other patients because you are a *priest!*" She always laughed at the privileges that priests were given.

She had missed me, and had gone searching my haunts: She had gone to the Misses Flannery and King at the Baggot Bridge

Bookshop, and then she said she had to go to the newspaper kiosk in the middle of the street outside the Intercontinental Hotel:

"--Where is that American priest who buys a paper here every day?" She asked; and the woman there said, "He lives over in number 67--- but he's up in Baggot Street Hospital now," for everyone in Dublin knows everything.

Anne Francis told me that my motorcycle was alright, she had gotten young Tom Campion to park it in the greenhouse at Haddington Road. She said "Sister Marie Pauline and I cleaned out your apartment for you. --The *grease* from all that bacon!

-- *No wonder you got sick*..."

I laughed. Her voice might as well have been saying, "Lazarus arises! Lazarus come forth!" That was what I heard. I had known that she would come. I knew that somehow she would find me. I knew that she would be there. *"For they shall love as pure spirits; they shall love all before the face of God, and they shall know, even as they are known."* We were always fortunate, the two of us, in one another. Sheep may safely graze.

Then, I did it; I was weak and wobbly, but gathered enough together to purchase a train ticket. I left my thesis and the few things

I owned with Anne Francis, I left my life with her knowing it would be safe. I remember accurately: I left Dublin at page 72, and headed for Rome.

I found myself back again at Brig, Switzerland, where the train rumbled into the Simplon Tunnel, into the darkness underneath the mountains. The train carriage went grinding down with us to Italy, rocking from side to side in the dark, the smell of the brakes burning back against the incline. The train circles three times, you know, inside the mountain, it is a masterpiece of engineering; the birds have found it; migrating, they go in one end and circle and circle, and come out the other; I have done it often --perhaps you might say, I have done it with the birds. It is something that Hendrick Ibsen told of, coming down out of North Europe in his time of black despair. He said that everything he ever wrote was only an expression of what happened in the moment of bursting out from that darkness into the warm light of day. He said that it was only about that, being born again out of the womb of Mother Earth. I remember, from deep within the tunnel, the sight of a trailing vine, shining in the sunshine at the mouth of the tunnel, a spray of waterfall playing with it, tossing it this way and that, the melting snows of the Alps splashing down in the Italian sunshine; unless it was Ibsen, and not me, watching it for mile after mile, watching it come nearer and nearer, until finally the train carriage broke out into it all, into the sun itself and the bright painted walls of Italy.

Unless someone else told me about it. It happens all the time; you are held in darkness, something will not let you go. You hope for a sign, that this sleep is not unto death. You listen for sounds. You hear the owl cry your name. You see light, and move toward its warmth. The past is a winding sheet at your wrists; it hangs on to your wrists as you would lift them to pray. Trailing behind you the winding sheets of the grave, you step out into sunlight, blinded by the brightness of life. Behold, I come.

"Hello. *--You are late. --You were expected much earlier.*" It was Father Mullahy who greeted me at the door, in steel-rimmed spectacles, pointing to his watch. His "Pontiff" brand plastic collar rose high around the chin, stiffly, his hair was parted exactly down the middle of his head, his voice speaking everything in a kind of iced holiness. He explained that he was now Assistant Superior. I had forgotten what they looked like; except for my two official visitors, I had not seen any of them for three years. I paused a moment in the doorway, fearing what was behind him, for it startled me, it all seemed to be trying get out, trying to flutter out past him, the pungent scent of years past: peeling paint of Corby Hall, used steam of chapel radiators, polished wax of long hallway floors, tingling feel of terrorized youth, stench of Little Sem, smell of Novitiate Soap, and the black serge of Final Authority.

I knew that I was back, back among them all; I was with Mullahy, I was back with iced holiness; I was back in the Bosom of the Community, where I had begun. It was the end of a journey, no mistake. That sheeted thing, my Soul, had flapped its way through the darkness to find it: the most high and palmy state of Rome.

16

"NO MORE WORDS!"

"Do you want to see the Holy Father? *Up close?"* Lou Coutu said. We would have to get up very early, for the "station" next day was to be at San Pietro in Vinculi. At dawn, Lou stood me there on the church steps. He knew just where to put me. "--*The Holy Father will pass right by here*," he whispered, "-- *You should be able to touch him!*". And sure enough a black limousine drove up, and out came Pope Paul the Sixth. I was excited to see Montini himself, I remember those ears, and the holy smile, for he blessed me and said I was a good boy as he mounted the steps to say Mass at Saint Peter in Chains.

I was not a Roman. To be a Roman was to know where the "stations" were. To be a Roman was to be fast track; it meant that you were, within the confines of the order, jokingly, but still very seriously, said to be *"papabile"* --that you were suitable material to be made Pope. That meant that one day they would see the white smoke coming out, and that you were Superior General, or maybe President of Notre Dame. It did happen; it happened to Tom Barrosse; he one day did become Superior General, even though he had been Chicken Man, and had worked alongside of me, killing chickens, back in the seminary. There was a short list of the *papabile*, but it was forever kept " *in pectore"*, in the secret breasts of those who did the appointing, and you knew you were not on it.

When I showed up in Rome, I felt like some creature from the Outback arriving, hopping into the center of things, like somebody from the Far Hebrides and the very edge of Christendom, knowing nothing, not even rudimentary facts, such as who was on the Holy Roman Rota, the marriage tribunal which presided over requests from all over the Christian world to dissolve marriages, to annul marriage vows. One Canon Lawyer who assisted the Court was called the *Defensor Vinculis*--the Defender of the Bonds of Matrimony, or quite literally, the Keeper of the Chains. "What God has joined together, Let no man put asunder" the Church believes, and so there is one figure at the court who resembles the Devil's Advocate, who defends the marriage contract itself, whose job is to keep any dissolution from happening, to keep people together, to keep the bonds intact.

Most of the priests at the house in Rome had been, at one time or another, *Defensor Vinculis.* The house was full of those who had protected the bond, keepers of the holy chains. There was Ed Heston, there was Monsignor Doheny, there was Bernard Ransing. Those had all been my seminary superiors; and I was still in awe of them. I knew I would never grow up until I would stop being in awe of them. Until as an adult, I beat them, at a game of cards, even, or was confident enough to able to joke with them about anything. Or even better, until I *did* something --like finish my thesis and get my Doctorate, or write a book. But there were smart new young ones among them, like Michael Novak and Dave Burrell and James Burtchaell who would go on to their own kind of fame-- the new young *papabile* of the order, and people like Charlie Schleik who apparently had popped out of his mother's womb a fully formed *Defensor Vinculis.* What came naturally to them never came naturally to me, or did not come at all; with ease they spouted the names of Prelates: Valerio Cardinal Valerian, Hilario Cardinal This and Aegidio Cardinal That, and there was at least one Settimeo -- all heads of various Congregations, they rattled off these names as if they were the names of baseball players: I'll trade you two Valerios for one Aegidio. I was back on the boat, back among the *periti.*

I however seemed like some ghost at the door from Ireland, from such place as they would never be caught in. They had made it to the center of things, their careers were marvelously on track, while I remained for them still a boy vaguely remembered from First Theology; poor at Canon Law, poor at everything; amusing, indeed, talented perhaps, but in unnecessary ways, even, granted, sincere, but really, almost, a fool. What was I doing in Rome with them? "--Why is he *here?*" They wanted to know; "--What is he *doing* among us?" And when they were told that I was recuperating, they dispensed me from their concerns, for I became a poor fellow, --what at Oxford is called a "sizar" --and being a poor fellow was sufficient.

If they had known that what I was in recuperation from....if Mullahy or Heston or Ransing had known that what the Community was spending its money and time on was my restoration from being surrounded by young beauty... But I refused to think about it; that way meant destruction. They would know nothing of my good intentions; they would not know about walking along Waterloo Road and Baggot Street, with Thomas a Kempis for a companion, turning myself upwards and turning myself downwards.. They would only hear scandalous reports of a cleric, frequently seen in the company of beautiful young women, and who, moreover, went around hatless.

The house in Rome was on the Via Aurelia Antica, a true Roman road, covered over with blacktop. It is the great road of Civilization, carrying things to Provence and Paris and London, before jumping across to places like Boston and Detroit and Spokane.

I walked out of the house, on great walks, along the Via Aurelia Antica. I was there to get better. I made myself think of other things. I interested myself in Roman aqueducts--the Virga, the Claudian, the Julian, and the fountains of water they served. "--*L'Eau Vive*," I said to myself. There was a college the order sent our men to, in Belgium, called "L'Eau Vive". Its name meant Living Waters, a phrase taken from the words of Christ, I think, when He says that every one who believes will have a Fountain of Living Waters within his Soul. Or maybe it is from one of those mentionings of a fountain of water in the desert. I used to spend long moments looking up at the living, thundering fountains of Rome. I loved the water; it did me good, it seemed to be flowing into my Soul and bringing life with it. I traveled to each of the Seven Hills of Rome, and even discovered a new one, never mentioned: Monte Testaccio, a man-made mountain composed from discarded shards of pots tossed off of bi-rimes and tri-rimes on the Lungo Tevere, which over the ages had mounted high, and now had a cross on it. But I never became a True Roman, for it is said that the test of a true Roman is if they can tell the waters of the different aqueducts simply by taste. I could not do that, but wished I could.

This time, I did not have to wear a Roman Hat; I did not have to clamp it down over my ears and have the prostitutes of the Appian Way yelling *"--Aie Padre!"* and laughing at me. There weren't any Roman Hats left; there were no Roman Hats on the ivory coat-rack, or anywhere else that I could see; those had all disappeared, along with much else. And I began to see that times had changed; I sensed, back in the House, that nothing was like it used to be; the whole world was changing. It was 1966; but what I had failed to realize, and was now only slowly beginning to understand, was that things were changing even more inside the church than outside. Those fellows on the boat had been right, when they had said, "Francis, we are changing everything! Francis, when you come back, you will not recognize *anything!*"

I walked and walked. I thought about Dublin, and wondered if I was getting better. I still thought of the various Julias and the Patrices, from time to time, but not as often as I once did. I wondered if I would be able to finish up when I got back into all that.

And I thought also a lot about Father Bernard Ignatius Mullahy, from Fitchburg, Massachusetts. He had been my teacher.

One of the things I always associated Mullahy with was a vivid story he told us, back in a course called Ascetical Theology. He hauled into class one day a great tome by Saint John Climacus, one of the Doctors of the Church, and read us a story from the *Divine Ladder of Ascent*. It is one of those handbooks of the spiritual life, it teaches you how to live the life of the Soul.

At Saint Catherine's Monastery, on the slopes of Mount Sinai, there was a holy man named Stephen. He was a Keeper of the Gates: the Ladder of Ascent, the way to sanctity, rose behind him, steps carved out of the rock leading up to the summit of the mountain, where God had appeared to Man, and it was Stephen who tested you to see whether you should be allowed to pass, to begin the ascent of Sinai. But on the night of his death, the story as told by John Climacus is that he was involved in a great and final dispute, with evil spirits tempting him; the other monks listened outside his door while he struggled through the night, they heard him saying "But it is true" and "--It is not true." Then in the morning they went to look, and found him dead, with his head held in his hands like a person thinking, pondering, like Hamlet, thinking himself to death. They left him there as he was; the dry air of the desert mummified him in that position. Tourists can see them today, the dry bones in the shape of a human, contemplating reality. James Joyce meant that, I think, when he said : "Stephen no longer interests me; he has assumed a shape that cannot be changed."

Mullahy had read us the story from John Climacus years before, in First Phil-osophy; it had rattled around in my skull with everything else I was taught. Whenever I thought of him, I thought of things like Stephen with his head in his hands, and the Ladder of Ascent; Mullahy was all my yesterdays rolled up together, or surely most of them.

I was out of step with the rest of the House; I would go out in the morning and walk on into the heat of Rome, while the Romans were wise enough to be moving toward their siesta. Storekeepers rolled down their metal grills noisily in front of my face, and I would keep walking. By the time they started cranking them up again, ready for business, it was time for me to go back to the House. As I came in from the heat of Rome one day, beginning to want to get back to Dublin, Father Mullahy was at the door of the Generalate, waiting for someone to who would talk to him.

"---They don't want to listen to you!" he was saying, to nobody, as I came in.

"---They just don't want to listen to what you have to say!" Father Mullahy kept repeating it, and shaking his head. I was taken aback; I did not know what he meant, and had to ask him who he was referring to.

"---Why, the *students,* " he said, "---They don't want to listen to your years of experience! I was talking with two of them yesterday, giving them the benefit of experience, and do you know what they said to me? They said ' *--No More words! --We have had enough words, we don't want to listen to any more of them!* ' Now what do you suppose they meant by that? *Where are they getting this*?"

He was talking about the seminarians. "-- They laughed at me, they just laughed, and told me they did not want to hear anything I had to say!" He shook his head, utterly unbelieving. "--They do not even wear the holy habit any more," he added, "-- Of course, I never thought that it was all that important in itself, either-- it was what it *stood* for..."

He was all my Superiors, talking to me, all the Superiors and Assistant Superiors I had ever had. I had had a lot of them; I think I had more Superiors over me than anybody ever had in the history of the world. But I was surprised; it was the first time he had ever really spoken to me. He was actually speaking to me on his own level, at last. It certainly sounded different. Of course, I was in no shape to think about this; I was still recuperating. You see, I was recuperating from something like the Tenth Century. You could say I was coming in from the cold; I was coming from as far back as the Late Middle Ages, at least. Maybe earlier; I think I may have been journeying from as far back as the Synod of Whitby, and the year 664. This may not mean much to anyone, but that's all right --all I am trying to say is that I think, maybe, I was worse than Mullahy.

I went out into the corridor that day, and walked into chaos: the seminarians were all painting signs. They were down on their knees painting huge protest-signs, and stapling them to poles, for they were going to march next day. When they held them up, the signs said,

NO MORE WORDS!

I still don't know where it came from, "No more words." I think the line occurs in Samuel Beckett. It is one of the passwords for the student protest movement of the 60s. It had apparently reached even the seminarians of the Church, in Rome. They were painting protest signs as I stood there, in the hallway of the Collegio di Santa Croce, on the Via Aurelia Antica, in the Year of our Lord 1966, with my eyes staring, trying to take it all in. It felt like being in the middle of The Education of Henry Adams, as he tries to make sense of what he is living through; I felt like Alexis de Tocqueville, observing the march of events, on his travels.

I wanted to know more, so I came over a little closer.

Two of the seminarians were from Germany. They were personable, and creative, and entertained us all. Their two names were Helmut and Heintz; I thought this comical, for it made me think of Hans and Fritz. They were from Berlin; I think they were the kind of young German boys of that period, the kind you saw in the famous picture of the boy hurling a stone at an approaching Russian tank during the uprisings. The boy in the picture is a European boy, with low cut shoes and short pants as though he has been mountain climbing, and you can see where the rock in his hand has come from: the street is torn up at his feet, they have been engaged in the old European custom of tearing up the street for ammunition to throw at the enemy. The tank is a Russian T-34, its huge gun aimed downward from the turret trying to get the boy in its sights. Maybe there is a laughing soldier inside, and maybe not, for the muzzle is menacing. And the boy is about to bounce a rock off the tank's sloping steel sides.

I wanted to gain some sense of what was going on. I went over to one of them--either Heintz or Helmut, I was not sure. He was painting a big "NO!". I asked him what it was they were doing? What were they going to do?

He explained that they were going to make a march of protest next day at their university ---"the Greg"-- at the Roman Pontifical Gregorian University, the *Gregorianum,* where the Jesuits have always taught the best students from around the world how to be priests.

I took me a long time to digest this. The brightest Catholic seminarians brought from all over the world to study in Rome how to become priests were going to go on strike against the Gregorian University? Where they studied Sacred Theology and Canon Law and Liturgy? The answer appeared to be, clearly, Yes. They were going to make "Demands". They were going to march "in the Platz" --on the square outside the Gregorian-- with their signs NO MORE WORDS-- and make demands upon the University. Which would have to be met, or they were going to go on strike!

I thought some more; I knew I was holding Helmut back, (he said he was Helmut) from painting more signs. But I had to ask. "What will you do if they refuse your demands? What if the Jesuits simply do not back down?" I asked, hesitatingly. It seemed the strangest question I had ever asked in my life. He waited patiently until he finished putting in a huge exclamation point, after " NO MORE WORDS."

"--Then we will pick up the Square and *trow* it at them!" he said. "We will reach down and pick up the stones and start *trowing*!"

I suppose I arched my eyebrows. I don't know what I did. I was in no shape for this sort of thing. I must have looked a lot like Father Mullahy.

What Helmut was telling me had a profound effect. He was saying that they were going to pick up the small streets and hurl them upon the great. I was not a Roman, did not know which square the Greg was on, the one they were going to pick up and start throwing, the next day, when they carried signs. I found out that it was on the Piazza della Pilotta. At first I thought it was named for Pontius Pilate, and that they were going to honor him by crashing stones through the holy windows of their House of Theology, trying to get the Jesuit's attention. But then I found out that it was named for a kind of ancient handball, which had been played there. Perhaps that was why the idea of throwing things came to Helmut's mind. Bouncing stones off the walls where generations of them had scrupulously taken notes-- taking notes on the doctrines of Merely Sufficient Grace, taking notes on The Deposit of Faith, taking notes on Canon 2342, ("Women who violate the papal enclosure of religious men in solemn vows,") or on Ex-communication ("Whoever lays violent hands upon a Prince of the Church," Canon 2343,) taking notes on the Binding Force of Conscience.

I began to think that it was all over, then. I began to hear the song of the woodsman, the twang of axes shaking the tallest of trees. The greatest one of all was falling, and its crash would resound through the forest, and shake the earth as it fell.

I had grown up among them from a little boy starting on the green lawns of Holy Cross Seminary; I used to think Mickey Fiedler was mad when he said, like ancient Laocoon, that it could all be taken away, that if we were not careful, it could all blow away. Now, there in Rome, I wondered if that priest of Troy had not foretold rightly, about the falling of the walls, and if I was not watching the prophecy begin to fulfill itself. I thought of Jeremiah the Prophet on Good Friday: "See how the City solitary sits" which had always made me think of Christ, weeping for Jerusalem.

Suddenly, an overwhelming sense of energy came over me. I wanted to go back, and finish, and do whatever it was that I had to do. I wanted to get out, to get out of this, to get out of Rome, and to return to my work. I wanted to talk with Anne Francis about it. I felt like looking for my things and buying a ticket.

Next day, they went marching off with their signs, to join the universal student protest movement of the 1960s, which had reached even to the seminary, which had reached even Rome, had reached up under the very eaves of the Vatican. I watched them go off, from a window.

But the Jesuits weren't Jesuits for nothing. They had handled the Reformation and had endured the Tower of London and Recusancy and Cathrine the Great of Russia, and they knew how to handle a parade of 60's seminarians. They simply declared a free day, in honor of Saint Fidelis of Sigmaringen, or somebody --perhaps one of their own Jesuit martyrs. It worked, the marchers threw away their signs. They went home and planned a house picnic. But I thought, if this had happened at the Vatican's own seminary in Rome, what else might happen? What could things be like in America? I decided I would think about that later.

The last morning at breakfast, I watched Mullahy. He had finished before me, but was just sitting there, hand to his temple in thought.

Bernard Ignatius Mullahy had always been present in my life, an eternal Assistant Superior to refuse permission and to say No to things. He had been Philosophy instructor, to cross out my essays, and Master of Ceremonies, to correct the smallest rubrics for me. But most of all, he was purveyor of the ways of holiness, for he had made himself or been appointed a sort of holy janitor--the door-keeper to the gates of heaven, to sanctity, and the Degrees of Perfection. Whenever I was in his presence, I thought I saw behind him, always, over his shoulder, the first step, leading up toward the top of the mountain, up to the site of the Burning Bush, to the tablets of stone and the thundering voice of Jehovah, telling us all what to do and what not to do. Of course I never survived his interrogations, I did not do very well, and it all seemed a horrible nightmare, one of those in which you want to move forward, to climb up out of danger, to be allowed through the exit and into safety, but your feet do not move.

I felt sad for him. He seemed to be all of the old things, everything I had ever known among them, mummified by events; he had assumed a shape that could not be changed; like poor Stephen, holding his head in his hands, his antique garment visible, with its ravelled sleeve of care.

That morning I was filled with energy, which had been coming back to me, and it had reached a point where I was possessed with the urge to leave. Suddenly I simply could not remain there any longer. I had to leave Rome, leave them to the sweet taste of their Acqua Vergine and the waters of the Felice, and get out, to return, to get back to what I had been doing for so long, to finish it, in the name of God, and go home.

So I said my good-byes to him, I said good-bye to Father Mullahy. But he paid no attention; and I left him there: propped up, guarding the gates of sanctity.

17

A BOWL OF SOUP

When I returned from Rome, the plane circled north of Dublin and I looked down through an opening in the clouds and saw the soft country-side around Swords again, and my eyes searched for the two famous villages of Hook and of Crook, the ones you go by way of, when you are trying to get somewhere, to finish something, and you say "I will do it --I will do it by Hook or by Crook!"

After Rome, everything looked gray and I knew that I was coming back among them. We plunged down into the clouds through the overcast looking like that stew of things they called "Shepherd's Pie", we came out into the night underneath the clouds, and then I realized that it was actually broad daylight, and was really only the usual gray. I was amazed at how all the same you could see through the darkness, there were the Wicklow Mountains and Great Sugarloaf, you were back very quickly, it did not take long as you saw North Dublin and the road into the city through Drumcondra and Killester, and you felt that you had never left, had not gone at all. I was both anxious to get going again and at the same time afraid of not being ready for everything. I was suddenly not so sure of things; all I knew for certain was that I was still at page 72 of my thesis

I headed straight to Donnybrook, to find Anne Francis. But first I stopped in at Mrs. Guy's restaurant in Lower Baggot Street. Mrs. Guy had some kind of connection with Irish dissidence, and her place had a reputation for being a hang-out for radicals and socialists, but it was cheap, and I needed food so that I could think straight. I sat down at a table alone, but after a while, I found myself staring across at a deferential little man in a dirty tan raincoat, who kept asking the waitress for more bread to go with his bowl of oxtail soup. He had slipped in to join me while I scarcely noticed. He kept me rather busy with questions. He asked what I was doing in Ireland? When I told him I was studying Irish Literature, he professed himself amazed, he asked if we did not have universities of our own, where I came from? He kept asking vague, general questions;

I was astonished at his fascination with my answers, for he always responded in a squeallyvoice "--*Is that a fact, now?*" or "--Is that *so?*" Then I looked away once, down at my paper, and he was gone. The waitress came and asked me "--Where did that one go?" that he had left without paying. I said that I did not know. She blamed me, saying *"But I thought that he was with you!"*

The little fellow might have been a gunman out of the Abbey Theatre, who had slipped out for something during Intermission. But perhaps he was the real thing, for if he was not a gunman, he was someone clearly on the run, one way or another. He knew about Mrs. Guy's famous restaurant; he had looked in the steamy fogged window, saw me alone at my table, took the empty seat, and turned me into a bowl of soup.

Having found myself used as a stage-prop, I knew there was no question that I was back. Perhaps that was his reason for existence, he was someone who had been sent, had stepped in briefly from the Other Side, to show me I was back, back among them and their little warm tricks.

At once I hurried out to Donnybrook to see Anne Francis. It was good to see her again. She welcomed me, relieved that I was better. I told her about Rome, and we began a conversation which we would often return to, a conversation which, you might say, would gradually turn into the rest of our lives. She told me about Dublin --a lot happens there when you are gone. She took me to my foot-locker; everything was all there: I looked down into it and saw thesis, note cards and typewriter. She had saved everything for me; she had saved it all.

I had taken it for granted that she would do so, would look after things. Seeing her again warmed me back into life, and I knew then, as I had known for some time, that we would never fail one another.

I walked the long walk from Muckross to Haddington Road. I would find my motorcycle; I would have wheels, and life would begin again; I felt that I was being warmed back to life. Turning up Pembroke Road, I saw the poet Patrick Kavanagh. The place was full of poets, you could not avoid them. I used to see him every day. I used to cross the street when I saw Patrick Kavanagh coming. He lived somewhere around Baggot Street, near the Grand Canal. He was a great friend of Misses Flannery and King. They said he threw a loaf of bread at them once. I knew I amounted to something the day Missus King pulled out her writer's book and showed it to me. She opened it to what "Patrick" had written. I remember it vividly; I do not remember the opening lines, which were a sort of compulsory note to the two lady book sellers, his patrones-ses. But I do remember what happened as the writing went on down the page: I saw the scribbled note gradually turn into something as I read, saw it turn into the beginnings of a poem, until he finally said, "--There I go, being profound again!" and I nodded my head in agreement, for I had seen the same thing he himself had seen, the moment of inspiration.

Patrick was a strange one; he wrote about frightening the little children up and down Baggot Street, and he called himself "a Queer One." And he wrote "Raglan Road--Raglan Road" about a love lost there, long ago.

It is too bad that I always crossed the street, I suppose. He had a poignant story. He was a farm boy; like every farm boy he considered joining the Christian Brothers. But they saw his ungainliness and would not have him. He considered the world of business, a piece of madness for Patrick; and if he tried politics, he certainly got no where. He wrote a poem about it, seeing his soul as a farm-boy would, as an old horse which nobody wanted. He had tried to sell his soul at the market, and the horse-dealers said it would make good soap and glue. Any prospects of human love having been rendered difficult, he had tried to sell his soul to the church, but those little men were not interested; then he went out even to the Tinkers, the Irish gypsies --who are used to taking and stealing everything-- but even they were not interested. At last he took the halter off, saying there was grass enough by the side of the roads, and with that his soul became young again and sprightly, it grew wings, it became

Pegasus, the winged horse of poetry, which took him everywhere he wanted to go. His poem is called "Pegasus", the poem of his life.

Later, when I returned to America I taught university students out of a textbook and began to see who Patrick was. "--My soul was an old horse," I began; I stood there, thinking of how, in spite of his strange ways, he was like all of us, so like all of us. I would start to feel guilty for having avoided him. And yet, if today I saw him coming down the street I would still avoid him; I would look to see if he was carrying a loaf of bread to throw, and I know that I would cross to the other side.

I dropped by the rectory at Haddington Road; the priests were glad to see me. One of them, a Father Kennedy, told me a very Catholic joke, about. General DeGaulle, suffering from sexual impotence in his old age. The joke was told in French, but it was an Irish joke, and I laughed too.

They sent me out to the green-house, and I found my motorcycle where Anne Francis had arranged for it. Little WZE650. I greeted it, I talked to it as if it were alive. It was covered with coal dust, and the handle bars were askew; but everything seemed all right. I walked it out into Baggot Lane to see if it would start and cranked it vigorously; after a few tries, it started up. Things were dark by now, but I knew the way; I wobbled along Pembroke Lane, the wet little service road in the backs of the great old Anglo-Irish houses, to get my life started again. I was back. I was back among them. My soul was an old horse, but I knew now that I would finish.

SEARCH FOR THE HOLY GRAIL

Humankind cannot bear too much reality.

--T.S.Eliot

The typist told me to get lost, to go away someplace and not to bother her. I had found her in Abbey Street, right next to the Abbey Theatre, and had taken my finished thesis to her, 311 legal-sized pages. I told her that I felt like Alexander the Great must have felt, after the Battle of Granicus. She told me to get lost, that I should go away for three weeks, and let her type.

I did not have money to go anywhere. But the small hotel said they could rent my room out for me, it being summer; that was all I needed.

You see, it was coming up to "Bloomsday," and I did not want to be around for that. Bloomsday is June 16, the day in the year when bus-loads of American professors were trundled through

Dublin, being rolled around high up in busses with huge rubber tires to follow the footsteps of Leopold Bloom and Stephen Daedalus. It was called "The Joyce Industry"; they came to search for the real Dublin, for real life, and it infuriated me. It was always fine weather, by the time they arrived; sitting high up in their coaches, pink and warm and well fed, pilgrims on expensive Sabbaticals, making a farce of what we had been through, while we, down on the sidewalk, might just as well have been corpses, floating in the Ganges River, for all that they would ever know.

So when the typist told me to go away, I went to see King Arthur. It would be my last chance to visit ancient Glastonbury, in England, where the legends and Fairy Tales come from. I could make use of that; I loved telling students of the landscape associated with the literature we studied.

I had some trouble finding it, it is a place at the end of the world, and the English did not know where it was. Little WZE650 sang along under bridges and over streams, on its last trip, to the Vale of Avalon, and the site of Camelot itself. Coming in along the Salisbury Plain, I saw off in the distance Glastonbury Tor, rising from the mists of the lowlands and pointing toward Heaven, the last remains of the Monastery of Glastonbury, the greatest of all English monasteries. King Arthur was buried there, with Guinevere, their

186

bodies found in early times, if you believed tradition, and then there was Lancelot and Galahad and all the rest. You see, Joseph of Arimathea had come there, after taking down Jesus from the cross, he had come to England and brought with him the chalice used at the Last Supper. That is what started the Grail Legend. Weary-All Hill is difficult to climb; and when Joseph of Arimathea climbed it, to look out over the site, he put down his staff, so that he could rest. But the walking stick had been made from wood of the thorn bush used to form the crown of thorns for the head of Christ, and when Joseph of Arimathea put his cane into the ground, it sprouted green shoots, and eventually grew into a large tree. This tree today is called the Glastonbury Thorn, and can be seen in various parts of town. It is quite beautiful, and does grow thorns several inches long; the lady in the bookstore pointed to one across the street; she said that it is unique, in that it bursts out into large beautiful flowers, two times a year.

Because it held the Holy Grail, Glastonbury Abbey became the most important monastery in all England, its Abbot a very influential figure in English history. Gifts were showered on it, as well as land-holdings, it became very rich, and it had the greatest number of monks and lay-persons. So when Henry the Eighth decided to sack the monasteries, the first one he thought of was

Glastonbury, with its shrines and jewels and precious reliquaries and perhaps most of all, its extensive land holdings. He sent his trusted man, a certain Jack Horner, to go get the valuables for him, and bring back the deeds to all the Abbey lands. And on the way home, on the way back to the palace, Jack Horner looked through the pouch full of deeds, and saw one he liked very much, and he pulled that one out, and kept it for himself. By the end, at the time of Dissolution, there were only twenty four monks left, and since they wore the black habits of the Cistercians, they became the Four and Twenty Blackbirds, baked in a pie. So that Jack Horner could rime, and say, "O what a good boy am I!" The last Abbot of Glastonbury was named Whiting; He was drawn through the town on a cart, in 1539; then he was hanged and slit open on Glastonbury Tor, his private parts taken off and burned in front of him. I remember the Abbot's name, because for years, in the seminary, we had a reader named Clair Whiting who read to us morning, noon, and night, in Refectory, Chapter Room and Chapel. He read beautiful books for us, books I might well have never read myself; he read Merton's *Seven Story Mountain* and *Seeds of Contemplation*, and he read *Death Comes for the Archbishop* and Werfel's *Song of Bernadette;* I can still hear the sound of his voice, as though my head still nods from sleep in Chapel at early Morning Meditation, or as if I am back in the Refectory looking down at my plate and at what has been placed upon it that I have to eat, or maybe I am even in the Chapter Room, where everybody will soon accuse themselves of their faults and kneel down to kiss the floor and ask forgiveness; the voice is reading from out of the *Book of Saints and Martyrs*, out of the *Book of Legends and of Chronicles*, it reads on and on, telling of things present, and passing, and to come.

I found Weary-All Hill, and from its top, I looked over what remained --mostly only the outlines of buildings-- and tried to imagine what it must have been like. I knew what I had come for. It was all quite obvious, for it made me think of the Notre Dame in which I had grown up, which was at that time still a monastery as well as a university. Looking down I could plainly see, along with the Chapter House and the Refectory, what was left of where the out-buildings were. It was what I remembered from when I first entered the Order, with the Brothers bringing to us milk each morning, rolling it in huge cans, the Brothers baking bread and the Sisters washing clothes and Brother tailor mending your clothes and Brother Boat-House guarding the lakes, with the rest of us in long lines, walking in silence. It made me think of young Brother Athanasius, who spoke with a Chicago Polish accent, who rose early in the morning to come with the smell of the bakery on him bringing Notre Dame Buns to us to break our fast after mass; he told me once that he had to rise at 3 am to do this and I still remember the smell of the fresh bread of the bakery falling from him as he told me, it was the world of Matins and Lauds, of Little Hours, of Vespers, and "Now with the swift departing light", the Night Prayer of the Church.

It was easy to hear the voice of T.S. Eliot, standing in such a place, pondering the remains of what had been before, in that rasping voice of his, about the desolation confronting him, going on about not knowing what it was you came for, about settling for "only a husk of meaning:" And saying

Dust in the air suspended

Marks the place where a story ended

I wanted to hurry home and be with Anne Francis. I suppose I wanted to tell her that I had been to a place, a place where the story ended. But she would not have had to go to England to know about such things, it was from her I got my Eliot: *In my end is my beginning,* she would say, and *Humankind cannot bear too much reality.* I wanted to speak with her about her future. I wondered what it was that I would myself be returning to in America, if there would be much left, there, either; and I wondered how my thesis was doing, if it was in the typist's typewriter, and if possibly she was typing it, at that moment.

I departed out along the sacred stream, mentioned in all the legends. I walked and walked, to see where it went, and found that it emptied into the grungy swimming pool of a modern English boy's school. So much for Camelot.

. I looked around me, at the outlines of it all, left for the archaeol-ogists, a museum to show the tourists how monks and nuns lived. A short, fat Englishman acting as a guide was explaining to the tourists what had happened at the site. He said we were standing in the Refectory, and showed us what was left of a Lectern, where a reader had read to the monks while they were eating. The monks were ahead of their time, he explained, they knew that having somebody read to them while they ate would assist them in their digestion. The tourists laughed. You got the feeling that he told this to every group.

I was about to speak up and say that I had been a reader in a refectory myself, standing at just such a lectern, and that it had nothing to do with digestion. It would be about Christ healing the Leper, or Francis, saying "Make me an instrument of Thy peace", or the story of Ignatius who prayed that he would be ground up by the teeth of the lions in the way that the grains of wheat were ground up, to become the Eucharist. I decided not to say anything, I would only end up addressing the entire crowd, and the fellow was plainly making a livelihood out of it.

Instead I thought of the two of us, Anne Francis and myself. We had both been faithful. But you heard things. You wondered if when you returned anything would be left of such a life, as well as much of your own life, or if it there would be only outlines of it, humps in the ground for archaeologists, with old Mister Eliot saying: *These fragments I have shored against my ruins.*

I wanted to hurry back and tell her what it was that I had seen. I thought some more, as I hurried.

It was not about Digestion. It was not about the body, and food for the body, it was of the Soul, and food for the Soul. If you abandoned it, you ought to know what it was you rejected. And it was not, even, about the Mind. It was about Spirit only, and what made the Spirit live. It was about the white-robed throng of martyrs, if it was about anything, those linked to us in their blood. You could turn you back on it, a modern person could dismiss it easily; but it was not about what the fat little Englishman had said to the laughing tourists. It was not about Digestion.

18

STAGE IRISHMAN

One wet day, also in that last year, Oliver Snoddy came up to me in the National Library and whispered, "It's raining out, I'm taking Thomas MacGreevy up to the Shelbourne; do you want a ride?" Oliver was an important figure who knew everybody, and I wanted to say Yes to him at once, but --- Thomas MacGreevy--- wasn't he the man that James Joyce had asked to finish *Finnegans Wake* for him, if he himself did not live? Yes, that was who Oliver Snoddy was going to get me into a car with, and I was not sure that I was ready for it. But I said Yes, gratefully. On the way out, however, things began to come to me. No it wasn't Thomas MacGreevy who was to finish *Finnegans Wake* --that was James Stephens-- but now I remembered: Thomas MacGreevy was the one who had introduced James Joyce to Samuel Beckett. Yes he was, and I was getting well beyond my depth. I began to become frightened, and wondered how was one supposed to act in such presence?

When I came out, Thomas MacGreevy was already seated; "Oliver tells me you write satire----Do you read Martial?"

I thought he said "Marshall", and the only Marshall I ever knew was Marshall Goldberg, who was a football player; but I recovered, I thought fast, ---This is the way they were, I thought, This is the way they all must have been-- and I said, hurrying to conceal my ignorance, "--Do you mean Martial, the poet?"

"Of course! --Marcus Valerius Martial! --'*Parcere personis, dicere de vittis*'---Spare the person, speak only of their vices! ---Who said that everything he wrote was nothing..." At that moment I knew myself to have tumbled into their world, a world I did not know, could never know, the world of people like him and Joyce and the rest of them. So this is how it was; you caught it in an instant, understood that everything was required of you, felt foolish and ignorant. I should have just said that I was a dumb American and had not read Martial.

He spared me; he asked me what I was working on inside there, what was I doing my thesis in? I felt relieved; he was asking me the only thing I would know anything about: "The fight over the Stage Irishman, " I said.

The Stage Irishman is the Steppin Fetchit of Irish history; he is like the Indian in Cowboy films, whose single line is "How!" The Stage Irishman goes around saying "Faith and Begorra," and "The Top o' the Marnin' to Ye", he has a clay "pippeen" out of his mouth, he drinks too much, and he gets into fights; you see him mostly on Saint Patrick's Day cards; I have often said that he is a travesty, but I have also been corrected by those who claim to know, and who say that he is close to the real thing.

Thomas MacGreevy was delighted. He bounced right up in his seat; "---The *Stage Irishman is it*? --Now you wait until we get up to the Shelbourne, wait until Oliver gets the machine up to the hotel, and *I'll tell you something about the Stage Irishman!* "

We helped him out of the car, at the old gates of the hotel entrance, and as soon as Thomas MacGreevy gave his wet coat to a porter, he stood squarely in front of me in the Shelbourne foyer: "It was right *here,* " he said, "right where you are standing, it was on that very spot, that Mr. George Bernard Shaw spoke to me. I was a young man and it was just before I was leaving Ireland-- about to take the ferryboat to Holy Head, and take the boat train from there into London. I had been introduced to him as a young man going where I hoped to make my reputation."

" 'YOUNG MASTER MACGREEVY!' Shaw shouted at me with that voice of his...'---Young Masthur MacGreevy--- They tell me that it's to England that you are going--- to make your reputation over there....'"

"He was wearing a cloak, Mister Shaw was wearing that great cloak of his, the actor's cloak, he was very impressive, and all I could do was nod in agreement to whatever it was he was saying ...."

I had noticed that McGreevy as an old man was short; it was easy to see him as a young man overwhelmed in Shaw's presence, quaking before the great man's voice. "And then he said, '----Well, *Masthur MacGreevy*--if its to England that you are going, if you expect to succeed over there, THEN YOU HAD BETTER START PLAYING THE STAGE IRISHMAN FROM THE MOMENT YOU HIT HOLY HEAD!"

MacGreevy acted it; he showed how Shaw had swirled away in that great cloak of his--MacGreevy imitated its swirl out over the Shelbourne foyer as Shaw marched off-- "Then he suddenly turned around, his cloak flew out in a theatrical gesture, and he pointed his finger back right at me! He said '----*BEFORE* YOU HIT HOLY HEAD!' He meant that I should start doing it on the boat, that it was never too soon to start....And he pranced off, for good this time, leaving me quaking in my shoes..."

It was a lesson. The English expected you to play the Fool; if you wanted to succeed, you had to do it. Who better than George Bernard Shaw to tell this: the Irishman who became more English than the English themselves, who turned himself into Henry Higgins and railed at them "Why cawnt the hinglish teach they-ah Children how to speak?" Who made himself their very own captive Irishman, and who made them laugh about themselves for a whole century.

At last I started to feel myself at home with Mister MacGreevy; we understood each other after all; we had some Powers Irish Whiskey and talked; and I was grateful. It was a private lesson, first from Shaw to MacGreevy and then from him to me; I was the only one who heard it, Oliver was still parking the car. I have told the story to years of students: that unless we are careful we are all Stage-versions of ourselves, and the world will ask us to play the fool.

The rain stopped, and I walked home, thinking. I had just bumped into George Bernard Shaw, in the presence of Thomas MacGreevy, just as it seemed I bumped into Gogol, when Frank O'Conner talked. It was as though they were all passing a message down from one to another, and that it had finally gotten to me, and that if I cleared my head sufficiently, I would be beginning to know what the message was. I had been surrounded with it, or something like it, ever since I had arrived in that place; Dublin had done something to me. But I was too busy now, I would think on it elsewhere.

19

MOTHER RO AND THE APPLE TREE

But one more thing happened before I escaped from that place --Ireland-- with what was left of me: there was Maureen, young Maureen O'Rourke. Full of life, she came in the mid-Sixties to Ireland, with a guitar, to work on Folk Literature. Her professors at Indiana University knew she was good, and had sent her to the Source, for Maureen was a swimmer, who dove from heights, and when she came to Ireland, she dove into the Gaeltacht----that is what they the area where the ancient Irish language is still spoken—she dove into it like a high diver, immersed herself in it and spoke it with the children, and three months later she came up spouting Irish, spouting the old tongue with those fresh accents that only children can manage. The rest of us were astonished, for it seemed no one should be able to do that.

She discovered Anne Francis at once, and sat on the floor of her room in the Convent at Muckross while the two of them ate cheese and drank wine and sang songs. They would get to talking, and they would talk of Maureen's friend Don, and of other things, far into the night. But the Convent doors were closed early, and were locked, and the grounds of the convent were patrolled by a night watchman, and once the doors were locked it was almost impossible to let anybody out, because no one is supposed to be leaving a convent, after dark. Maureen was in danger of being imprisoned inside.

But the place was run by Sister Rosario --"Old Mother Ro--" who knew everything, and who knew of the cheese and crackers, of the young American girl who sang songs, and the wine and the guitar, and who knew that a young girl would not want to be captured inside the convent walls.

Who was Mother Ro? The name Rosario makes one think of a Spanish or Italian background, but it was an acquired name, taken by an Irish girl when she entered the convent to give herself to a life of service, as they did in those days. She was an old aristocrat, there is no one who can be more genteel and human than the Landed Irish, they take what the English have brought and add to it their native Irish nobility, and in my experience with Irish gentry, it is something hard to surpass. You run into it in the person of, say, the prioress of

Kylemore Abbey or such, and it recalls to you something of the way things used to be.

But it is Mother Ro and the apple tree that I want to get back to, to the old branch that tells almost everything I have been trying to say.

One night, instead of bothering the night watchman and making a clatter with the front door, Mother Ro secretly whispered to them of a certain convenient tree, and took them both over to an apple tree at the back of the convent, which had a large branch that hung out over the wall. And since Maureen was a swimmer, and quite an athlete, it was easy for her to shinny up the old apple tree, she would crawl out over the wall, and lower herself down into Mount Eden Road, and return to her own digs. Anne Francis would wait to hear the sound of her feet landing on the sidewalk, Maureen would call back Goodnight, and everything would be solved.

I was not present for all this, I did not know Maureen then, I was busy finishing up, but I have heard its account often, and every time I hear it I think of Shakespeare's little story of Pyramis and Thisbe, where there is a wall, and even a character who is actually named "Wall". Wall strides out onto the stage, the way a wall does; he seems absolutely impenetrable as he comes between Pyramis and

Thisbe. But when the young lovers have to talk to one another, the player named "Wall" holds his hand up, separating his fingers with a crack, and they speak to one another through the crack in his fingers, through the crack in the wall. And it makes me think of Mother Ro, who knew how to deal with walls.

Sometimes I think it was a Midsummer Night's Dream for all of us, that time there when we were all younger. It seems to have been glorious summer, after all, with a backdrop as from the play, the field of ripening wheat rising behind everything, saying that it was the harvest time, surely, that it was the very peak of life, that life was at that moment whatever it is or was ever meant to be, and that we would never have anything like it again while we were still on earth.

It was a play made by the Master, with Snug the Carpenter and Peas Blossom with Cobweb and Moth and Moonshine, all of us leading The Fair Maid of Kent to safety, over walls and hills and woods, and it seems nothing else than our lives, the same story rolling on an on, through everything.

Years later, it would be Maureen and Don who would be the sole witnesses to our wedding, before the Justice of the Peace, in Hingham Massachusetts, in the presence of

J. Stanley Gardiner. Being married before a New England Justice of the Peace in Hingham High Street meant Automatic Excommunication from the One, Holy, Catholic and Apostolic Church. I knew that, it meant removal, I had arranged it that way, with full purpose, so that if there were any lingering doubts, our ships were burned behind us, and the drawbridge was broken—we were out, forever.

And when that happened, it was as though all present, all of us---even J. Stanley Gardiner--- had climbed over the apple tree, to get there. It is as though he were Wall, holding up his two fingers, with the split between them, for us to talk through, and it has become a dream, it is Midsummer, smiles of s summer night, for there is Wall, being most helpful to us, there is Maureen, leading the way, with Don close behind her, and there is the ripe field of golden wheat, which means it is time to harvest the harvest of our lives, and there are the two of us, following, and Stanley Gardiner, that true-blue Protestant escaping from a convent too, climbing up over the branch, all of us dropping down with Maureen safely onto Mount Eden Road, our shoes reaching down and touching the side-walk, while the Night-watchman stamps elsewhere, looking in the wrong direction.

20

BROOM MAN

It happened. I had done it. The typist handed 4 copies of my thesis to me. I followed the instructions I had been given; I took them to a bindery. Then, two copies were for the External Readers in England, at the Universities of Hull and Exeter; one was the official copy, to be deposited with the corporate body of the National University of Ireland. To do that, I had to go looking for a certain door I had been told about, hidden in the government offices somewhere around Merrion Square. When I found it, it turned out to be like those "drops" that spies use; it was a drop called "Theses." I looked at it. They expected you to just go searching for it, and when you found it --the door called "Theses"-- you were supposed to open up the little slot, and just dump it in. You were supposed to listen for the thump as it hit the floor, I supposed; it was very Irish. I felt like a young Mother abandoning her baby in an alley way.

I refused to just dump three years of work into a drop labeled "Theses"---the Irish probably had a man with a broom right behind it, sweeping it all up, sweeping every-thing into the dust-bin of history. I knew them, I had come to know them well ---I would not just throw my life in at them and listen to it hit the floor. I decided to knock on the door. A man came; he asked me what the trouble was, hadn't I seen the word "Theses"? I said that yes, I had seen the word "Theses", but that I was afraid there would be a man with a broom behind it sweeping them up on the other side of the door, and I did not want to have my work swept up. He laughed. "--There's no man with a _broom_ in it!" he said, "Just leave it here and it will be all right!" I smiled, and he allowed me to hand it to him, but I still thought he was the one, all the same, the man with the broom. _"It is finished,"_ I said.

One morning earlier in that Spring, at about 4 am, I had been awakened by a loud thump, it sounded like a powerful explosion. Later in the day the girls at my hotel desk told me what it was: the IRA had blown up Nelson's Pillar, in O'Connell Street. The Pillar was the very center of Dublin, it towered over everything, people used to say, "I'll meet you at the Pillar, " and it was a trysting place for lovers. I thought the IRA might have done something better to make their point. The bombers had not hurt anybody, a few taxicabs waiting in a rank were showered with pieces of stone. The gigantic nose from the statue showed up shortly in a Chicago bar, where you could kiss it, for a donation to "the Cause."

I had not bothered to visit the site, and examine it; the regular Army had cleaned it up within a few hours. But whenever I looked at downtown Dublin without the pillar, it didn't seem to be my Dublin anymore. It was like Washington D.C. would be, without the Washington Monument, I did not like it. I did not go near the site until I got on my motorcycle for the last time, little WZE650. After I dumped the thesis, I got on it and rode it up to Parnell Square at the top of O'Connell Street. I was getting rid of things. I looked for the motorcycle shop which bought old motorcycles, above Austin Clarke's Black Protestant Church. (The children had a saying: 3 times around it, and you saw the Devil).

The motorcycle man said he could only give me few pounds for my motorcycle; winter was coming on, and it was not the right time for one of these. He acted as though I had interrupted more serious work. I threw in the helmet, too. Poor little WZE 650; it had taken me everywhere; when I shook with the cold, I could feel it shake too, it was so small; as I left the shop I looked back and saw him putting it in with others, as though it was no different. Take all my loves; take this one too.

I now no longer had wheels; I would have to walk to the University for one last lunch with Julia; she had arranged it. She was back, to begin what we call the Fall Semester, what they call Hilary Term. It would all go on without me. My walk took me down O'Connell Street, past the gaping emptiness left by Nelson's destroyed pillar.

I looked at the site. There were some street sweepers sweeping around it, still sweeping there weeks later, as if to sweep away with brooms the last vestiges: Nelson's sword, his tri- cornered hat, his very famous nose. The dust-bin of history. They were sweeping away my Dublin: England expects each man to sweep up the pieces. I stood there looking at it. It was all gone, you would not think anything had been there. I walked off, to say good-bye to Julia. She was one of the last of the old crowd of them all. I looked back. The broom men were still at their work, sweeping everything all away.

She had arranged it. She showed up at Number 86, Newman House, the University Cafeteria. After I had dumped my thesis in at the door marked "Theses" in Merrion Square, after I had dropped off my motorcycle, Julia showed up with another girl, a hopeless little *gomme* of another girl, who did not know what was going on, but who was clearly under instructions on how to act. Julia was in a fresh new dress, with a sprig of something on her lapel. And as we ate, as though I might somehow not understand, as though I might not grasp the full meaning of what was going on, she managed to work in the word "Good-bye" quite a few times. We talked about many things, but "good-byes" kept inserting themselves.

After that was over, we walked across St Stephen's Green, past the duck ponds and monuments, and out the gate at the head of Dawson Street, and crossed. By now I knew it was the end; I had been told enough times. Suddenly she shouted to the other girl "Here comes our bus!" and the two girls jumped on the rear platform of the Number 10 Donnybrook. I do not think that it was their bus at all; I think it was just any bus that would do for her purposes. For her purpose you see was to leave me happy; Julia surely had said to the other girl Now look happy, and at a signal the two of them started waving "Goodbye, Goodbye-- Goodbye, Father, Goodbye" and twirling around the pole on the back of the bus. One last prank.

I turned into Stanley's News to buy an Irish Times. I glanced down at the Colonial Outfitters mosaic as I stepped over it in the entry, with its boots and saddle and map of the world. "The Wild Colonial Boy", it made me think, as it always did.

I never heard from her again. Whenever I think of her, which I do from time to time, it makes me think of the word "Unhouseled"" in Hamlet. That sounds almost like "Unhoused", but what it really means is to be without the Eucharist, to die without *Viaticum,* the thing that should travel with us on our journey, that journey we make at death, the last of all the journeys that we make. To housel someone means to give Holy Communion to them on their death-bed, it is what priests are for, and it is something you would not do, if for example, you left the priesthood. That other word, "Unannalled" means "unannointed". As a priest you were in charge of departures; if you left, how many souls would have to make their last voyage alone? When I think of Julia I think of all those unhouseled ones, who have had to make the journey themselves, and think if I am to blame for any of them.

I much prefer to think another way, to remember Julia happily waving to me from a bus at the top of Dawson Street, the way I am supposed to.

When I got home, I started cleaning out my room. I remember singing that old cowboy song, "--When the work's all done this fall."

21

DRUMLEEK

It was time for me to go. Anne Francis was in the Highlands; she was in Scotland with her sister's family at Dunoon, in Ayreshire, near the U.S. nuclear submarine base at Holy Loch. She had one more year in Dublin, to stay behind, after the rest of us had gone. But I would be returning by Pan Am from London. We talked on the phone, to say good-bye. The lines from Scotland to Ireland were weak, they seemed full of bag-pipes, the pipes were calling, and I could hardly hear her.

I had not planned to go there at all. I did not think I had the money to go to Scotland first before the plane in London. Yet we had been through everything together, we had always counted on one another; now I was leaving her alone. I did not want to do that. I was not sure that either of us could survive another year there; I knew I would not have been able to. Her voice was coming to me from a telephone booth in Dunoon; I could imagine her fumbling with English Shillings. The line seemed to be coming down under the Irish Sea, you could hear the waves trying to drown us out, her voice came and went.

The call was a last connection between us, we had agreed upon it. But it was not quite what I expected. When the phone rang I was surprised, for suddenly it seemed life itself that was calling to me. Take care, life was saying, Know what it is that you are doing. Do not let this slip away, for if this goes, all will go, there will be nothing, absolutely nothing.

I more or less expected to lose her. I had no long-term friendships; I thought this would be like the rest. Somewhere, I feared, ages and ages hence, I would be telling this: How once I knew another person, who knew me better than I knew myself. But it had failed. It had faded away in the name of something--- something called Holiness, perhaps, or Keeping the Rule, things which, in turn, seemed to be doing a good job of fading away on their own.. "---I knew a person once---" I would be saying, " --the finest I have ever known... For a while we were very close..." Where would I be saying this? In a bar? Trying to tell it all to someone who did not particularly want to hear it? If I could find anyone to listen at all. That sounded like me. Yet I was not allowed to do anything about it, I had disciplined myself not to dwell on such things.

I stood there at the phone desk in the hall of the little hotel. I held the plastic beige receiver in my hands. What would I do? She would be running out of shillings, we would be cut off. I knew what she was saying, though her words were not saying it; she was saying *If anything means anything, Come.* I decided to do it. Yes, I said, Yes.

I would take the Burns and Laird boat to Glasgow, I would leave on the night boat, from Dublin's North Wall.

I asked the girls at my little hotel about the Glasgow Boat. They said "Oh, Don't take *that*, Father! The *Burns and Laird boat*? You know what they say about it? They say that the seagulls follow all the other boats for the scraps, but they never follow the Burns and Laird boat, because it's too stingy to throw anything away!" I decided to take it, in spite of their warning; I still remember the fare, 4 pounds and a half. It was the Burns and Laird night boat, from the North Wall, for Glasgow, to Gourock and Greenock, to Dunnoon. I was leaving Ireland for Scotland; Ye Flowery Banks of Bonnie Don

The evening I left was a splendid one at the end of Summer. Everything had warmed up. The evening sun was going down over the Dublin Mountains. As the ship sailed out into the bay, I began to be able to see things. I looked back, saw the church steeples: the one in Rath-mines, then the Jesuit Church, and, rather easily, Haddington Road. I saw where Ranelagh was, with its St James Terrace. Over there somewhere should be the Shelbourne, "---*Miss-uz William*

Walsh! -----Miss-uz William Walsh!", Mary Lavin being called out

for something important, and there would be the Tea Time Express,

and the old Kildare Street Library, with its newspapers from 1904,

now without me turning them into more brown dust. It would be my

last look. I could plainly see the sweep of Mount Kippure, above

Sally Gap and Lough Tay, where I had heard the cuckoos as they

sang to one another across the valley. There would be Parson's Book

Shop on the bridge, the Misses Flannery and King; and old Mother

Murphy saying: *O Sister, any woman would love Father Francey!*

The boat slowly rounded the corner of Howth Head, at

Drumleek. Goodbye to everything. My lost walkings on the damp

sidewalks, the caked grease on the "Cookers", waitresses with that

habit of saying "*Now!*" as they set down your plate in front of you,

"the mist becoming rain", I suppose, on the screen of my little

Suzuki, out by Drumshauglin, on the way to Bective, the swallows

flitting on the Powers Irish Whiskey bottle, all gone now, or the

James Bond films seen enormously alone in the dark at the

Serpentine Cinema. Are they to be shouldered away, then, in the

Room of the Possibles? --Yes, shouldered away they were to be now,

fettered and forgotten, for they will have no mind to remember them.

If a thought has no mind to think it, does it exist at all? Ireland was

all barley-color as I left it; the little children would be playing in

Hebert Park, the low sun sending their shadows long across the grass.

It grew dark, and I looked out into the darkness very hard, I wanted to know if I would be able to see the Isle of Man in the night. I calculated by my watch where it should be: It was out there, an island in the middle of the ocean. That was the home of King Lear, whatever they say happened to him must have happened there: it would have been there he had been left upon the heath, to go shouting at the winds, and where he said, " a man may see how this world goes with no eyes." Where he said that the storm outside was nothing to the tempest inside him, and where, rejecting foolish behavior, he had said, "--That way madness lies." I looked out over the black water but could not see anything. I looked hard in the night, but I don't think I ever saw the Isle of Man. I turned away from the rail; it was a naughty night to swim in.

A new book had come out before I left Dublin, written by Brian Moore, called

"I Am Mary Dunne"; it was about a strange lonely Irish woman named Mary Dunne, brow-beaten by parents and by life, the kind of girl who stays home to take care of her aged parents and who has no other life. (I had seen them; Ireland was full of them; that was all Mary Lavin ever wrote about.) In the end, she has to have an operation in the hospital, to which there is some danger attached: the doctors warn her that she may not come out. No one will watch her go under, no one will be waiting for her to come out. She has nothing left, her parents are dead, she no longer believes in the Sacred Heart of Jesus picture on her wall, she is not confi-dent in the doctors. But she talks to herself, as she is going under, for possibly the last time. She repeats to herself who she is: she says it, over and over: I am Mary Dunne, I am Mary Dunne. And that is the way it ends. as she goes under on the operating table she has nothing left to hang onto except for the Sacred Heart of Jesus over her bed, her name is the one thing she has left of what she has been, so she holds on to that, for her salvation, she keeps repeating it: "I am Mary Dunne" she says, and as she goes under repeats it, " --I am Mary Dunne". You know she will be lost.

There, on the boat, headed past the Isle of Man. I was nervously patting each of three pockets, of course; I had a habit when I traveled of checking over and over the passport-pocket, ticket-pocket, money- pocket. I decided I was the person pictured on my passport, that was who I was. " I am Mary Dunne. " I said to myself, peering into the darkness.

For you see, there really was a Mary Dunne. She was a real person that I used to notice. I used to often pass a youngish Irish woman in her early forties; after a while I knew she was always headed for a pub at the top of Baggott Street. It was called "The Crookut Bauble", for you see by this time, Dublin was beginning to be coy about such things. In the past it would have simply been called something like McCabe's or Quinn's, but now it was "The Crookut Bauble." Anyway, it had its supply of drink, and like all Irish pubs, there was a "Snug" at the end of the bar where you could ring a buzzer and be served, privately; it was a kind of Carry-Out, and every time I saw her, it was where she was headed, and though I did not know what her name was, she was certainly Mary Dunne.

At this time, I was not drinking myself. No-- that is not true, I was only beginning to drink, and so I was still in a position to look down at those who did too much of it, who were unable to cope with it. This was good for me, as I was moving around in my black suit and Roman Collar, and it was meet and just that I should be able to look askance.

One day as I was walking in Baggott Street just below the Crookut Bauble carrying some brown paper bags full of groceries in my hands back to my apartment--though there may have been a bottle inside, too-- stiff and formal in my black suit and collar-- I saw her coming, I saw Mary Dunne, and she passed me. And as Mary Dunne passed me, she said, loud and very clearly "--Oh, What *beautiful hands!*" I arched my eye-brows, I suppose, I certainly looked askance, I pretended, I think, not to have fully comprehended what my ears had just heard.

She turned back as she passed, and repeated more loudly, " I SAID 'WHAT BEAUTIFUL HANDS!'" and continued on to the Snug on the corner.

Priests are supposed to have beautiful hands. Irish culture is laden on the subject. There are holy cards with verses about the hands of a priest. Their hands are consecrated at ordination, to be used for anointing people, blessing them, and holding the chalice. Many priests are far removed from hard physical labor --though by no means all-- in my case, the hardest work I did was pound typewriter keys.

But she was saying "Too bad you are a priest. Too bad we cannot all love one another. Too bad we are all lonely on this planet, and I have to drink.'"

It took only three seconds; I continued on my way; I managed to look like someone going to afternoon tea, at the Vicarage. Or hurrying home to the Sacred Heart of Jesus. I remember considering it as a compliment: that I indeed did have good hands.

But the three seconds held too many worlds to be accounted for. No matter what I looked like, I was myself very like her. Too bad we all can't say what we think. I might have spoken. She was a painful case. But then so was I.

As the boat turned its head toward Scotland in the night. I patted the pocket with my passport in it. I knew who I was; I was the one with beauti-ful hands, the one with the hands of a priest. Mary Dunne had told me so. And if you had asked me, I might have said that I was going home, to please my Legitimate Superiors.

Yet a man can see how things are going with no eyes. I was headed toward Anne Francis, that was what I was doing; I had always been headed toward her.

I looked out into the impossible night, toward where I thought Man might be. It was a naughty night to swim in.

22

LOCH LOMOND

Give me liberty or give me death. We were standing on American soil, Commander Chuck Diem explained, even though the deck of the submarine-tender at Holy Loch was clearly made of steel. I looked down at the two nuclear subs tied up along us: one was the *USS Patrick Henry*, the other the *USS Nathan Hale*. One had said "Give me liberty or give me death"; the other was famous for "I regret that I have but one life to give for my country." Both ships were ready to blow up the world, or a good deal of it, in the name of freedom.

Chuck was married to Sally, the sister of Anne Francis, who we were visiting. He continued: "--Patrick Henry said other things, too; he said, 'If this be treason, make the most of it!'" and he also said ' I know of no way of judging of the future, but by the past' "

He pointed out things to us. Each submarine had two rows of Polaris Intercontinental Ballistic Missiles, hidden under its hatches; some of the hatches were open, and you thought you could see their tips. Chuck said they were manned by either the Blue Team or the Red Team; whichever team was in port, he was the dental expert who did their teeth, as an officer periodontist, so that when they went out for long sorties under the Polar Ice Cap, no one would have tooth trouble.

Anne Francis's sister Sally had a large family; little Cathie, a beautiful child of four, looking like a young Anne Francis, had been brought along, and had been prompted to help me with my suitcase at the landing. The two of them had a poem they recited to one another, I had been told about it:

I love you,
You love me--
--We are friends,
Can't you see?

For the next few days, we all did together what you do in Scotland; we looked at the moors and the heather; and thought we heard bag-pipes, coming over the glens.

The visit was a somber one; it was obvious to the two of us that those last warm days of August and early September, with the sun shining down upon the ripening grain, would be our last ones together, at least for a long time, and possibly, very possibly, for ever. We were trying to do something difficult, to remain close friends within the rigid confines of the religious life. That is allowed, of course, within limits, there is considered to be nothing wrong with good friendship. But the religious life is a life of separation, if it is anything it is that; we knew there was a very real chance that we would not see each other again.

When it was time to leave for the airport, Chuck said that we would go out by way of Arrochar and Tarbut and Loch Lomond. I asked in disbelief if that was the real one, the famous Loch Lomond of the song?

"It sure is, " he answered, "-- We'll be going out that way--I'll show it to you, I'll show you the High Road and the Low Road, and the bench where the guy sat who wrote it, too!"

We did go out that way, when the time came. Little Cathie, Anne Francis's favorite, was selected to accompany us. And we actually did drive, for a long time, past Loch Lomond, on a beautiful summer's day: its bonnie banks and its bonnie braes filled with flowers bending in the breeze.

We were quiet by the time we reached the town of Linlithgow, half way to the airport. It had public restrooms in the middle of the square; the Men's was sufficiently horrible, everything broken and worse than in Ireland; but Anne Francis refused to have herself and little Cathie even use the Women's. I said that the Men's was not that bad, and that I would stand outside and guard.

She was still wearing her magnificent black Mercy habit; I wondered what Scotland thought when they saw her. She would look like Mary Queen of Scots to them; I doubted if many of them had ever seen a Roman Catholic nun, walking their streets. The last one had probably been hanged.

In the car, leaving, I looked over at Sister Anne Francis; she was in everything so much exactly what I was myself. She would be left alone, now, back in Dublin, facing the same old things, but now without the two of us side by side. I hoped that no matter what happened, the two of us would remain somehow together.

I was leaving, all the same; there always seemed to be a demand for more leaving. Parting seemed the national industry of Scotland; it was the land of the parting glass, the stirrup-cup: *"just a wee drock in dorra --- just a wee bit, that's aw--afor ye gang awa"*. It was full of benches where poets had sat and where you could sit and ponder it all. Ponder what? The Sweet Afton, I supposed, flowing gently. It all sounded like verses from a Gift Shop.

As we approached Edinburgh everything grew dark---*dour,* I suppose, is the term, the word surely comes from there. Everything turned into the gray stones of John Calvin. At the airport, we finally said goodbye. Little Cathie surprised me; when I bent down to her, she suddenly reached up and hugged me by the neck and would not let go, and Chuck said "Cathie, that's enough!" He said he was worried about the child, but I knew she was just doing what she thought should be done.

People used to stay around and wait for planes to leave, you know, much more than they do now; you waited for passengers to press their faces against the glass, saying "--I'm here, at this window, count fourteen back from the front of the plane! Don't you see me? I am waving!"

I did what everyone did; I pressed my face against the glass. Trying to show them where I was, I waved at the two of them, at Anne Francis, and little Cathie (*I love you, you love me*) who was a copy of Anne Francis; both of them waved and waved, but I could tell that neither of them was able to see me, and by God, I thought it a cold strange way for things to end.

23

THE HOLY GROUND ONCE MORE

There is an Irish myth about a poet named Usheen: he falls in love with a fairy princess called Niamh. She reaches down and swoops him up behind her, upon the back of her fairy horse and together they go galloping off, and they ride through seven centuries, while Time stands still. But then one day he reaches down to help a human struggling to carry a load, and it is all over, he has made a mistake, he has touched the things of earth, he lands on his rear in the middle of the road, he has fallen back into Time. He is no longer living in ancient Ireland, he has fallen back into Now, and he does not recognize anything. When I landed in New York, I felt like Usheen, dumped in the middle of 34th street, all done with my own galloping around.

New York smelled of subway, the whole place smelled like the IRT; there was a constant noise to everything, which began close to you with the noise of taxi wheels driving over manhole covers but then moved off into the entire roar of the city, the total of all sound in

Manhattan and the Boroughs, made up of everything, the sound made by racks of clothes being shoved around the garment district, the sound of dancers shuffling in lofts, and the yells of option traders, and paper getting stuck in copy machines, and agents breathing on writers and the swish that bar-tenders make wiping off bars, and bums sleeping in dumpsters, and paintings being mounted and taken down at the Museum of Modern Art, and sopranos practicing up and down their scales, and cop whistles, and of course steam rising out of holes in the street, the roar of Funland. I was back in the New World, but I was not fast enough for it; I was not even quick enough to go through its swinging doors. It was like always, when I came to New York, no matter when I came, I was centuries behind, and I had to learn everything all over.

The first thing I did was to go out into Times Square and order a hamburger and a chocolate milkshake. I was nervous about everything. The person ahead of me said in an impossible New York accent "khawfee and a dhawg," got what he wanted at once and was gone with it; but when I ordered distinctly a chocolate malted and a hamburger the man behind the counter did not know what I was saying, he had to ask me to repeat, and seemed annoyed at having to deal with someone like me who was taking up his time. He finally gave me my milkshake and hamburger; and even though he hated me

I had been waiting for that taste for three years, and when I swallowed, I was proud to be an American.

As I came out of that place, whatever it was --Orange Julius or something-- a crowd had gathered; at first I thought it was only New York, that it might be just the ordinary sidewalk crowd, but no, they were all watching the police. A taxicab had rammed into a long row of parked cars. Someone explained: the cabby's fare was a drug-addict and had stabbed the driver; the driver was only able to come to a halt by ramming his taxi into the row of cars. A tall young man in a beige suit and a good hat, holding a briefcase, was directly behind me. "----Dis *fuckin' city!*" he said with disgust, shaking his head. That was the first violence I had run into in three years, and I was concerned that it had happened in my first few hours in America. But I did what I always did when I came to New York: I took the subway down to South Ferry, paid my 5 Cents and headed toward Staten Island, out with the shoe-shine boys and the flute players, and the garbage scows and work-boats; I breathed in the oily smell of the harbor, I saw a plane rising out of JFK -- it had been called "Idlewild" when I left--- I looked far off and saw the Verrazano Bridge and remembered the cable that had fallen down behind us as they were building it; then I hurried over to catch the return ferry, so that I could watch Manhattan rise again before me.

When I arrived at Notre Dame, there was another surprise: the Moon was in the Seventh House, and Saturn was aligned with Mars; for it was the Dawning of the Age of Aquarius. There was hair all over the place. Even the professors were wearing their hair long.

You saw headlines. Army Private Dennis Mora jailed for three years hard labor for refusing Vietnam service. Group of Negro Children Taken to All-white School in Mississippi. US Bombs Friendly Village Killing 28. I tried to pay attention, but there was too much going on in my own life, for you see I was at last back in the bosom of my community, I was back among the Magnolia Trees. Somewhere the voice of Joan Baez was singing a song: "*Have you seen my dear companion?*" she was asking.

I was back. My brethren were not absent any more; I sat at table with them, listening to Dick Downs talk to Charlie Weiher, about "the Really Real," which was what they had been talking about before I had left. I knew I was back, for I saw Chester Soleta walking on the Main Quadrangle; I waved excitedly and called out to him, but he did not hear me, he was walking away from me in the opposite direction with somebody he knew.

It took me a while to feel fully returned. Football started immediately, and on home game weekends Corby was full of visitors and cigarette smoke. The main corridor of Corby was full of Monsignors, priests with Irish names from places like Buffalo or Lackawanna, and with people of connections, like the young Peter Grace, of Grace & Co, people who had football tickets waiting for them. I found myself more and more not liking it. I was amazed at the campus on football Saturdays. It struck me as an enormous Potemkin Village, full of ruddy-cheeked citizens, acting the way you are supposed to act when you are being Irish. Everything was more full of Leprechauns and shamrocks and green beer than I remembered, I kept hearing the voice of Bing Crosby, asking "How are things in Gloccamora?" I wondered, What had ever become of the Notre Dame of my childhood? It had turned into a huge Fairy Tale, it was one big Bloomsday. But then I had a thought, a very strange one: What if it was really the same place that it had always been? What if it had not changed at all? What if it was I who had changed?

* * * * *

I went to the bookstore to see if my texts had arrived. That was now far different from Brother Conan's little hole in the wall that I grew up with. To get to the textbooks, you had to pass through aisle after aisle of merchandise--the bookstore was filled with Notre Dame sweatshirts and Notre Dame sports jackets, all bearing the mono-grammed initials "ND", and coffee mugs, with shamrocks and leprechauns, and pennants with a big "Number 1" on them. The color green was prominent; money was involved. I had come into the real world, and thought of Warren's scurrilous comment about the Holy Ground not being quite what we thought it was:

And still I live in hope to see The Holy Ground once more.

I pushed my way past the shillelaghs with green ribbons tied to them; to where I hoped my books on Joyce and Lady Gregory and the Abbey Theatre were. They were not there, the books I had been careful to order from Ireland, and I was furious; there were plenty of shillelaghs, but not the books I had ordered from Ireland! Some of them were eventually found, and I quieted down. But it made me wonder if this was really the best place in the world to try and start Irish Studies, or the worst, for it was clearly the same old shillelagh my father brought from Ireland, and I began to wonder how long it would be before they would want to be rid of someone like me.

I was surprised to find that my first class in Irish Studies had been assigned a room over in the old Little Seminary building. That

was all but abandoned, it had been closed down while I was away ---
the Little Seminarians were gone, gone forever, my friends on the
Leonardo da Vinci had decided that it was wrong to put little boys in
such places to grow up and be priests. There would never again be a
Little Seminary, the building was now just extra teaching space.

I wondered, who had thought of putting my class there? I
walked towards it, walking backwards through my life, crunching
through history on the same old paths. I decided to enter by the side
door. I knew well enough where it would be.

Other Voices Other Rooms. This was where the Trojan War
had been fought:

I had been assigned the exact same classroom of creaky
wooden floors where we had laughed, as Bill Finn imitated the old
men looking down from Priam's walls at beautiful Helen as she
walked by. It was a place where disembodied voices hung in the still
classroom air, quoting Virgil to the smell of chalk and dried
inkwells. Anyway, I knew how it all ended, it ended with the death
of Hector, the first hero, it ended with the simple epitaph, "--*And so
died Hector, Tamer of Horses.*"

I did not like trying to teach there, and requested a change.
Were there any other classrooms available?

Of course there were: there were rooms available in the ROTC building.

It did not occur to me to ask why there should be space in such a nice building. But it was September of 1966, the very middle of the Sixties, and my mind was still back in old bloody Ireland, or with Hector, maybe; I was thinking of the wrong war.

As I began my first class -- while I was telling the students of the distance their minds would have to travel from the life they led to understand another culture-- the fire bells sounded and we were routed outside; a bomb threat had been phoned in: the ROTC building was part of the military establishment, you see. Though no bomb actually went off, I felt bombed out, I looked back as I was leaving and saw a Quarter-master securing the top of the building; he was silhouetted against the sky as he looked for anything suspicious.

Father Hesburgh's response to student unrest was his famous "15 minute Rule" He was not going to have the students at Notre Dame acting the way they were acting everywhere else. He said that the place was "private property," and that they did not have the right to be there if they did not behave. If they acted up, he said that he would explain it to them, that Notre Dame was private property, and they would have fifteen minutes to reflect upon this. After which, I supposed, he would make sure they would be gone. I was not happy about student unrest, either, but felt that it was unfortunate that it all had to come down to real estate, it seemed strange for his response to be based on whose property it was.

The students needed background. I told them about "The Wild Geese". I told them how, when Ireland was finally conquered by the English, the Irish nobility fled to Europe, to the Catholic armies of France and Spain and Austria, to continue the fight against the invader. This was called The Flight of the Earls, or The Flight of the Wild Geese. That was at least a start; The Wild Geese was a beginning.

I told them fairy tales, too, which are at the basis of much sophisticated allusion. There was that one called The Golden Ball. A fellow is falling asleep by the fireside in a little town near Stepaside, and is suddenly awakened from looking dreamily into the embers by a beautiful golden ball which comes bouncing in on him. Shortly after, it is followed by an agitated creature "from the Other Side." A Fairy Visitor comes looking for it; the golden thing is their football, they have been playing football with it, and it has gotten away from them, and has bounced out of the Other Side, into what human folk call Reality. The fellow by the fire wakes up enough to realize he has something good in his possession; he refuses to give it back, he holds the golden ball for ransom by the Fairy Horde. He demands a ransom, and makes the *shee* pay up. They do, but in the end, although the Fairy Visitors honor their word, and grant him what he asks for, you can be sure, that as they go bouncing and kicking the golden ball on their way back to Fairyland, it is they who are laughing, and not the poor fellow at the fire.

And, of course, I had to teach Joyce. I had not bothered with James Joyce in Dublin; I had determined not to read him, so as not to let him destroy my own experience for me. I kept bumping into him, of course, but the Irish set no store by him. Now I had to teach him, and I was astonished, for there in his lines was the very place I had endured: "Oysters in the Red Bank", Leopold Bloom thinks to himself. The students wanted to know what that meant. "He is complaining about the well-off, how they eat in such places. " I said. The Red Bank was the first good Dublin restaurant I had eaten in; it was too rich for my budget, too; it closed during my second year, along with the fine Russell Hotel. There was mention of the DBC-- the Dublin Baking Company, and the River Dodder, and The Tolka running through everything, the rivers which ran through life. Leopold Bloom especially seemed fixated with my old neighborhood: "Rich ladies in the Clyde Road", he would say, which was around the corner from me, next to the new US Embassy, and he complained, "--Where were the police when you needed them? Walking two by two out in Pembroke Road!" Yes, that would be right, Pembroke Road was the place the police would be protecting, out with the likes of us in Number 80, and T.W. Rolleston up in 104, not down in Night-town with Leopold Bloom.

A student read out " -his sister had the organ at Haddington road" and wanted to know why Joyce talked that way. I said that Haddington Road was actually a church, that the Irish called churches and hospitals after the streets they were on, and wanted to add that it was a good place to park your motorcycle. They asked about Donnybrook, and I told them it was now a neighborhood of Dublin, but earlier had been the scene of an annual roustabout fair, which had given its name to all such melees. What else was I to tell them, that someone very dear to me lived there? I was back at Notre Dame, back in South Bend, Indiana, looking at my students; my Soul was hearing that poignant line from Gounod's *Faust,* where he looks up to see the home of Marguerite: "*Behold the street where she lives.*" There are some things you cannot explain to anybody.

The students were bright, and quickly became obsessed with Joyce; I watched, as they determined to rebuild Dublin for us brick by brick. I could not keep up with them, and their demand for specific details. One of them asked about the "River Dargle," and I

237

said it was a small river which flowed down from Mount Kippure through Enniskerry to the ocean at Bray. I described it and its place in Joyce's story, keeping out of the answer all mention of its place in mine, of going out through towns like Golden Ball and Stepaside to walk on its banks, and the lapping sound it made as it flowed to the sea, and the way you felt, riding home from there on lonely Sunday afternoons in the top of the double-decker bus, swaying in the rain, for that was not part of the question.

One day I saw something scribbled in the margin of my book: *The loved thing has many names*, it said. It was then I began to wonder privately if it had all really ever happened, if anything I thought I remembered had actually ever happened. If it was true that I had sat one day and listened while old Jeremiah Hogan had approved my thesis topic and sent me to the library for three years of tunneling in the dark caves of Irish history, if I was the same person who had bought "streaky bacon" in the alley off Haddington Road church, if there had ever been a Bewley's, and even if it was true that there had ever really been an Anne Francis I had talked with, when, laughing and wet, we both came in from the rain.

No one else in the English Department seemed to have found it necessary to go through anything like what we went through; they had gone to good schools, yes, they had taken their courses in Wyatt and Surrey, and had been inside many classrooms. Wyatt was fine enough, of course, (*They flee from me, that sometime did me seek*) and they were competent enough, surely, yet they seemed to have escaped, supremely innocent of that thing, the unnamed thing which we had fought so desperately to achieve. It made me wonder, how there could be such two different types of reality. And they certainly knew nothing about me; for when they asked me what my field was, and I said Irish Literature, they said Oh yes, and I could see the space behind their eyes fill with leprechauns and sweatshirts, placing me among the coffee mugs: Oh yes, they knew all about that, from the football stadium.

I became angry: I said in my excess, *'"All men are liars!"*

I began to feel compelled to set everyone straight. When anyone asked me if I had been away, I would start to speak, and then find that I could not stop talking; I wanted to stop, but could not. I wanted to make them all understand. I became an Ancient Mariner, holding people and thumping them on the chest and saying "*There was a ship!*" (-*His eyes,* they said, -*Beware the flashing of his eyes!*)

"---*There was a ship!*" I wanted to say, and go on, about where the ship had taken me, and what had happened there, about things, and then more things, to which they should raptly listen. I must have sounded to them like that fellow who had escaped up out of Plato's Cave, the one who alone had seen the Light, and had come back, to tell them about it. Indeed, what <u>was</u> I doing? Trying to stand up for Baggott Street? What was it that I was trying to tell them? To say that it all had truly existed, that it was I who knew about the Really Real, that I had had more than a brush with it, that I had seen it and tasted it and smelled it and sopped it up? It must have been something like that. I wanted to shout "*I am Lazarus, come back from the dead! I shall tell you all!*" Of course we all know that when Lazarus comes back, nobody believes him.

So they had a point, therefore. It is true, I was only pretending to be among them. I must stop this, I thought to myself. Perhaps I should feign madness, to pass among them unscathed.

"Come on, come on!" they shouted at me. "-- There's a game Saturday, aren't you going to use your ticket? *What the hell happened to you over there?*"

* * * * *

Finally, I received word that I had got my degree. A little cockeyed mimeographed sheet from Earlsfort Terrace arrived announ-cing that the Board of Governors of the National University of Ireland had granted the undersigned the degree of Doctor of

Literature, let it be known to all and sunder, --an exotic envelope with that old world print on it. *I had won!* My thesis had been approved by readers at the Universities of Leeds and Exeter and every place that mattered, with a few carping English-sounding criticisms-- it had been accepted, I had received my Doctorate.

I wanted to celebrate, but there was no one. I went walking, down along the twisting footpath around the lake. "Have you seen my dear companion?" a woman's voice was singing again, probably Joan Baez, it was popular. Alone, I wondered where she walked now? What she was doing now, with her small pence finding some fresh fruit in some hole-in-the-wall grocery, walking down Leeson Street with her satchel. It was she who seemed to inhabit the real world, while I alas was clearly walking in my false one.

I wanted to be walking with her, and walk with her along those streets paved with gold through seven centuries with the Shee turning open those old brass knobs on the doors of Dublin for us, those doors through which we had walked together and had come into life, those doors which opened to us under fanlights into their cold ancient hallways -- back into that circle of friends beneath the green lampshade where the light shone down on our new faces, that first, bright, spinning place at the beginning of the world. *And behold I open:* gray doors green doors golden doors and one heavy, heavy door with bronze polished handles, the one to life itself, to your own life with numbers 80 or 67 or 72 on them, so that you would have them doors of Bramante -- The Doors of Paradise. You talked your head off, boring everyone. But people were kind, they said He has been away some place he has suffered much he will get over it

But you would not get over it. Why would anyone, once the ghost begins to quicken, allow it to be laughed away, or even merely talked away? And as I fell asleep each night I wondered if I would ever be able to do it, ever be able to live now with them back in what they had chosen, back, indeed, in what we had all freely chosen, I as much as any. I tossed and turned, listening to the migrating wild geese over Corby looking for a place to land in their eternal migrations. I was thinking of something; I was thinking of all that could happen, in my life, if only a certain few conditions were met, if only a person had the courage, and if a person were not, after all, a coward.

"Away! Away!" the wild geese honked as if flying to Glencullen and Glencree, as if searching for dear companions

There is a line from Holy Job; he cannot sleep; in his pain he prays,

242

" I turn back and forth on my bed in the night, like a door swinging upon its hinges. How long, O Lord, wilt Thou let me to swallow down my spittle?"

We do not talk that way today; but he was talking to God, and that is how he saw one's life on earth: turning like a door on hinges, as you try to figure things out, back and forth, back and forth, on your bed at night. You know that you have only so many turns in you, you understand, you are allotted only so many, this way and that, before it is over. And swallowing down one's spittle, you have only so many swallows in you, too, I guess, before the earth itself opens up and swallows you. No wonder you want to ask the Almighty that reasonable question: How many swallows have I been allotted? *How many swallows have I got left?* And as I found myself thinking this way, as I became a squeaking door turning back and forth making a dry sound on its hinges, I found myself thinking also of Frank O 'Connor and those things he told me, about that old Gogol of his, that fellow in the frigid overcoat walking down from Raglan Road to Merrion Square, that one who looked so much like me.

25

LAST OF THE BLACK-ROBES

Her letter came into my life like a golden ball, bouncing from the Other Side, as though it had caught me dreaming before the fire. I held it in my hand: she was real, then! She had been real all along! She was not going to be one of those who came and went, who became lost like all the other friends I had ever made. She was not one of my Absent Brethren, absent to you even when they were present, who absented themselves away even as they called themselves your Brethren. She said she missed the sight of the little motorcycle, that she had gone to visit old Mrs. Murphy from downstairs, who said "We have lost our dear friend..."

She would be starting Hilary Term. She would be taking her tuppence and buying a fresh apple in Morehampton Road, and then walking all the way to Kildare Street. Up past Lyster's marble tablet at the top of the stairs, to desk number 76, if it was open.

And if she was real, what about my own Soul, then? I had begun to believe that such a thing had not existed, that maybe I myself had not existed.

I heard her voice come to me in the written words, my own real world had found me again, had established contact, it was a note in a bottle: Whoever finds this... Say, *We are two boys and a man, we are off Gibraltar, it is the eve of Europe.*

I carried her letter around with me; the letter was proof to me that it had happened; I felt like waving it at people, saying that I had been right, that I had proof that it had all happened, that I was a real person, and not that gibbering scarecrow which walked among them instead of me.

But they knew, I think. They already knew. He wants to go galloping off with her, they said, He thinks he wants to be swooped up out of time again, and live a life no man has ever enjoyed; of course it is all impossible, O yes he thinks he is back on Baggot Street, --where he was never happy-- he thinks he wants to go sloshing along the damp pavements to Mary's place and drink with Frank O'Connor and Gogol, chat with Elizabeth Bowen you know, breathing out and breathing in, all that strange air. Well surely. Let him knock around with the likes of them; he's not doing much here.

What made things worse was that I was one of the last persons who still went around wearing the holy habit, too, outside of a few old timers who had been stashed away over in the Community Infirmary. Sometimes I would forget that it was Saturday, and would get caught in my habit, out on the campus. I was the last of the Black-robes, you see, and Tourists would come, whole families of them, running, to ask me "Which way to the stadium, Father?" I knew I should be kind to them --I had been one of them myself for so long a time. It was all still the dream of many people, still fond of a kind of childhood. "We have grass from this place, at home!" a mother had told me; she was hoping her child would go there. "--And don't say it's not possible!" she warned. People were like that, they wanted grass from the place, a piece of sod, some holy ground. But I was not happy there. I was kind to them all, but it had a strange effect on me; getting caught on the campus with my habit on kept making me feel like a telephone pole, stuck out somewhere, for dogs to piss on.

So I stopped wearing the holy habit on football Saturdays. I stopped wearing it to class, and then I stopped wearing it completely.

When I stopped, it seemed to me I was the last one to do so. I must have been among the very last; I think I have as much claim as any of them to have been the last real "Black-robe" there, the last

Black-Robe at Notre Dame; I certainly often feel like it, that that was the way it had been. I stopped going to games, too. I overheard someone say, "Keep an eye on him, --He turns in his football tickets!" I went walking down by the lake, instead, to see the frogs.

It had been a mistake; they had made a mistake, ever letting me out to see the hawsers drop. I would not get over it. What was bothering me was more than Ireland. It was not just Ireland, and it was foolish to get things all mixed up with the smell of a peat fire. It was not Dublin either--- Dublin was not entirely wonderful. Instead it was a something, a something that one loved but could not give a name to.

I have tried to do this, to name that which cannot be named. It presents itself as many things. Sometimes it is a breath of moist air, fresh on the face, and taken into the soul. Sometimes it is a lone figure, seen from far off yet recognized at whatever distance. And sometimes it is only a voice coming over the meadow, *"the mist becoming rain."*

25

THE MOTHERHOUSE

Old Father Matt Coyle and old Father Charles Doremus had a fist fight in the Corby elevator one time; people said it was only about which floors they should stop at, but I often wondered if, in some way, it was not over Notre Dame itself and about much deeper things. The place had originally been a French foundation, the early people had French names, and Father Doremus was the last of them, he was the end of all that "du Lac" business that was in the official title of the place, he spoke French and only managed English with a pronounced accent, he was the end of the French connection, whereas Matt Coyle was from maybe Chicago or someplace, at least he was very Irish- American, and represented to Father Doremus, and maybe to a few others, what the place had become. I suppose old Pere Doremus got the worst end of the fight; he was a small, intense man, with exquisite taste in cooking, whereas Father Matt Coyle, well, he was a very physical fellow.

This was a long time ago; I mention it mainly because of certain things that happened in my own life. I was not in any elevator fights, but there is a connection.

One day, years before I ever went overseas to study --- long before Ireland, long before Anne Francis-- Joe Hoffman passed the broccoli to me at table, and I refused it. "-Oh--" he said, crossing his hands mockingly over his chest, and managing to sound like The Lives of the Saints, "--*Blessed Francis did not like broccoli!*" Everyone laughed, and for a while Joe took to calling me "Blessed Francis". It annoyed me, but it gave me an idea. I wrote a piece about a vain religious who hoped to be canonized a saint, one day, and sent it to the *New Yorker Magazine.* I called it "Story of My Life".

The New Yorker wrote back and said they had found it "amusing." I was astonished; they said that if I signed my name to it, they would accept the piece I had written for them. I was reluctant to sign my own name --for reasons which seemed compelling enough, in that very different time-- but I finally did so. Waiting for it to appear made my days exciting; I was fulfilling the expectations of my teachers all the way back to Freshman English to appear in such a magazine. I can remember the particular smell of the proofs they sent to me for correction, it filled my head as I walked around the campus, waiting for the story to appear.

249

But something else happened, as well: the magazine took liberties. Without asking me, an editor there, in the interests of clarification, had referred to Notre Dame as "the Motherhouse" of my order.

That was a mistake. As soon as my issue of the *New Yorker* appeared, in the campus magazine rack at The Huddle and in people's mailboxes, I was told that there was a phone call for me from the Provincial House. It was from Father Mullahy (who had not yet gone to Rome.) Father Mullahy wanted to speak with me at once. It was the first time I had ever gotten a phone call from the Provincial House, and Father Mullahy had not wanted to talk to me before. When I picked up the phone the first thing he said to me most emphatically was that Notre Dame was _not_ the *Motherhouse* of the Congregation; and that I was wrong to think so, that the Motherhouse was not at Notre Dame, it was on the Via Aurelia, in Rome, Italy, and that I must have the New Yorker correct this most unfortunate mistake immediately. I did what I was told, I informed the editors, but they said there was nothing they could do, and did I have anything else to send them?

And not everyone was impressed. There were some tough old members of the community who actually hated Notre Dame; they talked of "being screwed" by the place, or by "the bastards who run everything". You might be surprised by them, and by how tough some priests can be.

Some of them started speaking loudly of "the Motherhouse" in my presence. It took a while for me to catch on, but when in the coffee room I heard it again and again, I realized that they were referring to Notre Dame. And you could tell from the way they said it, they said the word "*Muth*-a-house" in such a way that you knew they meant something else, and some of them deliberately called it "*Da Muddahowze.*" I tried to tell them that it had been a mistake, that it was not I who had called Notre Dame The Motherhouse, but it went into their language anyway, they liked using it. After a while, most of them forgot how it started, and that I had anything to do with it. But there were those in authority who did not forget, who associated my name with that deplorable tone in which the term "Motherhouse" was uttered; it was felt that I had presumed in some way to actually speak for the place, and everyone knew that there was only one person who spoke for Notre Dame. And I always had the feeling that at least some of what happened to me later on went back, one way or another, to that unfortunate mistake.

A literary agent in New York called Naomi Burton contacted me, and it quickly became clear that she was Thomas Merton's agent. She was famous for an anecdote, which she repeated to me in her

New York office, about the time at a cocktail party when she first heard that the young Merton, one of her prized writers, had decided to become a monk, and was going to enter the Trappists. She said she almost spilled her drink, and said, "*My God --He'll never write another line!*" Then he went off and wrote *The Seven Story Mountain.*

I felt that I should be congratulated; after all, it was the first time a Catholic priest had ever managed to appear in the New Yorker, ("Xavier Rynne" would come later), it was the culmination of what Carl Hager had taught us. I talked to myself; "--*You have the same agent that Thomas Merton has....*" I said. Then Harcourt Brace asked permission to use the piece in their Rhetoric Casebook, a text used to teach writing in college English classes and which was used at Notre Dame.

I was invited to Madison Avenue, to the Curtis Brown literary agency, and to Farrar Straus and Cudahy publishers. I thought I was something, or at least thought that I was becoming something. I saw myself as the kind of person who made New York his oyster, while still all the same remaining a faithful religious.

And so I tried to make New York my oyster, by doing the things I thought such a person as I should do: I mastered the subway,

I went to hear Cesare Siepe and Renata Tebaldi in the old Metropolitan Opera, from far up, standing in what must have been the seventh gallery. I took the Brooklyn train and headed toward Borough Hall, to visit the Oriental Museum. I knew I was on the rise; I was at last becoming the kind of person I had planned on becoming, when I was little and stayed home from school to read my brother's books with the blueprints of submarines in them and the facade of Rheims Cathedral in France. One day walking down near the Hudson I saw a huge ship of the Italian lines at its berth in 59th street; it was called the Julio Cesare, and they said it was headed for Argentina. It made me dream of taking a ship some place, that instead of just standing on the pier and looking at the gigantic hawsers running up to it, that I would be on such a ship, I would be leaving, and going somewhere. And I even discovered where the Algonquin Hotel was, where the famous writers congregated, but did not have the nerve to go in, for I was afraid I might run into Ernest Hemingway.

On the train leaving New York, going up the Hudson past Tarrytown and Peekskill, every passenger around me started singing "There was a Wild Colonial Boy", and I realized they must be all Irish working girls off for the weekend. I understand now that the wild colonial boy was a lad on a chain gang --"the iron gang" in Australia-- who escaped and robbed the rich to give to the poor, but then I had to struggle to make sense of what the girls were singing. I had never wanted to be Irish, but listened, enthralled by what was in the voices of the young girls. On the long way back to South Bend, I thought of all that had happened in New York, and in between thoughts I hummed the song over and over until it made some sense, and remembered the voices singing about the lad who was born in Castelmaine, his parents pride and joy, and that *"never iron on earth could hold the wild colonial oy."*

I tell such things because of what was going to happen later. Though my Superiors had not been much impressed with what they called my "modest literary success," it seemed to me that I should see if I could write something else. The How-to-do-it movement was new, and it was sweeping America. I decided to write something called "*How to Found Your Own Religion.*" It purported to be a hand-book --that a person could do _that_, too--but was not meant to be taken seriously. It was the work of a little smart-aleck; I am ashamed of it, for it did such things as condemning Jazz as an instrument of the devil

Still, it was a book. I suppose I always kept waiting for a comment from Hesburgh. I thought he might come by and slap me on the back, and say " --You're the kind of young man we need around here!" He never did speak to me. But shortly after the book came out, I heard from a friend that he had said, "--If that young man wants to found his own religion, then perhaps he should go out and get himself crucified, first!"

This happened, as I say, rather early, before I ever went to Europe; I offer it after the manner of one of those Profiles that are used by the FBI when they are tracking down someone they are looking for; long before they ever actually get their man, they know exactly what he is like, they know the things he does, what kind of candy he eats and which TV programs he watches, the places he is apt to appear, and the offenses he is likely to commit. I always felt there was a file on me; and of course, there certainly was, we all had a file; only that never bothered some people at all, it seemed to only bother me.

But one more thing flowed from the *New Yorker* piece. Father James Burtchaell --always said to be in direct line for Hesburgh's Presidency-- had long wanted someone to do a piece about the contribution the order had made to Notre Dame. He asked me to do this for him, and I thought about it. I understood, he wanted someone to write an appreciation for those who, after giving their lives, lay in long silent rows, out under the oak trees in the Community Cemetery, behind the Little Sem. The effort was laudable, they deserved it. But he seemed to want a kind of Gettysburg Address:

That these Unremembered Dead shall not have died in vain. And I could tell from the way he talked that it was going to be called "Giants Under the Headstones." I knew that it did not sound like me, that I could not write *Giants Under the Headstones* for him, without abandoning much else, I honestly did not think I could do it. I looked at Burtchael and said that I was sorry, and suggested that he might try doing *Giants Under the Headstones* himself, but I must have put it badly, for as soon as I said it I began to sense that my future was being chiseled out in cold stone for me, and from that moment on, when I awoke in the night, at times when I was not sure of myself, it seemed to me I heard the activities of Brother Cemetery, over where they prepared such things at the place behind the Community House, who stayed up at night preparing your gravestone for you, with your name on it, old Brother Cemetery chiseling away, chip-chip, getting your name correctly into the stone, with the letters "C.S.C" carved neatly after it, so that whenever the right slot out there called, they would be ready for you, so that there could be no question of who was positioned in it, deeply buried among them. When I woke up from this half-dream of mine, it made me feel that something was going to happen; I would always have trouble getting back to sleep, for the night seemed full of burials.

But I was wrong to say earlier that it was Father Doremus who lost the fight in the elevator. He stayed on for years at Corby, you could smell the Norman and Breton sauces simmering on a hot-plate in his room. It was instead Father Matt Coyle who was sent away, he was sent across the railroad tracks to be a chaplain over at Saint Mary's, taking his boxing skills with him; but of course, it was always clear that Charlie Doremus was not likely to hurt anybody, and I have always felt that the Superiors may just have been looking out for themselves.

26

THE KNOWN WORLD

I made certain that I would be waiting for her on her return, with a car at Pittsburgh airport to drive her up to Mercyhurst College, in Erie. And then after she was back a while, I invited her to visit us at Notre Dame, and found her a room in Lewis Hall where the student-nuns stayed. It was not new to her, she had visited it for conferences on the Religious Life and lectures.

I decided to do things properly, and introduced her to everybody. I said that Sister Anne Francis was my good friend, who meant a lot to me. But I did not sufficiently anticipate the response this would bring. The response I received at introducing Anne Francis to my community is difficult to describe. It had the effect of making me feel a regular Marco Polo of a fellow, come back from his travels, as though I had come back from the Silk Road, returned to the Known World with Treasures from the Orient. It was not as though I had introduced a person to them at all, it was as though they had been presented with Silk, Fireworks, Gun-powder, and maybe

Chinese noodles thrown in. I could not have surprised them more if I had shown up with Gold, Frankincense, and Myrrh. Father Paul Duff was an athletic, angular man; when I asked if he wanted to be introduced, he said, "--Don't *crowd* me. --You're *crowdin'* me!" as though he felt backed into a corner. I decided to go see Father Bob Griffin, and try again; he would certainly be different, for he was a life-long friend that I could count on; I wanted *someone* there to properly greet the person who had been through so much with me.

It went off alright, the two of us chatted with Father "Heavy" (that was what we called him, "-Heavy" -he had a weight problem) about life in Ireland and I thought it went well because of the way he entered into it. But afterwards, he almost could not wait to get me alone. *"---Well wouldn't you know!* " he cried as soon as he saw me, " *--Well, wouldn't -- you-- just-- know!"* He shouted it out angrily at me, whacking a magazine noisily on his leg for emphasis; he seemed to want to both congratulate me and scold me at the same time. At first I did not know what his tone meant, and only slowly began to understand. Heavy Griffin was telling me, Wasn't it to be expected that you would be the one to show up with someone like Sister Anne Francis? Had it not been predictable all along that you would travel the world, only to arrive back with such company?

259

After a while I began to know, well enough, what he was thinking of. He was remembering back to the time he had seen me off, on the slanted deck of the *Leonardo*; at that time he had acted as though he had caught me sailing away with the Province Pension funds, as though I were running away with everyone's retirement monies. I had actually been behaving myself perfectly, but he pretended grandly that they had all better watch me, had better keep an eye on me. I treated him to a drink, and as we drank a parting glass, the "All Ashore" warning sounded, he looked around him at the Grand Salon of the vessel; and then Heavy had to finish his Manhattan and walk down the gang plank, while I stayed on board, hugging the Future to me in a kind of ship-board romance, as though I were running off with Zelda Fitzgerald. Standing before he left, he looked back once more at that carpeted sloping floor; then he turned to me and said, " ---You clever fellow.....I didn't know it was like *this!*" I think he never forgave me for it, for telling him he would have to get off; it was as though I was making him walk the plank, you see; he always remembered, he said it was as though he had been made to walk the plank, while I had sailed off with Zelda. That was why he was now saying "*Wouldn't you know!*" once, and then "*Wouldn't you know!*" again.

But it was not what he imagined, at all. Anne Francis had faced everything with me; she had gone through exactly what I had gone through. No one there could know what that meant. When I thought about it I realized that Bob Griffin's response was close to what I should have expected; it was not all that surprising; I had been like that, too; I had been just like them, and just like Bob --only if anything, more pronounced. I supposed that I would just have to let them keep their Zelda, and have it that way.

But there were others who might be expected to react. Father Ferd, the Local Superior, always scrutinized any religious who he thought was pulling things under his nose; he might he expected to ask his usual questions, as though something were going on. But he said nothing. Altogether, the visit was an education, for it straightened out some things for me, and I should have been grateful.

We did meet one warm response. I used to play cards with Old Father Tom Brennan. I enjoyed him for his sense of humor. He was from farm country, and in his old age, planted a special kind of corn, up at the house in Lakeside, he tended it and watered it, so that he could enjoy the taste of what he remembered as a boy. But we lived in a community, and it was difficult to keep others from meddling in what you were trying to do. Young Tom Engleton came along, and seeing the freshly prepared plot, unheedingly proceeded to plant beans in it. I was there when it was told what had happened. Father Brennan sat there disconsolate for a while; then he said, "-Hell, we're not going to have *corn* at all, --we're going to have *succotash!*"

Tom Brennan took to her at once. We chatted about everything, all the different ways of saying "good morning" over there, about Mrs. Gavin Duffy's Turf Fire Restaurant, about climbing Great Sugarloaf in County Wicklow. I got her to tell him things I thought he would appreciate. I asked her to tell about the old Veteran from 1916 who used to wait for her. Father Brennan laughed and laughed at the old gentleman. "--Still some life in the old boy yet, wasn't there? --Still some life..." he said. And I got her to tell about the odd fellow in the library, who wanted to tell her future for her. And when Anne Francis said "I never give anybody my longitude and my latitude!" Old Tom Brennan laughed and laughed, about the longitude and latitude.

We talked about the Irish way of saying things. Anne Francis told about "one arm as long as the other" A little girl was looking out the front window of her home when she saw her Aunt Gertrude coming. Her mother called out to ask if Gertie was bringing anything? And the little child looked again, and then called back, "No she isn't---*One arm is as long as the other*!" Father Brennan thought about it, and then said "--So if you show up and don't bring anything, they say your one arm is as long as the other, is that it? -- There's nobody quite like them, is there.." He laughed.

We talked about pubs and the bodrum music and the Battle of Mount Street Bridge; he wanted to hear more and kept us as long as he could, he did not want to see her go. He was a veteran himself, one of the very finest. " Thank God there are a few of us left!" he would say to me at the liquor closet. And he used to say "--I'd do it again, *but not for money!*" He was getting old, and I knew he was afraid he would die without ever seeing that distant place we were talking about. He did get back, the following year, and then he died shortly after. When I think of him, I still hear him say "Thank God there are a few of us left!" and raising a glass of Irish Whiskey. I was glad I had found someone to welcome her at Notre Dame.

Afterwards, I took Anne Francis to Chicago O'Hare, and drove back alone. It had been what life was intended to be, having her there. I thought of that old war-horse of a Mother Superior, at a conference of all the big-shots who were running things for the Orders, saying to her, after she had given her own report on the status of things, "--Darling,--- where did they ever find *you*?" as though she were indeed a treasure beyond reckoning, it was a usual reaction when people met her. And Heavy Griffin had been right, his

263

response had been true enough: to those living there, Notre Dame was simply The Known World; yes, that was right, that was exactly what it was; I was headed down the Indiana Turnpike, back to the Known World, back to what was, for certain people, their very own Frog Pond.

Maturity is not easily come by; some of us are mature in one respect but not in another. Thomas Jefferson as a middle aged man fell wildly in love with beautiful young Maria Cosway. He was greater than any of us have any hopes of being, yet his foolishness when infatuated was also great, he went riding around Paris with Maria Cosway, who was a married woman. I was entering into the one abiding love and friendship of my life; it was not just another piece of foolishness, I had to put foolishness behind me, and learn to treat what was happening differently than anything that had happened before

I thought on my way back alone on the Indiana Turnpike: Wouldn't it be lovely if we could be, somehow, together? If we could somehow just burn up the Mortgage that they seemed to hold against us, and own our own life? Yet the answer was No. It would not happen; not in that place, certainly, with Assistant Superiors and Local Superiors and Provincial Superiors hiding among the Magnolia

Trees, expecting to find *Gone With the Wind* taking place under every nose.

No, certainly not in The Known World. Elsewhere, perhaps. "Away." Where? Just "Away" that's all: *A way a lone a last a long:* like the River Liffey flowing out to sea, to meet her cold mad feary father. Some place else. Not there.

27

THE WHISKEY REBELLION

On a late afternoon back there in 1968, we were all told to gather in Corby Recreation Room, to hear something that Father Hesburgh and the University Lawyers had to tell us. When we came in, there was Father Hesburgh, and the Provincial Father Kenna, and the Local Superior Father Ferdinand Brown, there was the University Lawyer, Mr. Ed Stephan. And then there were the rest of us: the young, the old, the wise, and the foolish, and we were sitting there, along with I think what was left of the Lay Brothers, who were quiet, as usual. I remember thinking that the four personages lined up that way facing us had a strong resemblance to the four main turrets on a battleship, say something like the giant Bismarck, slowly turning its guns around, and looking for a target; but I was only day-dreaming, my mind was always thinking of things like that, when it should have been thinking of something serious.

Father Hesburgh spoke; he spoke as he always did to us, as someone just come in from the great world outside, who knew how things were, out there, stopping to speak to people who had remained back home and found themselves confined, and of very limited experience, and this tone of his you would have to say was based in a kind of reality, for it was, to a great extent, true.

He began by saying that the time had come to speak of certain things, specifically, of the relationship of the Province and the University, of a financial settlement which the Trustees had deemed advisable, that the way things were going it had seemed advisable, that most of us had wrongly assumed that the university *belonged* to us, to the Province, whereas in actual fact the university belonged to the Trustees, and not to us. He introduced the university lawyer, Mister Ed Stephan who would fill us in.

Ed Stephan said the same thing. He said that though it might come as a surprise to many of us, the Congregation of Holy Cross did not actually own the University --the campus, the lakes, the golf course, or any of the buildings-- with the possible exception I think he said, of Sacred Heart church and of those community buildings on the other side of the lakes. And that the University Trustees had decided at their recent meeting, that in order to preclude any misunderstanding which might come up in the future, a settlement had been already arranged, by which the University would pay to the province the sum of I think he said 18 million dollars in 1968 money. And that this should be sufficient, if laid aside, and handled properly, to provide for the retirement of the members of the congregation who were still living, etcetera, etcetera.

Mister Ed Stephan talked like a lawyer; he used words like "deeming", he "deemed" a lot, he talked about the absolute necessity of it, he explained in a careful manner to the old priests assembled and to all of us that the world was changing, that things were changing, and that though he was sure that we had always assumed that everything---the classrooms the library the stadium the paths, the ball-field we had grown up playing on, the laundry, and such things-- that they all belonged to us, as the legitimate successors to the founding Father Sorin and the seven lay brothers who had tracked up into the woods before the Civil War when it was Indian country, whereas in fact Notre Dame did not now belong, in fact never *had* belonged, to us, it had always belonged to the persons hereinafter referred to as The Trustees, the aforesaid Trustees being in perpetuity and so forth, it had always rightly belonged to people very much like Mr. Ed Stephan, very much like him, and not so much like us as we might have thought, not very much like us at all. At least, that is what I heard him say..

And so on.

The amount of money which would change hands, he was sure, the Congregation would find very adequate, even generous, he said; although he anticipated that some among us might feel some uneasiness about the prospect. It had to be done, he repeated.

I think it was then that Father Hesburgh got up, and repeated: You have heard everything that Mr. Stephan has said, he said in effect, and he said that he agreed with it. And then he asked were there any questions?

Did I look out the window, past the peeling yellow paint of Corby, and wonder what I was doing there? I think I probably did. I may have thought of things like flying gliders out in Baldonnel, of climbing around Howth Head, thinking maybe of desk number 26 at the Kildare Street Library, and the Misses Flannery and King at Parsons Bookstore, of the old transcribings of Irish monks, and of Sally Gap. I may have even thought of Father Sorin and the seven brothers coming up through the snows in that first winter. And of how circuitous the windings are that bring us to a certain place. But to be accurate I do not know what I thought then, only I know now what I might well have thought.

Some one rose; I think it might have been Ed O'Connor; he had a way of asking questions which had just been answered. He asked if, then, the Trustees of the University were proposing a final settlement with the Priests of Holy Cross? All four of the heads in the front of the room nodded Yes; Ferdinand Brown nodded Yes too, and you could tell he felt honored to be there to say Yes. Ed O'Connor thanked them and sat down, he was glad he had gotten that straightened out.

Old Father Minnick arose after him, ---simple, kind, gracious--and asked the same question, still asking again for reiteration, and explanation, possibly trying to make sense out of what had been the years of his life. Hesburgh and Stephan repeated for him what they had just said, and he slowly sat back down.

Another arose, getting more trenchant, and asked if we were not giving the whole place away? If it did not amount to "a great big giveaway"? I forget the answer--perhaps it was that the place was not ours to give, and so that what was happening could not properly be called a "Giveaway".

There was a long pause, during which it seemed that no one really had any questions to ask. All the people who always talked had already talked, and it appeared that we were all going to go back to whatever it was that we were supposed to be doing. But before that happened, Father Lew Thornton got up.

Father Lew was a Southerner, from I think North Carolina; he never spoke much at meetings; he was genteel and very easy going. But this time he got up and asked firmly if it was expected that the priests were to accept the eighteen million as final payment in full, and that the order would from that time forward in no way be said to own the University of Notre Dame?

There was some little show of deference between Hesburgh and Stephan as to which would be most qualified to answer that. I don't recall which of them finally responded; it really didn't make any difference: the answer was, pretty much, Yes.

There was another dull empty pause full of stale Corby air, as Father Lew pondered what to say, before he sat down. Finally he spoke. "---*Then you better buy a <u>whiskey distillery</u> with the money!*" he said, and he sat down.

It seemed final; it certainly was the end of something. We were expected to leave. This was a real nice clam-bake, I said to myself.

I looked out the window. I thought of those famous Four and Twenty Blackbirds, baked in a pie, and what had happened to the Abbot Whiting of Glastonbury.

I looked around the room; there were certainly more than twenty four of us present that day, listening to Ed Stephan talk about who now owned the property. But it was clear to me that we were blackbirds, all right, the kind that Jack Horner was going to have baked in a pie. No one was actually hanged and slit open, I could not in honesty claim that, and that other unmentionable piece of business was not performed on anybody, in actuality, but in most respects I thought the words of the rhyme were fully honored. I looked up at our Superiors; they all seemed happy, honored to have been included.

But Hesburgh asked one more time if there was anything else anyone had to say--as if there were anything anyone could say.

I always said nothing at community meetings; I always sat in the back row and remained silent. But this time I surprised myself; I felt myself getting up; my throat was a little hoarse from nervousness as it always is when I speak in public; I have always been considered a quiet person, and I was very surprised to hear the sound of my own voice speaking to them.

I said: "--This money that is going to be paid... Is it real money, or is it going to be 'Funny Money?'"

I have never claimed to be of great intellect; I know certain odd things, small facts, which clutter my mind. I know for example that the battleship Bismarck had 8 fifteen-inch guns in four turrets, she weighed 52,600 tons in fighting condition. And that her crew had given each turret a name, the forward ones were called "Anton" and "Bruno" and then, since it was alphabetical, three and four had to be "C" and "D," and were called "Kaiser" and "Doris."

And so as I sat there in Corby Hall Recreation Room waiting for a response to my question about how things were going to be done, I could not help feeling that what I was facing was Anton, Bruno, Kaiser and Doris. I had been nervous when I had risen to speak, when I felt myself standing up, to say something, and when I heard my voice start to speak. Now it was more unnerving as all four turrets began to rotate, to see if they could find where the noise was coming from. The first forward turret Anton rotated, then Bruno, followed by Kaiser, and finally of course Doris, which I took to be Father Brown, four huge turrets looking for a target that was too small for them to be able to hit.

Ed Stephan looked at Father Hesburgh; Father Hesburgh turned and whispered something to the Provincial, Father Kenna. Father Kenna had been my old seminary superior, it was as though I were all his fault, you see. His thick spectacles appeared to be made of bottle glass, and I had always been afraid of him and his glasses. His eyes went looking for me in the room, I was his responsibility. He finally found me, and he asked me what I meant? What, exactly, did I mean by the term "*Funny Money*"?

I had often heard from people who worked in the finance office, had heard repeatedly, that each year when the University and the Indiana Province settled up accounts between them, there was often some small discrepancy, and to remedy the situation there was an old practice that one of them would sell back to the other the ownership of the Grotto---the Grotto of Our Lady of Lourdes. I knew nothing of the great goings on at that level, but someone who had been part of it had assured me that indeed this was so; I do not think I would be capable of thinking up such a concept myself, it is something I would have to have been told.

I suppose I knew, right then and there, or certainly should have, that I was completely finished at Notre Dame; from what I had already said, I knew that in one way or another there would be an end to me. But shy people are often brave-- inordinately and even foolishly brave, for after remaining in long silence they sometimes blurt out things which they can no longer hold in, things that no one else would ever blurt out, and they generally do it at the wrong time.

I knew I was speaking at the wrong time, about something that no one would be expected to speak of, but somehow I refused to back down. I said to Father Kenna:

"--You know...like when the Grotto of Our Lady of Lourdes is sold, back and forth between the Province and the University, to settle accounts. Is this real money we are going to receive, or is it going to be that kind-- *Funny Money*?"

This question of course was coming to them from the one responsible for the unfortunate "Motherhouse" terminology, which many of the men had taken up; Hesburgh looked at me as though recalling that he had been right in his original assessment that I should hurry out and get myself crucified. He did not have to take out a note-book and take my name down; they say he never forgot a name, he held things as Rome did, *in pectore* or "in the breast," and it really should not have been such a great surprise to me two years later, when I found myself kicked out of Notre Dame.

Somewhere in there, while Ed Stephan was talking, I had a strange sensation, a hark-back to another time: I thought I was standing in ancient Pompei, in the Street of The Bachelors, maybe, or the House of the Tragic Poet, or someplace like that, and I was looking at the tortured remains of what used to be, of people contorted and of dogs even, buried in the dust, that moment when I had heard the great horn of the *Leonardo da Vinci,* leaving, out in the harbor, leaving me alone with my thoughts, on a new continent and without any other humans, and solely with whatever came next. I do not mean that he had a foghorn of a voice as he droned on, --no, I think I was not concerned with him or with them, up there, but with something more like what Virgil called "the Tears of Things"--that everything, everywhere, actually weeps, if you listen closely, and sometimes you don't even have to listen very closely at all to hear it do so.

I do not know what will become of my old Congregation, if there is anything left of it; I find myself wanting to call it the Little Congregation from Kingdom Come. Perhaps it will return to its former place full of grace and truth, and young people will flock, to take home grass from the place. But it makes me feel the way I felt that time coming up through the Campagnia from Terracina on the road to Rome: the arches of the old aqueducts are still there, they run along beside you, they cease awhile, for they are often broken, but then they start in again, they rise and fall magnificently mile after mile, as if still hurrying to bring water to make the fountains of Rome thunder; only nothing is running through them, and the water to feed them no longer exists.

As I left Corby that day, I thought and thought, for the whole process had reminded me of something else, something unspoken that had been going on, something very present but which had not been mentioned publicly.

And then I finally knew exactly what it was. The whole thing had been as though Hesburgh had gotten up and applied his famous 15-Minute Rule to us-- the one that had been read to the students, during the protests of The Sixties. It was as though the Community itself had been read his famous "15 Minute Rule" and had been given time to come to our senses and to think about the consequences. And it did not matter whether it was he himself who read it or if Ed Stephan had read it for him, what had happened was that they had gotten up and said to us, "This place is Private Property. You may have thought that it belonged to you, but it belongs to someone else, now. It never belonged to you, anyway, this was a misconception, for it always properly belonged to the Trustees. We will therefore give you fifteen minutes to reflect that you are standing on Private Property, so that you will have time to come to your senses. Etc,etc...." The community had arrived in the snow of 1842, without

277

the help of lawyers like Ed Stephan. Now the community was being told, in effect, that we had fifteen minutes to think about things, and to come to our senses, fifteen minutes to get off the property.

Yet it was Father Butch Davis who shocked me. He was a tough guy, and a good chemist; he worked away at patents for Eli Lilly & Co. in the Notre Dame chemistry labs, something having to do with detergents, he was in the long line of Notre Dame chemists stretching back to Father Niewland, the pioneer of synthetic rubber who gave his name to Neoprene for Dupont, and to young Knute Rockne, Niewland's talented student. Butch knew his stuff. I ran into him downstairs afterwards in the coffee room. He was saying

"--I signed up to be a Notre Dame priest. If they give Notre Dame away, I am going!" He pronounced it "Dey" as he always did. He was very angry.

It shocked me, because we all had vows, and priesthood, and those things had little to do with Notre Dame. You were to go where they sent you, the place you lived was beside the point. Your vows and the priesthood were between self and God; even if Superiors did something you thought was foolish, your job was to keep your vows, and to obey.

But Butch left. He left not only Notre Dame, he left the priesthood too. And he married the girl next door. The Congregation --as part of all the changes taking place, had decided that the members ought to have a recuperation house, far from the campus where they could get away from student water fights and bed-checks, up to Lake Michigan, in a place called Lakeside; it was just an ordinary house, but it was on the water.

There was a girl next door there, a young woman, really; we would meet her on the beach, our two property fronts ran down to the water; some of the men chatted with her, she was a nice person. She was also exceedingly wealthy. She was reputed to be the heiress to the Crackerjack fortune, I guess the one built upon the little prize inside the box; I don't know, but we used to refer to her as "the Crackerjack Heiress" or the "Crackerjack Princess". Anyway, Butch Davis left, and married her; and when it became public that he had married her, I saw a lot of our fellows nodding their heads knowingly, and smiling, as though *they* could have had a chance at that sort of thing too, if only they had *wanted* to, and they would go away shaking their heads, as if they were saying the word "Crackerjack, Crackerjack," to themselves over and over. And I know what most of them thought; they thought that while they had been faithful, had remained in spite of everything, Ralph Davis, poor

Butch, had failed, had faltered, had married the Crackerjack Heiress, he had actually gone out and married the girl next door! It was really too much!

I remained friends with Butch, though I did not see him often. The more things kept going the way they were going, I used to want to get away by myself and go up to Lake-side. I would turn in my football tickets at the Superior's office, to be used by persons entertaining visitors. So then on Saturdays, instead of all that drum-thumping and cigarette smoke and the trample of feet and the sound of cars parking in the various assigned parking lots and the screaming frenzy that seemed to be sending your blood pressure up inside your chest until you wondered who you were and why this was happening and what in the name of god you were ever doing there, I would sign up for a car --there was now one available on football weekends-- and in the late morning before things got impossible I would see if I could work my way out of the campus by the Juniper Road exit and bounce up and down along the ruts of Douglas Road out to the Dixie Highway; I would turn north, among the autumn leaves, and cross the river into another state, and I would have some peace up at the lake, watching the waves still warm from the late summer roll in on the sand as they always had, for millions of years, before any of us where there, and watch the last few Golden

Monarch butterflies beating their wings south, to Mexico, to that mountaintop in the Province of Michoacan, where they would hang high on the trees waiting for the return of the sun to warm them back to life, and to the mystery of being alive.

I went up to the lake in the very depth of winter, too; I looked forward to frozen January; I would bundle up and go for a walk on the frozen sand of the beach in high boots, along the great piles of ice thrown up by the wind into pressure ridges, just like waves caught before they crashed. Grains of brown sand went scudding along the ice like hailstones against your ankles; it could not have been colder or more desolate at the earth's two poles.

And one time, I saw a black figure, off in the distance; someone like me who was going for a winter walk alone. A thought passed my mind; the figure looked awfully black, like me; and sure enough as it came closer it turned out to be Butch Davis. We came closer and closer, each slowly beginning to recognize the other, each wondering if the other would want to stop. We stopped and talked, there on the ice and frozen sand. He said that now instead of doing Chemistry research he spent his time keeping track of her investments. : "--_Boy_--it's a lot of work! Its _hard_!" he said. And as his figure comes to the mind's eye, I see that he is wearing black, yes --Butch is still wearing almost certainly the last of his priestly overcoats, with a black hat pulled down over his forehead to his eyes; he was the eternal Little Seminarian, he had been raised that way from the Little Seminary first by Father Fiedler and Father Grimm, and after that by Father John Hoy Murphy, and endless superiors, and also by old Father McElhone, with the hearing aid, they had each left their mark on him, and you could see that things were really not going to change, all that much.

I think of this period as the "Time Between the Chairs." There used to be an old priest at Notre Dame who studied the weather. He is surrounded in memory with the sound of ancient radiators hissing, against the yellowed paint of Corby Hall, in one of the parlors where I received Spiritual Direction from him.

I came for spiritual advice, but got other things. It was often winter when I came, and he used to say to me, over and over, "--The worst weather of winter comes between the Feasts of the Two Chairs ---*the worst of winter always comes between The Chairs!*"

(He meant the Chair of Peter in Rome and the Chair of Peter in Antioch, which used to be celebrated toward the end of January..) But that period is also called The Great Stillness by bird-watchers, it is that time of year when every bird that is going anywhere has flown away, and there is nothing to look for. And sometimes, remembering that Spiritual Direction, I consider that the Great Stillness can also be within the Soul itself, a landscape where only stragglers peck for sustenance, lone wanderers who have lost the urge to fly.

28

THE AGE OF STEAM

The effect of this on me was to keep pushing my mind back to an earlier time. When we were little more than boys, those in charge of us tried very hard to keep the world of the football stadium away from us: we were there to become priests, not to follow football. We were permitted to go to two games a year. To do this, we wore our black street suits, and stood in discreet little batches of four and five, up near the concrete columns at the top of the stadium. We looked strange in our black suits, but no one noticed us, everyone was watching the field, and so were we.

The Rule, however, said there was to be a Holy Hour in chapel in the presence of the Most Blessed Sacrament exposed upon the altar, at 5 o'clock every Saturday. Can you imagine little boys marching from a nationally featured football game straight to a Holy Hour? The Rule, made for us in France, was really the Rule of Saint Benedict from ancient Subiaco and Monte Cassino in the Fifth Century; it did not say anything about football games.

284

So you cut things close. You hurried home from the wafting cigar smoke of the stadium, made your way out past the press box where the reporters were filing their dispatches to the New York Times and the Chicago Tribune, you slipped around the edges of the crowd, hurrying like good rule-keepers past the Grotto, around the curve of Saint Joseph Lake, toward the yellow bricks of Moreau Seminary. You rushed up to your room to get out of your black street suit and back into the holy habit, tying your cincture around you as you skipped down stairs. You were lucky if you arrived on time, not to have to get down and genuflect on two knees for being counted late, in time to hear the voice of Father A. Leonard Collins majestically beginning The Consecration of the Human Race to the Sacred Heart of Jesus:

"--Sweet Jesus, Redeemer of the Human Race!
We are Thine, and Thine we wish to be..."

Was that really me, kneeling there? It is so long ago that I find myself doubting how it could have been, and so to make certain, I do a strange thing, I search with my tongue for that missing tooth of mine, the one the dentist pulled out, as though with my childhood. It

285

is easy to find, that empty space, for I know exactly where it is, and I confirm beyond all doubting that it was me, and not another, it was me, attending Five   O' Clock Holy Hour in Moreau Chapel, with the Monstrance holding the Host all in gold, surrounded in a cloud of sandalwood smoke rising from the thurible, and Father Collins praying to the Sacred Heart *"for those deceived by erroneous opinions, whom discord keeps aloof"* We knew who that was; we knew who we were praying for; we were praying for everybody, for Protestants of course, for Agnostics and Atheists, for Baptists and Episcopalians, Methodists and Presbyterians, so that they would see the light, so that they would all be saved. There was concern uttered *"for those held in the darkness of Idolatry or of Islamism."* And, in the end, of course, we prayed for the Jews-- a prayer not for what might happen in this world, but in the world that was to come:

"Look finally, with eyes of pity upon the children of that race which was for so long a time Thy Chosen People; -- of old they called down upon themselves the Blood of the Saviour -- Let it now descend upon them, a laver of redemption and eternal life!"

It was a long time ago. But it is not what I am remembering, chiefly; what I am remembering really is what happened next, what always happened next. For it was about this time, it was almost always precisely at this time, when we had gotten to the place where

286

we were asking for a Laver of Redemption and Eternal Life, that the trains began to start up, the great special trains which had brought the football crowds to the stadium. They would slowly begin their business of grandly backing out along the Steam-House spur, the bells of the great steam locomotives began to clang loudly as the locomotives backed out along the tracks which ran behind the rear of Moreau Chapel, making the old disused cross-ties creak and scream under their unusual weight, the chuffing and clanging and creaking of one train after another, leaving after the game, backing out to return to Bloomington and to Ann Arbor and to Champaign Urbana, their sounds mixing in with the darkness of idolatry and of Islamism, everything inextricably mixed with the Laver of Redemption and of Light.

It is all gone with my missing tooth. It was truly of course the passing of the Age of Steam that was going on out there, indifferent to us, the great steam locomotives backing out to the highway, their tremendous weight making the tracks squeal, the engine bells clanging and clanking, and all the while excess steam hissing out around the boiler and the piston rods and elsewhere, rising to heaven, stopping traffic out on the Dixie Highway as each train crossed. We tried hard not to think of the game we had just attended; *Sweet Jesus, Redeemer of the Human Race--,* we prayed, *--chuff chuff, clang*

clang, creak creak-- the receding black hulks interrupting the voice of A. Leonard Collins, the occasional blast of a train whistle, which the old yellow walls of the seminary could not seal out, drowning out everything, the trains full of cigar-smoking sportsmen, many of whom surely deceived by erroneous opinions. We prayed for them all, to save their souls for them.

Hear the train blow. My knees still feel the hardness of the wooden kneeler; I can still smell the cigarette smoke which drenched the cuffs of my sleeves from the game, as I prayed for those lost in darkness. I do not disdain it; for though I have knees like a camel from all that kneeling, it is good for a man to kneel. But did we not know then that we were passing, too? Our way of life and our Notre Dame was clanging out backwards with us, thing of great beauty, and we ourselves were passing out of time; it was all passing away even as we were making the Consecration of the Human Race to the Sacred Heart of Jesus, with its *Many indeed have never known Thee.* Those locomotives, of course, were headed to the Elephant's Graveyard, they were working their way to some siding or other, where their black hulks would slowly rust into scrap; and as for the rest of it, that panoply of devotion going on inside, that way of life and that way of looking at things was headed to a place of tusks and skulls and dry bones as well. In the name of God, did we not know that we were going, too?

29

YOU BEST KEEP ON RUNNING

"My affairs are everywhere going smoothly."

-- Cardinal Wolsey, in a letter shortly before his fall.

Andy Smithberger was an Indiana farmer who smoked a Meerschaum pipe as he sat behind his desk as the Assistant Chair of the English Department. He wore red suspenders over checkered shirts, and would recite "The Boy Stood on the Burning Deck" or "The Village Smithy" and you might easily dismiss him as foolish, yet he ran everything for the department.

The department was having trouble filling its courses. By the end of the 60's, students were demanding "Relevance" and voting with their feet, the kind of courses Andy and his friends had taught all their lives were dying. Each day during Registration week, the department counted up totals feverishly, to see which courses and which teachers were going to survive; indeed there was some concern even for the department itself.

I experienced no trouble, yet considered myself a demanding teacher. One day I came up the stairs to the Department Office and saw a list taped up on the door jamb: "Courses Filled" it said, and listed the courses which were filled and could take no more students, and the first three courses were mine, the first to be closed off due to over-subscription, they each had my name behind them. Seniors were filling up my Introduction course, leaving no room for the Freshmen. As I walked into his office, Andy took his Meerschaum out of his mouth and said, "Father Phelan---Father *Phe*lan! Such popularity with the students in the year 1969 is *unbelievable!* It beggars the imagination! Your courses are over-subscribed! We have to *beat* the students away! " Then he added, rolling his eyes "--That's *good!* --That's *very* good..."

I should have noticed the way he rolled his eyes. I tossed it off as a compliment, but I should have known better. There were many professors who could not fill classes; indeed a new art-form had sprung up, the art of inventing courses which would "go", and the giving of exciting names to them. "Sex in the Elizabethan Age", say, or "Poe and Pornography" and so on. Any popularity a teacher maintained thus became suspect; it implied that you were not delivering *Content,* were not a demanding teacher.

It was a difficult time, you saw your own old wizened-up professors, the ones who had taught you, who had been autocrats within their classrooms, who had frightened you into learning by threatening to fail everybody. You had learned your Hamlet from them, as the ancient *Brudermorder* play, about a man willing to kill his own brother to get the throne, about what brothers do to brothers. They now moved along the corridor clinging to the walls as though afraid for themselves, as though they might be reciting elegies. Indeed, nothing was certain.

But Andy was pleased, I was a bright light for them. The situation made him lean back in his chair, and take his pipe out; it reminded him of a story, he said, he was going to tell me one of his stories, a most illustrative story. "---There was a young lady once," he began, avuncular.

I stood there, listening.

"-- She went home and told her mother that she was going with a wonderful young man. The Mother arched her eye-brows and said, ' --That's good..." but continued her sewing. Then the girl said, 'And I'm *pregnant!*' The Mother paused, and then managed to say '---That's good' in a less than convincing voice. Finally the girl announced, '--And we're getting *married* on Saturday!' The Mother dropped her sewing, jumped up, and said in a loud voice, 'Now *that's* good! Oh, that's *very* good!'" Andy laughed and laughed, and threw his head back, opening his mouth so that I could see far in, even to his bouncing Adams Apple.

I laughed, too; I thought I had a good sense of humor. But I did not know what I was laughing at. What Andy Smithberger, the suspendered Assistant Chair of the Notre Dame English Department --who was in on all meetings and knew everything-- was telling me, was that it was all well and good for someone like me to pursue a

293

noble career in letters, but that my situation was very much like that of a young girl who was in love and pregnant but with no prospect of marriage. He was trying to tell me that it was very good for me, very fine indeed, that I was so overwhelmingly accepted by the students and that the department could see that all my courses were filled --- that was very good news. But he was also trying to say that if it were not for such signs of success in my work, I would almost certainly already be on my way out. When I recall the way he told me this, in that twang of his which sounded like it came from "The Grapes of Wrath" and took me back to the days of the Dust Bowl, it reminds me of the line spoken by the old Mother in a famous gangster movie: "--You best keep on runnin', Bonnie and Clyde!"

* * * *

You had to get Tenure. Not getting it was much worse than losing a job. If a person is fired, there is still a large world out there, they may even find better work elsewhere. But if your school refused tenure, no one else likely would have much to do with you. It is a small, tight system, and persons refused tenure find themselves classed the way carriers of infectious disease are, to keep whatever it is from spreading. Moreover, that particular period was a terrible market to be dumped into. I stood there feeling sorry for the ones it would happen to. I did not have to think much about it, I would just keep on working. But Andy shook his head. "--What's happening today.... it reminds me of Felicia Hemens' poem, _Casabianca_ --do you know that one?" Of course I didn't, I didn't even know who she was, so he started reciting:

> _--The flame that lit the battle's wreck_
> _Shone round him o'er the dead!_
> _Then came a burst of thunder sound;_
> _The boy,---oh! where was he?_

--It _applies_," he said, "--It's like what's going on today! Everything's _exploding_ all around us!"

I stood there, waiting. I did not see why he was speaking this to me.

My degree was as good as anybody else's-- probably better, I thought-- they had not done what I had done; my service to the department was pronounced, I had started the prestigious Seminar in

295

James Joyce for them, where eight teachers each applied a special interest on one subject; I had brought Distinguished Professors to the campus, and distinguished writers; and my own work had not merely been published, but was contained in the Harcourt Brace Rhetoric Casebook as a model of good writing; none of the others had anything in a textbook assigned by the department. Every course I offered was over-subscribed. What possibly could be wanting?

Perhaps something like an instinct for survival. The kind of instinct that had brought Andy Smithberger behind that desk, red suspenders, checked farmer shirt, meerschaum pipe and all, so that people like me stood in front of him, listening to jokes about pregnant girls, and hearing him recite his favorite verse.

I turned to leave, to go back to my classes. Andy called out to me, "--That's from Felicia Dorothy Hemans-- She has another one called _Landing of the Pilgrim Fathers_: He threw his head back, holding his pipe in one hand, and recited again:

"--_Ay, call it holy ground, The soil where first they trod!_"

I began leaving while he was still reciting. He called out behind me as I left the office, "---She was pretty good, old Felicia! --

She was right bang on!" I heard him still reciting as I was going down the stairs.

Six weeks later I was terminated, and more fully understood what Andy Smithberger had been trying to tell me.

30

CASE HISTORY

One football Saturday morning, after I had stopped going to the games, I worked my way through the usual hubbub in Corby's front corridor past people with green hats on and scarves saying "Irish!" and "We're Number One" to the office where the mail was left. I had heard that the new announcements of promotion were in the mail, and mine had not come, it was late. But there was no mail to be seen; usually it was stacked there on Brother Cy's desk. I looked and looked, and almost gave up, thinking there had been no delivery that day.

But just before I left the office I saw that the telephone had been moved; someone dealing with such things as football tickets had nervously and very neatly, as they talked, placed the phone base down perfectly on a little square stack of letters beneath it. I was annoyed, I could imagine the voice of someone saying "Two seats behind the Goal Line!" as they pushed the mail aside. I placed the phone back where it should be, shot through the stack, and saw a letter to me, from the English Department. I swirled away   into one

298

of the front visiting parlors away from the noise, tearing it open so that I could read it alone.

It started out with a quote from the rules: The refused person will have the reasons for refusal explained to him. No explanation followed, however; the matter was declared confidential. The letter was from Jim Robinson, new Chair of the Department; it said that I was "very talented" but that I was being refused tenure. I looked at it, but could only see the words refusing me tenure. It went on to other things: if this inconvenienced me, I could ask to be permitted to remain on for another year, as a temporary appointment. I had been terminated.

I cannot find words for what I felt, reading the letter there in the Corby Parlor; it is not really possible to describe the moment.

Tolstoy was right: your own death occurs in the interstices of someone else's life; your end is in the nature of a footnote at the bottom of the page of some much larger story; you are not important to someone else's living and breathing, to their sex lives or their constipations, their coughs and tickles; there are too many people on this earth for you to matter much, there just simply are not sufficient resources for you to be taken that seriously. You, and the end of you, and all you stand for are matter to be stacked neatly under the telephone used for someone else's phone call; the call is important, it is about football tickets, for there is always some Purdue Game or other going on. My time in that place always seems to me to have turned, somehow, into one big endless Purdue game.

I had been faithful in a strange land, I had fought fate and cold and time, and in the end had won, against loneliness and fear. There should have been witnesses. I had won fair and square, honest witnesses should arise to say, He has done well, He has in fact excelled, displayed outstanding steadfastness in the pursuit of truth; we were there, we witnessed it. But there was in fact only me reading the letter, and if anything good was going to happen it was only me that could do anything about it. I suppose I should have started to do something right away, like stand up, to see if I could still stand, and then after that, try to walk, get in those first wobbles, toward wherever I was going.

But I did not feel like putting one foot in front of the other; I did not even feel like breathing. Carlyle in his classic The Everlasting No, says: "Do first that thing which lies nearest to Thee; the next will manifest itself." But I saw no first thing. I did not want to tell Anne Francis. That was the last thing I wanted to do; I could not bear to bring this thing upon her.

It was what was being referred to as "the worst market ever" for college professors. And it had been done to me at an age when I should not be out looking for a job. Besides, I was by now a specialized creature; I had been systematically developed to be a "priest-professor" such as exist mainly at a place like Notre Dame. There were scarce few other places like that; what other place, in the name of God, would want to hire a "priest-professor"? Why should they? I was in a very tight fix.

And I should have seen how things were going. The other person up for tenure was a young man named "Little Dorrit." That was not his real name of course, only how I remember him, for he spoke constantly of Little Dorrit, and must have done a thesis in Dickens. There was nothing wrong with him, but all year whenever I passed the door of the Faculty Club, Little Dorrit would be talking, over drinks, with Jim Robinson, the Chair of the Department. Robinson always seemed to be looking across at the young man, regarding him as his spiritual heir. The two of them had gone to the same college--- called Walnut, or something. In truth I did not know much about Little Dorrit, yet he was the other one up for tenure, and as I saw them talking intensely each day I should have known that it would not be possible for me to compete on a level such as that.

What you do, when you start thinking again, is to start looking for employment. You look at what are called Tombstone Ads, those dumb square announcements which seem so like a gravestone, with the name of the deceased upon them. You buy books on how to find a job. If you still want to live, you begin to pay attention to the How to Succeed shelves. You understand that much of what you are doing is useless, is throw-away, but you become wise: if you do not start somewhere, you will not start at all; these first beginnings may be throwaways, but you want to get rid of what you have to get rid of early, so as not to toss something later that is important. You have to become good at Disaster.

I became good at Disaster. First, I made myself two rules. Rule Number One: Look people straight in the eye. Keep your back straight up, and fear to speak to no one. That was a good rule; I am glad I made it; it works well even outside of calamity.

Rule Two: Don't Drink. I kept this one, too. The Community had gotten to the place where there was a Sunday evening cocktail party before supper. The next day after being fired I could go there, if I had the courage to appear in public. It was an open bar, you could pour yourself as many stiff ones as you could consume in forty-five minutes, and you could bring the last one with you to the table. I used the finger-and-a-half rule: one drink of scotch, no more than one finger and a half. I kept the rule faithfully, week after week. I finger-and-a-halfed my way on and on through everything. (Anything else that happened between me and drink took place a good five years later, after it was all over, after I had begun to think I was safe.)

Of course, your hair will feel like it is falling out, and may actually be, at least it will be turning white. You have to expect this. The people who did it to you expect it, too. They will say, "He is looking old and gray--" as though they were concerned. Your forehead will become red and tender, because it understands what is going on, your own body feels sympathetic to you. A ridiculous amount of courage is required just to stand straight and have good posture, when your hair is falling out and you have a red face from worry. You need good posture to get a job.

A person on the inside of things inquired about my case; it was the only reliable intelligence I acquired. He was told that I had been considered "a very talented candidate" but that the year before I had come up, the university had fired a young man with a family, and the English Department was determined that laymen were not the only ones who could be put out into the street.

Another response came from a fellow teacher. It was reliable in its way. One evening before it happened I had been sitting at the Faculty Club with Lew Soens, an old friend, I had been his guest and had eaten at his table many times. But that night, Lew had had a few drinks. He started saying "Fuck you, Frank Phelan, Fuck You!"

I listened to why he was saying this to me.

He explained that a person like him struggled to write an article, say, on Sir Phillip Sydney, in the hopes that "lightening would strike." He meant that as a scholar he dearly wanted to write a piece which would electrify his field, and be acknowledged as a stroke of genius. But it had not happened, he said, that had never happened. "But it has happened to you--- it has happened twice," he said. He had read two of my short stories that had recently been published, and said that what he wanted to happen had actually happened to me, and so he was not worried about me. It should be enough for me, I could look out for myself. That was why he kept saying "*Fuck you.*"

It was only afterwards that I recalled that Lou was on the Promotions Committee; and then I understood what Fuck You meant:. It meant Fuck You, the committee has already met, it meant we voted, Fuck You, you have had enough good fortune, and can shift for yourself. That is what it meant, and it required a few drinks to make it come out. It is what I called my "Fuck You Moment", when I at first was beginning to understand what was going on. I heard from psychologists somewhere a wise state ment: "Stress begins to alleviate itself with the first steps taken to deal with its causes." It is a strange way for life to unfold, but all of the really good things that have ever happened to me started with the words "Fuck You."

And so I began to live among the tombstones--. I lived among them, you could see my hands coming up over the backs of the stones, in ceme-teries, on dark and stormy nights, scaring the dickens out of people, like some escaped convict in the rain. You would wonder what it was that I lived on.

I marked those ads which had anything to do with my field. Each time I penciled one in I looked to see where the place was. I remember one from the University of Hilo, in Hawaii. As I held my pencil in the air, I thought of teaching Irish Studies at Hilo, where the warm surf crashed in and where the teachers wore Hawaiian shirts. Then I told myself to move on, to get going, and keep answering ads. Nobody wanted me. (A monk should not be found answering want ads.)

I bought books on how to write exciting resumes. I developed a style; I discreetly explained to schools across the country that they would be getting not only a qualified teacher of literature who had published and had studied overseas, but a person with two Master Degrees, as well as a Doctorate, who was even able to fill their class rooms for them. I smuggled in everything. I mentioned that I was a member of the Dublin Gliding Society. That should strike somebody's fancy: What a specimen he must be! The University of Houston would not be expected to have any teachers who had gone soaring at Baldonnell; I must apparently be in good shape; I must be exciting to be with; I was a learned scholar, yet one whose work had also appeared in the *New Yorker,* whose name was in the very anthologies used in their courses; I would add an international dimension to their department. I was a breath of fresh air.

I hated those who had done it to me. Being rejected by the Notre Dame English Department was like being rejected by the Mormon Fruit Growers Association. The department was average, there was nothing wrong with it, but it was no great shakes, it was scarcely what the place was known for; to be rejected by the people in it was especially humiliating. And I became quite selfish. I remember turning for consolation to the tv Evening News, because it was always so full of other people's disasters.

You have to find where the bottom is; you have to figure out the point below which things cannot fall any further, it is only then that you can start thinking if they will ever start upwards again.

I found a bottom. That Christmas, two months into the middle of the disaster, I went to visit my sister in Pittsburgh. I did not tell her anything; I used up my energies being cheerful. She put me up as usual in my old room, the one I had grown up in, which still had nautical decorations from my Clipper-Ship Period, and a lamp with a ship's wheel for the on-off-switch. As I came in with my suitcase I looked at it. I said to myself, "You are no farther ahead at this moment than you were the day you left this room as a boy." That was it, the lowest moment; and it almost destroyed me, but there was value in discovering it.

One day someone told me, "--There's an opening for a High School Chaplain in Laredo, Texas. The Brothers at their school there need a CSC priest...." This was said to be kind, it was a long lariat dropped down to rope me up back onto the wagon, in Laredo, Texas. I thought of myself advising high school students on their sex lives. And I wondered if they dealt with only the upper crust of Laredo or maybe the border-crossing Hispanics. As soon as it was suggested, my mind took me to walking the streets of Laredo: "*I see by your outfit that you are a cowboy*" it sang to me, and that was a mistake,

307

everything became all wrapped in white linen, and covered with clay. I decided to hold out, for something else.

And something strange happened. As it moved through channels, my affair somehow became Burtchaell's business. He seemed to take it as his own. By this time Burtchaell had become the Black Prince, he was now a Royal Pretender, with Right of Succession. He had been appointed to a new position, Provost, which appeared to have been created especially for him, and he was going to succeed Hesburgh.

That was not helpful to me. As I searched down alley-ways and long corridors, hoping to find some solution, my problem always seemed to lead only to Burtchaell, he seemed now to have become the problem: no matter where I arrived, I would look down and always discover the two big feet of Father Burtchaell, sticking out from under every curtain.

By this time the Province had designated a Father Mike Murphy as a kind of Court-appointed Lawyer to defend our rights vis-a-vis the Univer-sity. Father Mike Murphy said that he had remarked to Burtchaell that the graduating seniors in their exit reviews frequently mentioned my name as being among the best teachers they had had in their four years. Burtchaell waved his hand in the air. "---*Oh!* " he said, "---*That's the easiest thing in the world! It's the easiest thing in the world to get a lot of students to be crazy about you!*". That was a most prescient statement out of him, in view of what later happened in Burtchaell's own relationship with students.

And I discovered Sophocles, too. He said that even in the most awful and terrible of tragedies, there is always some opportunity for good. I did not believe him then, of course, or anyone who talked that way, no matter who they were, for I had not a crumb of comfort. But it is true; based on my experience I would say that----with the exception of certain very final things like being decapitated or being vaporized in an explosion-- disasters often do have good effects, and I think it may even be true that the worse the disaster, the better chance you have ---if you are still living and moving-- of starting completely over with things, and doing things the way you should have in the first place,

If you had been sagacious. Once you have been tossed out, and have to clean your desk while everybody is watching, it is not all bad, it can be motivating. You may end up with your own skyscraper, somewhere else.

And I read a story by Alice Munro called "The Moons of Jupiter", about a woman walking away from the hospital, right after the death of someone near. She finds herself passing a planetarium, with many school children waiting to see a projection called The Moons of Jupiter. She decides to go in, even though she expects the place to be filled with active children. She sits there in the darkness, among school children, and eternity. The universe is projected up on the screen in front of her, the deep encompassing universe. I remember her watching The Giant Red Spot, a storm which has troubled Jupiter for century after century, the same big storm, without ever dissipating. She sits in the darkness, watching the four moons in orbit, circling, as they always have. I sat with her, in the darkened place; we both looked up, and watched it all go round and round.

A few places seemed interested. Someone at The University of Southern California became interested in me, "because of your combination of scholarship and novel writing". And another at the University of Houston said I would "add an international dimension" to their department. Grand Rapids, after first showing no interest, got back to me later and asked if I was still searching? But I knew all along what was going to happen. I might have saved my writing paper, and not bothered to create resumes. I knew from the beginning that the only places with real openings for such as me would turn out to be the sister-institutions run by the Congregation, Kings College in Wilkes-Barre or Stonehill College outside of Boston.

Each night I sat up straight, and paid attention to the Evening News: three million cans of Coca Cola had been recalled as unsafe, the columnist Walter Winchell had died, the former Cunard liner Queen Elizabeth had caught fire and sunk, in Hong Kong harbor.

Then Kings College offered me a contract, and then Stonehill College did, too.

I was grateful to Kings, it was the first indication that I would not have to go insane; but I could not bring myself to return to the coal fields of Pennsylvania; Kings was a good place, for someone else; but not for me. Ed Haughey at Stonehill had carefully told me: "We have two positions; but in one case the individual is having emotional problems; and that position has to be held open for her; but Jeanie Rosenbaum is likely not to return her signed contract, and if she does not, that position is yours." And so it was April 1 when I waited for the call. Ed Haughey said that Jeanie Rosenbaum had not returned her contract, and that the position in the English Department was mine if I chose; he would send the contract. I agreed to go to Stonehill College; the hateful period was over, it had lasted five months and nine days, which in my straightened condition had seemed longer than the Siege of Leningrad.

But back while I was still lost, I used to go for drives, to get away and think of something else; I took Walter Goff with me, who could not drive and who counted on me to take him out. One day, before anyone had offered me salvation and before I knew what was going to happen, driving west of South Bend in the brown slush of an early February evening, I had to swerve suddenly to avoid a Greyhound Bus coming past. I always look up to see where buses are going. It sprayed brown slush over our windshield, and I had to start the wipers to be able to see. "BOSTON" it said, as it nearly ran me over, "BOSTON". I looked over at Walter; he had not noticed anything, except that he had not gotten run over. But it meant that I was going to Boston, you see, and I smiled inside me. I thought, What if I am going to Boston? I still remember the frozen South Bend slush.

"--Well of course..." my Sister said when she heard where I was going, "--Boston is where you should be, it's more like you. If you don't mind my saying so, I always wondered what someone like you was doing in that place out there, anyway."

As I signed the contract Haughey sent me, he said "We've got 300 Harvard Ph Ds standing in line out there waiting for a position; you wouldn't have had a chance except you have that 'CSC' after your name." I knew that was true; and I smiled. By that time, my face had cleared up, my walk was no longer tentative; I knew I had earned whatever I had gotten.

My time of trial coincided with the period in which the country was taken over by the Watergate affair, which made my own problems unimportant. It was terrible for the country. But it was the only time during the day that I did not have to think of my own troubles. I found it diverting as I watched the evening news, and for selfish reasons I made use of it, I badly needed a release, to keep from thinking about myself and going crazy. You would not like me; I needed Richard Nixon to keep my hair from falling out.

There was Haldeman, and Erlichman, and the round puffy face of John Mitchell, "the Big Enchilada" and squeaky little John Dean, and the clammy, quiet Hunt. I spent the full hour trying to comprehend that such persons did exist. I watched and watched, I heard how they spoke, for they reminded me of someone, and my mind kept asking:" Do you not know these people? Have you not come u pon them in the corners of your own life?" There was talk about "deep-sixing" documents, about letting someone squirm and

313

twist in the wind, about "stonewalling'". One of them said, " *We could do it! ---It would be wrong, but we could do it!"* Eventually, when Nixon finally gave his victory signal, as he got into the green helicopter and swirled off, all that was a long time later, and I was safely somewhere else, away from them.

And so Robinson, Soens, and Collins: in spite of efforts to dismiss them, they have somehow come to occupy a place in memory as my own Watergate Burglars. I have tried to remove them, for I know that it would be better if they were forgotten, but I do not succeed; I cannot always help it, when I get too tired, or cannot sleep, I still find myself listening for them, I am afraid they may still be running around in Nike sneakers, carrying flashlights and black tape, down in the underground of life, down where the bugs are, near the sump-pumps, down in the cellar. And my mind began to repeat a line from Robert Frost: "What to make of a Diminished Thing." I did not know where it came from, and cannot say I knew what it meant. But it started saying itself to me then, when I needed it, and it has kept repeating itself to me all through the time since.

I am not certain if we are supposed to know the answer.

314

31

HISTORY OF FLIGHT

Spring came that year, though I do not remember it. There must have been a moment, after I had signed a contract, when I saw what I thought were buds appearing on the ends of branches, and went over to examine them, and found that it was true, that the new growing season had begun. Botticelli's Primavera must have been smiling out flowers and green things from the upturned corners of her mouth, spreading life once again on Southward-facing banks and along the edge of woods, perhaps she was even smiling at me. There surely had been a moment of what is called "Just-Spring"; yes, certainly there had to have been, the force that through the green fuse drives the flower, the force that drives all of us, you know ---it had to have happened. But I had not been able to pay attention to such things.

I wanted out of there. I was allowed a small car (a Chevy, actually) so that I would "not be a burden" to the new Province. It

315

only took two hours to pack my typewriter and books. I remember wedging the two speakers of my hi-fi in against the backs of the front seats. I got myself a sandwich; and at the refrigerator, I ran into old Father Doc Ward. (We used to play cards together; I found him hard to beat.) He had earlier surprised us all by publishing a piece called "*Suckled in a Creed Out-worn*" about growing up in the old ways. You wondered: did he feel that what we all believed in was gone now, gone with the changes? This wise old man, like the rest of us, must have been wondering where the beliefs of his childhood had disappeared to. But I was not concerned with what he believed. I was full of what was happening to me. "--I'm leaving now", I said. "--I'm going-- But I want to tell you that I think for life-time averages, you were the winner, at the card games." He looked up, he did not know what I was talking about, did not grasp at once that I was leaving, but he recovered, he would not allow me to credit him with victory, and said like a gentleman, "---No, I think we are rather even there..."

During all this, crunching out on the gravel with things to pack the car with and glancing over across the lake to the grassy knoll where the Little Sem had been, I was thinking of what it was that I was actually doing: I was leaving the place. I wanted out of there badly now, and yet it had been the joy of my youth. Other young boys had parachuted into Salerno and had been wounded or were dead, while I had been protected, planted in a seed-bed for priests. The place had been good enough then. But there was enough not to like; there were things like that endless line of Assistant Superiors, saying No and then saying No and saying No again, dead butchers of the soul, an endless line of them, until I felt like Macbeth crying out : " ---*I'll see no more!*"

As I opened the car door to take off, I felt a piercing pain in the middle of my back, right between the shoulder blades. I had been hit by something. I looked back towards Corby, where I had lived with my brethren, and then up to the Presbytery behind the Grotto where some important persons lived, for it seemed to have come from there. I rubbed my back, and I looked around the car, and even in the bushes; the way it felt, it had to be a missile, maybe something shaped a little like a flying battle ax... Whoever threw it knew precisely what he was doing, and had awfully good aim, if that was what it had been. But I couldn't find it, I could not find anything, and decided in the end that I had been mistaken, that no one had thrown anything at me and hit me in the back as I was leaving, at all, I only felt that way. It was instead probably only the first sign of relaxation setting in to the muscles of my back, I had kept them pretty stiff, standing up straight and looking at people in the eye for over six months, for when the muscles finally start to release the tension in them, you are bound to get a few hitches and spasms, while things return to normal. As the old waiter says in Hemingway, after all that "Nada" business: *It is nothing; many people must have it.*

It was a fine June day as I headed East toward New England. I turned on the car radio, to catch the last of the classical music station WFMT coming from Chicago, before it faded. Norm Pelligrini was playing Jazz, Jelly-Roll Morton and the Dead Man Blues, followed by The Dippermouth Blues; out there along the soy bean rows, out there among the Clabber Girl signs on the barns for baking powder and the Bull Durham and Mail Pouch Tobacco signs. I had not expected to be so happy; I could never have expected to be that happy again. Then later, the music changed to something from Arcangelo Corelli, and suddenly I was able to fly, Man Flies, we have lift-off, we have true flight, (you know the feeling, when the weight of body at last begins to be borne by the arms and their undersurfaces and no longer by the soles of the feet, it is The Lark Ascending, O the achieve of, the mastery of the thing! Sophocles had been right, all along, some good always comes out of bad, all those experts on silver linings had been right, my symptoms were dropping away from me, they were dropping off, into the cornfields around Elkhart and Fort Wayne, the last of them gone by Toledo, my face was shiny now, I was no longer splotched, I was going toward Anne

Francis, and life was being played to the music of Arcangelo Corelli. I would stop off and visit Sister Anne Francis. More than anything I wanted to be with her. She would be happy to see me still in one piece. We would both be happy to be with one another. I leaned forward to hear the last of Chicago, fading and returning, until soon that went too, all of it was fading and fading, along with even the Midwest itself where I had grown up, fading away into the past of my life, like the paint of the Bull Durham signs on the fading red barns.

Of course, neither of us could know what faced her, and how much worse what she would go though would be than anything that happened to me. She was about to enter the fiery furnace, like in Melville's Tryworks on the rancid deck of the Pequod, that fable of seafaring which is meant to show us how everything of us, all of us, will be cut away with the flensing knives, and burned away, also, until nothing is left but the soul, which will then be seen for what it is.

I remained at her college for two days, there in the Chaplain's Quarters. That is allowed, there is an ancient tradition of life-long friendships between men and women vowed in the religious life: Saint Benedict and Scholastica, Francis and Saint Clare of Assisi, great Teresa and John of the Cross. In that tradition we talked for two

319

days, about Leeson Street and cups of tea and scones at Bewley's and Ladd Lane and Mary--always about Mary-- and Bective and the Misses Flannery and King, of the Baggot Bridge Bookstore. But really I suppose we talked about life and its meaning. I don't think we talked about leaving. Perhaps I was beginning to think of it as a possibility. We did not know the future; we did not yet know what they were going to do to her; she still had energy, the strength to do the impossible. But we must have known something was coming.

She had saved me. In the end, I had told her about everything, and she talked me through it. She had always saved me. It would soon be my turn now. I would be given the chance, I would have to be strong for both of us, and I would have to be found not wanting.

We all say certain things. We say, *Stand up and be counted,* don't we? We say, *Screw your courage to the sticking place,* we say, *These are the times that try men's souls,* we say. We sound like Vince Lombardi, we say, *When the going gets tough the tough get going,* and we say, *Run for Daylight,* and *A good team makes its own breaks.* We say a lot of things, but we often don't know what it is we are talking about until the thing actually happens to us. We hope that by saying certain words over and over, by reciting, we will be inoculated and ready when the thing comes. And we are full of hopeful imaginings, each of us is, until the very moment when life depends on it and we have to do it. It is like what I have heard of crash-landings: after that long slide along the runway when the plane breaks open, when the fuselage cracks down the middle and we start looking for the openings through the black smoke, when it finally happens we are afraid to move, and we will be lucky if we move at all, if we will manage to grope for our seat belt, unfasten it, and get out. I promised her support in whatever it was that she would be facing. We waved each other good-bye, each one waving the other on to a separate life. One thing more must be said; it should have been told earlier. In actual fact, the very last thing I had done back there, before getting into the car and leaving Notre Dame, was, of course, to stop at the Grotto of Our Lady of Lourdes, where I had stopped once as a boy with a missing tooth, and where I had wanted to remain for the rest of my life. I could not think of anything to say. So I just waved goodbye to her, and left; after 29 years of visits, of faithfully seeing her once each day. What I remember is standing there in the Grotto of Our Lady of Lourdes, looking at the sad weathered statue, and saying goodbye for good. I wondered who she belonged to now.

IV

32

OPEN THE WINDOWS

"Thou takest away their breath from them, and they die"

--Haydn, *The Creation*

"The spirit breathes where it will", we say, spirit and breath go back to our very beginning. If one believes anything, it is that we have the breath of God breathed into us; that is why we act the way we do. We think of God as a spirit, a wind, a breath of fresh air, which allows us to be what we are, and without which, we die.

Good Pope John knew this. He told us to keep the windows open. During the days in which he was elected, the Sistine Chapel was locked and sealed, as the custom is. No new air was allowed to come in to the Electors, so that what was left of the breathable air would every day become more unbreathable and stifling, so that it would become difficult even to think, and so that those inside would want to finish up, and get out of there. John was a fat old man, with big ears and a big nose, who looked like Santa Claus driving his sleigh in July. He choked his way through that suffocating election; he must have melted a little, each day, as the Roman air became ever more fetid and unbreathable, under Michelangelo's ceiling: under God separating light from darkness, up there, under God dividing the waters from the land, under the prophets Jeremiah and Joel, under the Cumean Sybil, and the punishment of Haman. "--*I will put up here the things they should be thinking about,*" Michelangelo said to himself as he painted, up in the dark of the ceiling, up where the candles sent their fumes. And John, as he struggled to breathe, and looked up at it, must have thought: This place needs some fresh air. Let us have more air. The human race needs to have the windows opened. We need fresh air to think with; we need to breathe in the spirit of God. And so when he came to power, the first command he gave was "*Open the windows, and let the fresh air in.*"

Soon after she returned to Mercyhurst, Anne Francis was elected Superior General of her community. That was a hard thing for her; after three years in Dublin, she was exhausted and deserved a rest. All she really wanted was to teach, to teach poetry to young people. Her motto was a humble line from Geoffrey Chaucer, and I often heard her say it: "*Gladly would I learn, and gladly teach*".

But Bob Dylan was singing, "The times, they are a-changing," and everyone sang it with him, the whole country was singing "The times they are a-changing." A new constitution had been called for, her order looked for someone to lead them, and they selected Anne Francis to see it through.

In electing her, however, they were also deciding to replace old Mother Eustace, who had been Superior for a long time, for as far back as anyone could remember. She has often told me about this. "Sister Eustace had been my teacher.....She had helped send me on for further studies, " she says. "--I think she always looked upon me as a candidate to follow her---- But in *literature,* not to follow her, I think, in something as important as running the whole community. "

"...The Order was split;" she says sadly, "We were split into factions from the very beginning, and there was much hatred between them. Eustace was leader of one of the factions...."

They disagreed on things. Anne Francis described how Sister Eustace scolded her, after she was elected: "--She was angry with me. She said, 'The difference between you and me is that you believe they are *educable,* and I know that they are *not!'* ---Sister Eustace was in office for a long time; she felt that they needed her to tell them what to do. I thought it was time they think for themselves."

So when Anne Francis was elected, it would be fair to say that Eustace and those around her were not pleased. "You have to understand, " Anne Francis said, " --Even after Eustace was out of office and was not Superior General any more, she still went by the title 'Mother', she was still 'Mother' Eustace, it was plain to everyone that she relished being called 'Mother Eustace' and that she would appreciate being in power, once again. I knew what I was up against."

There was good reason for change. As soon as Anne Francis took responsibility, she saw that the nuns could no longer support themselves by working for nothing. They had done everything for the church, they ran hospitals and schools and colleges; they did innumerable things for the Erie diocese, and though the diocese pronounced itself grateful, the arrangement was not working: the nuns needed money to live on; the old ones especially, were not going to have any retirement, they faced the dangers of old age without proper medical care and even shelter. "So I went to see Bishop Watson, to ask him to contribute something toward retirement facilities for the nuns who had so long worked in his diocese for little or nothing...."

" You have no idea of what it was like, " she told me once. "--Anything good given to the nuns always went straight to the

Episcopal residence, as a gift to the Bishop. It was for 'good will' -- very political." As a young nun, she mentioned to her family that her convent room was quite cold. They sent her a hassock for her cell, to keep her feet up off the floor, while she studied. "--But as soon as Mother Superior saw it, she said '--That will make a nice Christmas gift for the Bishop!' and whisked it away. I never saw it again."

Her goal for her nuns was reasonable, but she could not expect much help. When you are used to having people working for free, when over the years they work and ask nothing, not to be clothed or fed or for any of the other basics, it must be a great bother when they finally show up at your door, and ask for something. It must have been a bit like those days right after Lincoln's Emancipation Proclamation, when the former slaves who had worked for nothing first took the long walk up to the front doors of all those Ante-Bellum mansions and said: "Is the Master in? We have something to ask of the Owner."

I know Bishops; I have known a lot of them, including at least one Archbishop, and several Cardinals. Bishops drink Scotch; I have been with them enough, don't try to tell me they do not. I remember McShain the Builder (he built the Pentagon) at Archbishop O'Boyle's table; those two knew how things worked. Even I knew that if you wanted to get anywhere the proper thing was to leave them some Haig & Haig Dimple Scotch. (It would be Single Malt, now). I do not know much about Bishop Watson, whether he smoked or drank at all; and so cannot hang that on him, but a lot of them did, back then, and they certainly liked their good cigars. And so when I think of this now, when I remember the way some of them acted, I cannot help but be reminded of that old saying among real men, men who run the world and who know what is going on: "--A woman is a woman, but a cigar is a *cigar!*"

When Sister Anne Francis went to the Bishop and asked for some help in pro-viding retirement facilities for the older nuns who had worked so long, and money for them just to stay alive, Bishop Watson was not very helpful; it was at that moment when he uttered his statement, that if he did give anything, he hoped the money was "*not going to go for panty-hose!*"

We tried to keep in touch by phone. Anne Francis would tell me about what was going on. She was concerned for the older sisters. "I worry about my dear old girls" she confided, "--It isn't easy for them, you know, " she said, "--it's *hard.* "

"Some of them entered the Convent as young girls," she said. "They have lived as nuns inside that habit through youth and middle

328

age, through Depression and War, and all the booms which came after, and the recessions".

"--The old Mercy habit..." she said, " ---They had fed the poor in it, they had run hospitals in it, they were nurses for soldiers, wearing those starchy old habits in the muck of the battlefields.. Now, because of '*Aggiornamento*', they are being told to come out of it, to just step right out of that old thing, and to turn it in for something more current, something that an airline Stewardess might wear!"

"--The poor things," she said, " They think everyone is laughing at them. *You would too.*"

I smiled; it was true, I was afraid of the word "*Aggiornamento*" myself. And I thought of the old Mercy habit; it reminded me of Leeson Street, and having coffee in Bewley's.

But Anne Francis was not afraid; much of what had to be done was simply common sense, and she did what she could to save them. She took down old paintings from the convent walls and had them appraised; then went to art dealers to have them sold, to get money to take care of the old nuns. "--There were few new young ones coming, " she said, "and we have this brand new Novitiate being finished. I thought of all the various needs we had..." She

329

ended up by turning it into a Center on Aging, to take care of the elderly. When she used the word "Aging" like that I had to ask her to repeat, because it was not in common use, then, but she attended Workshops and knew what was happening.

But there were still plenty of Eustace supporters around; there were still hangers-on who had done well by the old system, who had been happy to run errands for it.

"When I walked into my office that first day," she says, "there was a letter waiting for me on the desk. It was from a nun out in one of the smaller convents, and it reported on everything and everybody in that convent, and what they were doing. It was the work of an informer and a sycophant What I remember is that it ended with a post-script that there was a sale on women's shoes at a local store there, and that she would get me a pair, if I sent her my size!"

Anne Francis wanted to stamp out such activity; it was the way things had been done in the past, under previous administrations, it was the sort of thing she was determined to get rid of. She told the nun to stop sending in such reports, and that she did not need any shoes from her. She would not owe her soul to anybody, even for a pair of shoes from the Company Store.

But that would by no means be the end of it. "The old system produced such persons," she says. That is true; you cannot stop people from behaving in the way they have been trained to, you cannot announce that everyone is to be treated the same, and expect nothing to happen, you may be sure that you will pay for such notions. Change makes enemies.

During her first term, Anne Francis worked in concert with the other Mercy Superiors to renew her section of the Mercies. "Renew" and "renewal" were terms very much alive then, when everybody wanted to put into practice the exciting new directives of the Vatican Council.

"Our whole purpose was to achieve consensus," Anne Francis says. "It was hard work, mostly meetings, endless meetings, in conjunction with what was going on in other communities. Everyone was encouraged to come to Assembly, everyone urged to attend meetings to come to consensus on the election process, so that everything would be available to everyone."

Along with other orders, her group had hammered out new constitutions in line with the directives which had come from Rome, and had submitted them to the Vatican for approval: to the Sacred

Congregation for Religious, which had sent out the directives which they were following.

She was determined to lead them in doing it right, so she did it in a professional manner, she went out and found Canon Lawyers, experts in the law of the Church, and hired consultants to help them, so that Rome would approve, and things would not fail. .

But trouble was coming. One small faction refused to take part, and refused to participate, they simply boycotted the proceedings. Yet each day, word was nevertheless rigorously reported to them of everything done at the assembly, for no one was to be left out. I called her on the phone, trying to keep close to her, I am glad I did. She would tell me of their progress; she would say "--I consulted Sister Jacqueline Rumley today, she has helped over 250 religious communities go through this process; she is skilled in 'change' and will take us through everything. And our own Canon Lawyers have showed us every step of the way, so that the Vatican will be sure to approve it." What they were doing seemed to me to be wonderful, it seemed like what John Adams and James Madison and were doing in that hot summer of Philadelphia that brought us our freedom.

From some reserve of strength still inside her, after the exhaustion of work overseas, Anne Francis managed to pull them together. "All we wanted was to implement the demands of the Vatican Council." she says. "-- We tried to do everything by consensus; more than anything, it was all done to achieve *consensus*. For well over a year we had daily meetings, and everyone was invited to attend and participate. It was *consuming*!"

Finally it was done. When it was all finished, the new Constitutions were ratified by a large majority of all the nuns, over ninety percent, and in the first election according to the new Constitutions, Sister Anne Francis was reelected Superior General by a wide margin. All members were informed, including those who had refused to attend meetings.. "Everything was submitted to Rome," she said, "and at last we were able to recuperate. *We were all exhausted!*" They had reason to feel that Rome would be pleased and give its blessing, for they had dutifully followed its guidelines.

Those were the days, my friend. It was an exciting time. I felt like a bird in a bush, watching; I could not help, but prayed that nothing would happen to her. Freedom was coming, those in power were going to be convinced that people should now start to be considered. Far away, I had my hopes. But to tell the truth, to my ears, nothing that I heard sounded very much like Rome, at least not the Rome I knew.

And it had taken time; it was long and hard hammering out such matters, and by the time it was all finished and ready to be submitted to Rome, kindly old Pope John was there no more, that saintly man had died, and Paul the Sixth, a new pope was on the throne.

I remembered him; I remembered that time he had looked at me and told me I was a good boy; he was still the same small man with those big ears of his, which looked as if they might be caught up by the wind and go sailing away with him. He looked scared, he looked frightened of everything that was happening; he seemed to be throwing up his hands and saying "*What have we done?*" and the look on his face asked over and over, "*Where will it all end?*"

What John had given, Paul began to take away. The open windows started to be closed. You could hear them being slammed first and then hammered shut, doors and windows all over the Vatican. The fresh air was gone, replaced by what was there before, captured and sealed in once again, just as it always had been. People were not going to be as happy as they had thought they were going to be. It would be like the green mantle that spreads over the surface of a pond.

Breathers of the Past came streaming in from banishment, career people immune to plague, they sat down again onto those little *"misericorde"* seats provided by the Church for their saintly behinds; they got themselves fitted out with grand new robes from ecclesiastical tailors near the Via Conziliazione, they made themselves comfortable, and they started running things again. Rome was still Rome.

33

THE SCREAM

"I know exactly when it was," she says. " --I had just made a retreat with the Jesuits in New York on 98th street. The Retreat Master told me that I was in need of a respite from convent politics back home, and said that while I meditated and prayed, I should also go on long walks. "I Have a Dream" was blaring out from across the street--Martin Luther King had only been dead a few years--"

So she walked the long city blocks of Manhattan. One of her sayings is that when she goes to great cities like Milan, she does not at first bother with the museums, instead , she walks: the city is itself her museum. "I walked and walked, looking in at the art of the window displays; I would stop sometimes and have a cappuccino. I went to films; I went to Bergman's "Cries and Whispers"; and I walked all the way down to Amsterdam Avenue, to see "Lady Sings the Blues".

When she returned, there was a phone message for her: *Ciaran Ryan was dead.*

"--The message was maddening." she says, " --It just said that he was dead, nothing else..." Maureen and her husband Don had been set to arrive after her retreat to take her out with them to Seacliff, on Long Island. That is the Maureen of the old apple tree, and the convent wall at Muckross. Good. She was in capable hands. If anyone could be with her, they could.

At Stonehill I got a telegram in the late evening. CIARAN RYAN DEAD STOP WE ARE BRINGING MAUD GONNE STOP ARRIVE MIDNIGHT.

That was a joke, a sad one; it meant that I was the poet Yeats, which I am not, and that Anne Francis was his great love, Maud Gonne. Perhaps it was meant to be a code language: I did, after all, live in a religious house of men, and you want to be careful about who is arriving at Midnight.

Before starting, Maureen had first called Dublin, over to Muckross. In Ciaran they had just lost their chaplain; they had lost a deep friend as well as a brilliant man. Sister Benvenuta recalls: " '--That will be Anne Francis now' , I said, when the phone rang." Ben described walking beside old Mother Rosario, holding her up in her grief. Beautiful, lofty people: I see the three figures mourning Ciaran in my mind: Mother Rosario, Benvenuta, Anne Francis herself, I am

337

reminded of that stark pre-war photograph from London, called Three Queens, figures in black captured in their moment of mourning. O Weep for Lycidas, dead before his prime, who hath not left his peer.

" Do you remember 'Big Alice?'" Anne Francis asks, sometimes, now. I still do. Big Alice was the name of Don's vans they all traveled in. "--I was all right at the beginning. But then as we drove I got sick. They had to pull over." I would know about this. We had been through a lot, and we all responded differently.

I ran to my Superior, a kind old fellow, named Father Tom. I told Tom what happened. He said certainly, that I should find them rooms among the empty ones in the house.

They arrived a 2 am. Don had his dog Skippy. The rest of the house was asleep. The dog Skippy escaped while I was showing them their rooms. Skippy ran into one room, which was the Superior's room, and went in under Father Tom's bed, and Father Tom did not wake up. My memory of that night includes many things: the telegram, Big Alice, and also Don trying to pull Skippy out from under the Superior's bed.

But the evening was about Ciaran Ryan, and how he died. Maureen repeated for us what had happened, how Ciaran in Switzerland had gone hiking in the Alps with a friend. The friend fell into a crevasse, and was injured. Ciaran did what he could to help him, but while running to give help, himself fell into a crevasse. It was a lonely death indeed.

He would never have been the one for her, she often said. He was a troubled man, too closed in upon other concerns. But the death coming at this moment, when she was trying to meditate for herself and find a meaning, to have him flung down from an icy mountain while trying to help someone, and to be left to freeze alone there in the dark at the bottom of things, it was very hard.

We then put her up in the Essex Hotel on Boylston Street. And each day, after teaching, I would drive in, to be with her. We would walk, and eat at such restaurants as we could afford. We spoke a few times of Ciaran Ryan, did not speak much of us. She would have to go back, to return to what was making her sick. We would be together, doing what we could, for only a short while. I could think of no solutions; neither of us could.

We were walking down Boylston Street, near the Copley Cathedral, when it all became too much for her: Ciaran Ryan lying in the ice, dead in the darkness of the Alps. What will we do? What will we ever do? And she cried out against it with her whole being, sending out a cry from her deepest self, there in Boston's Boylston Street, a great cry out against all that was happening wrong. You have seen the painting by Edward Muench, "The Scream". One human cries out. The cry enters into others. They turn, and wonder.

The cry certainly entered into me. I turned, I wondered. Nothing was certain. Our future could not be foreseen. I thought of how long it might be before things got any better. I remember wondering if they ever would.

34

YOU HAVE AN INFORMER IN YOUR RANKS

She went back to face it once again; I was determined to keep close to her at this time, at least by telephone.

But when she returned, she received word that her presence was required at the Diocesan Chancery. "I called a friend there to see what was happening. He told me that 'A missive' had arrived from the Holy See, by diplomatic pouch... It said on its front that it had come from 'the desk of the Holy Father' and it was all covered with red sealing wax, and had all these-- *red ribbons*-- falling out behind it....". Her friend, Father Hastings, the Vicar for Religious of the Erie Diocese, was the one who told her what it was." You have been reported to Rome. Someone in your order has reported you," he said "--The complaint passed through the Chancery; the Bishop sent it on, forwarding it by diplomatic pouch..." He thought for a while, and then he said, "-- You have an Informer in your ranks."

Someone in the alienated group, the ones who had been invited but boycotted the meetings, had protested the election to the Vatican, claiming that they had not been allowed to vote. The matter had made its way to Rome through the Bishop's office, and the news came back that way, by way of the Chancery.

The Informer's name surfaced, after a while. It turned out to be the nun whose overtures had been rebuffed, the Shoe-salesperson. She had reported Anne Francis and the rest of them and their new constitutions and all their talk of "personal responsibility" to Rome, which would know what to do about it. She was still the letter-sender, only the addresses had changed; now she was addressing her reports to "the Local Ordinary", the Bishop of Erie, who could be counted upon to send them on to Rome.

"Monsignor Hastings was my good friend," Anne Francis said "he was a very good person. He was on my side, but he said that because the protest had been lodged she would now have to send a Canon Lawyer to Rome with a copy of all the data, all material connected with the election, it would all have to be gathered up again, to defend the election process....He thought that we should hire a Canon Lawyer, and that I would not have to go myself."

But Anne Francis made the decision not to be absent from their case, she chose not to be represented by a Canon Lawyer. Why should they be absent from their own hearing, why should good religious become absentees, and be represented at the See of Peter by someone else?

"I decided that, with the documentary backup provided by my Canon Lawyer, I would go to the Sacred Congregation myself. We had a Canon Lawyer from Toledo, a very big one, who documented every step of the process; he prepared my presentation, and sent it all in two months ahead, by diplomatic pouch"

That would be a surprise for them. They would not normally expect nuns to show up at such a hearing.

What they expected would be one of their own, perhaps someone they knew from the Seminary, one well used to breathing in the air of the Vatican; someone a little more redolent of the Old Testament. They did not expect anything like Anne Francis; she did not look like someone who would darn their sox for them. They would be uncomfortable dealing with a woman in their presence, actually facing them. "Some nun--" they would call her, "---some nun." --As in "Some nun is waiting out there." In abundant red piping, looking down on her from up on their dais, they would think, what insolence is this?

Old Bill Garvey got it right, he said it better than anybody; a history professor at her college. I don't know what his specialty was, but he always struck me as having done a thesis in Tammany Hall or the Tweed Ring. I was wrong to think of him as a Democratic ward-heeler, for Garvey was a shrewd observer who saw things through the eyes of the historian. He had watched her as she had performed, over the years. He told everybody what he thought of her on one occasion. " --She is a real thoroughbred" he said

, "--She is like a fine race-horse. *But you cannot race her every day!"*

The Greeks had a word for it: *arête*. That word refuses be defined, the best you can do is look at one of their marble friezes of horses running, with manes out, and blowing in the wind. I agreed with Garvey; I knew that what she was and what she had done should stand up well under any kind of scrutiny.

Yes, indeed she was quite fine. But she was up against the Romans. Only God could save her now.

35

FINGER EXERCISE

What, just exactly, is a Roman? Little lamb, I'll tell thee.

One morning, long ago, in fact in the year just before I was to be ordained, I was serving an extra mass down in the Crypt, when I felt Father Bernard Ransing come into the crypt behind me. He was Superior over me, and I had developed a sense of where he was at all times. You see, I wanted to be ordained, more than anything on earth, and since I was only a year away from that --or hoped I was-- I did at all times what was expected of me.

But I was not very good at the Sacred Liturgy. I was especially poor at what are called "Rubrics" --those detailed rules dictating the proper way of doing anything around the altar. Indeed, for one with my expectations, I was not confidant around the altar. I always seemed one step away from a stumble, and sometimes, I actually did stumble, tripping over the skirt of my cassock. (I would hear gasps though the chapel: *He is going to fall!*)

As soon as I felt the presence of Father Ransing behind me, I straightened up, kneeling fiercely on the first altar step, even though I had already been kneeling up quite straight. You see, I did not want to seem lacking in the presence of the Superior, as I had many times before.

My fear radiated out in all directions; radiating across the crypt was my great desire to be ordained; my fear of not being "approved" must have filled the crypt. Father Ransing was an expert on Liturgy; he was Master of Ceremonies for all the big functions in Washington, over at The National Shrine; whenever there were visiting Cardinals; when dignitaries like Valerio Cardinal Valerian came to visit the Apostolic Delegate, Amleto Giovanni Cicognani, Rome's chief representative in the New World, it was Bernard Joseph Ransing who was called in to turn the missal pages for them on the altar, to bow properly to them, to lift the hems of their vestments for them. He knew my weakness very well, and he was also expert at knowing my fear.

That morning I felt him enter the crypt; I could sense him drawing closer; I felt him standing behind my back; I knew he was observing me from behind, looking me over to see how I was doing things. I stiffened even more, determined not to be found doing things improperly; yet all I was doing was kneeling as straight as I could, and holding my two hands fiercely clasped together in the attitude of prayer. There was not much that I could be doing wrong.

You can feel the warmth of a human body when it gets that close. Father Bernard came up right behind me and paused. And then quietly he reached over my shoulder, with his thumb and forefinger, without saying anything, without tapping me on the shoulder, but in complete silence; using his own thumb and forefinger like a tweezers, he reached down to my clasped hands and picked up my left thumb from over my right thumb, and then he took my right thumb and placed it over my left thumb, and fixed it there. He paused, to look at his work. Then he left me, and hurried off. I had been doing it wrong, you see; all along --since childhood, I expect--I had been clasping my hands in the wrong way: the right thumb was to take precedence; it was to be placed over the _left_ thumb, it was proper liturgy and proper rubrics to do it that way. I should have known that. I had been corrected. It was a monition before breakfast. In the future I would be expected to do it right. If I wished to be ordained. And I could be certain that I would be observed, for a long time.

I should have left right then of course; I should have just gotten up and walked out the front door, and let someone else serve their extra masses for them. But in fact I would not leave for another twenty years. Father Bernard was a good man, so were they all, they all did a lot of good in this world. But you see, he was what we called "a Roman". To my way of thinking he seems right out of a Panzer unit, a figure well suited for standing at attention under one of those steel helmets the German Wehrmacht used to frighten the world with, and when I think of him I hear the old marching songs, about closing the ranks, and stepping in file, and putting the world into a new order. *Panzerman, Panzerman.* Years later, after that whole way of doing things seemed long forgotten, I would run into him, after I had grown up and become a man myself; whenever I ran into him, my Soul wanted to cry out at him and ask, "--*What!* ---Are you still with us? *I thought you were lost at Stalingrad!*"

Of course, it should not be a mystery. Over the twelve years of training, as young boys grew up to be priests, if they were not careful they gradually turned into little "Infant of Prague" statues. You can still see these in certain places. In Boston's North End they are in store windows: the young Boy Jesus in satin and velvet, and rosy cheeks, with the whole world in his hands, dressed in garments as extravagant as the devoted seamstresses can sew them. It is as things should be, to the one who sews, for it means that the boy Jesus is still with us, that we are all safe. I was an Infant of Prague myself, they made a fine one out of me, for a good while I was revered as a walking statue among them; it made me uncomfortable, but that did not matter, you were saving them, you went around as if you were wearing a long pink baby's dress, holding the world in your hands, for all of them. And those Romans on the Sacred Congregation for Religious would have had much the same experience, they were all boys become men, who knew, without ever having to think about it, what religious women were for, and what kind of life nuns ought to be made to lead.

Most of them are Canon Lawyers. Canon Lawyers find themselves generally freed from the burden of dealing directly with conscience, what they deal with are the Canons the Almighty has set in front of them. They pursue always "the Mind of the Law-Maker." They come to know the law-maker personally, and though he may be dead in his tomb for centuries, they know precisely what he thought, in his own time, they think as he did, in that other era; they find him in the "Censures' and "vindictive penalties" he has left them, and they follow him everywhere, among such concepts as that of *grave fear* and *the enclosure of religious women* and *the exemptions of the clergy,* and they are very much at home with what they call "*the chains of marriage.*" Society has always had such persons; they go far back, they ran the Pyramids for the Pharaohs.

It was their world she now stepped into. The Sacred Congregation for Religious was a body of men qualified to judge women, competent specifically to judge Religious Women.

I have known quite a few Romans personally. I knew Monsignor Doheney, powerful man, Keeper of the Chains at the august Roman Rota, and little Billy Hogan who did Dispensations for them, and Ed Heston, The Chest himself, and of course Bernard Ransing, Finger-Man, as well as Charley Schleck. (Needless to say, they were people who knew their Acqua Felice from their Acqua Vergine.)

When Anne Francis told me who some of the men were she was going to have looking down on her from a dais in Rome, I thought I heard Ransing mentioned, and thought I heard Schleck too, and a few others; I knew there was no hope; there would be little hope for any breath of fresh coming in through the windows, there would be little hope for her constitutions, and, of course, no hope for herself. It would be a finger exercise; it was going to be all one big finger exercise. I knew what would happen. She was going to be destroyed. If she had been the Maid of Orleans, great Joan of Arc herself, shining in the Lord's own armor, they would have run and gotten faggots and tied her up and burned her at the stake, for her own good.

36

GALLILEO'S DAUGHTER

I think her trouble with the Vatican was that they thought she was trying to convince them that the tides of the ocean were influenced by the moon, or that the planet Jupiter has four satellites, or maybe, that the earth really does move around the sun, for that is the way they acted.

Perhaps it because I have been reading *"Galileo's Daughter,"* for the book reminds me of her; every time I read what that child and parent wrote to one another, [*"Dear Father, in the tempest of our many torments,"* and *"As I struggle to understand"* and *"To have the truth seen and recognized,"*] and hear the trouble that the great scientist suffered at the hands of Rome, and which his daughter a nun in the convent at Arcetri suffered along with him, both trying to defend themselves against savage authority while at the same time striving to preserve their ancient faith, in spite of what they saw arrayed against them, I keep being reminded of all that Anne Francis went through, against that very same power, in the Twentieth Century, from her own narrow convent cell in Erie, Pennsylvania. For it was the same power, precisely, and she was devout, too, every bit as devout as Suor Maria Celeste, that other nun was, and she observed holy obedience with the same fervor. You would think that history had not moved on at all in the Vatican, that they were still suspicious of new things. Only the new things were no longer inanimate telescopes and astrolabes and chronometers; they were quite other things, such things as strong women who looked them straight in the eye, and who were as educated as they were. The only aspect that seemed any different was that Rome did not put her under house arrest, they did not actually try to put Anne Francis in jail.

And that is the kind of nun she was, much like the one secretly buried under the great man's tomb. For you know, instead of being buried in the Convent burial ground, Sister Maria Celeste is in there with him, in Galileo's tomb, where he is buried in the church of Santa Croce, with the other great ones of Florence. They say someone found her, and secretly placed what was left of her in along with the famous father, someone who probably risked their neck to do it, but who knew the reality, who knew the silent secret daughter, Bride of Christ and God Anointed, who he could not openly acknowledge, that she rightly belonged with the man she loved and saved so patiently through life, for they saved one another, with apples and gifts of fruit and glazing for windows to keep the cold out, and in death, in eternity they live on together.

"--*And yet, it does move,*" he was heard to mutter, as he left the trial at which they condemned him, " --*I still say it moves.*"

37

THE TRIAL

Oh, Who will deliver me from the body of this death?-
                                              -The Apostle Paul

First they would make her wait; while they took their siestas.

Rome has its own ways. It has long been a place of plague, which comes up to infect it on dangerous winds from *The Mezzogiorno*, --:from "the Land of the Middle of the Day.". In order to fight the effects of the Noon-day sun and the dangerous heat, those clerics assigned to the various Vatican bodies have learned to protect themselves and wisely seek to escape, by taking a nap until it is over. People have always had a name for this breeding infection, simply referring to it as "Roman Fever".

What is it? Some say that it is of the body only, but others say that it is more, that it affects the spirit also; it does seem something that has been with us always, has come along with us from the beginning, a sickness unto death.

Where does it come from? *Death in Venice* says it best; in that story Thomas Mann tells of what an old professor is fighting against, that interior infection of the soul which has come to him from afar, as though it had blown up on the hot African wind to come into his spirit and make him think wrongly, and in the end, to kill him. He is surrounded by beautiful Venice, there on his beach, which he is attracted to by its warm southern light, for old man needs warmth. But something is wrong; the lagoon is sickly, the waters of the canals rancid and pestilential. The concierge at his hotel tries to tell him urgently that it is the Plague itself, that infection has come to the pastelled city, with the small waves lapping, and that he ought to leave. The Plague is described as coming from the East, where it had bred in the hot moist swamps of the Indian deltas, carried by sea to the Mediterranean shores, to Palermo and Naples. It comes up through the Mezzogiorno, the Pontine Marshes, and finally to Rome. He perspires painfully, his chest becomes heavy, the canals sicken him, and the fever-breeding vapors drain life from him. He speaks like my old teachers, Romans speaking the old Latin words for us: *stagnans, paludae, foetidae.*

And in the end of course, it conquers, it kills the old man, it kills the old professor, he dies in Venice. It sounds like a something we all have to fear; for Thomas Mann makes it clear that the man dies from something inside his soul.

The childhood rime "Ring Around the Rosy" really is our memory of the Red Death: we make a ring around the red-faced one, who is going to die. But first we carefully fill our own pockets full of various herbs, pockets full of posies, we hope they will protect us from catching it ourselves. Then it **is *Ashes! Ashes! and All Fall Down!*** We kill ourselves laughing at Death.

The men smiled down at her. "There were nine of them, up on a dais, well above me" she said, "--Most of them had red peeking out, from under collars and things..." This nun, whoever she was, would be set straight; they would act according to the canons, set for them by the Almighty She had prudently arranged to have 250 pages on what her order had done sent to them in plenty of time; but when she got there, the men up on the dais said that they had not received any of the material which had been sent. They said they had not read any such material. They said they had not seen anything that had been sent ahead in the diplomatic pouch. And so they made her start at the beginning, and take them through everything, line by line, as though they had never heard any of it before. (Her own canon lawyer later said to her, "*That is an old trick, Sister.* It is called 'denuding the witness.'") They insisted that she go through everything page by page for them, questioning her which took from 5 in the evening until around 11 at night. She went through a book of over 250 pages detailing everything they had done, in accordance with Vatican.

I call it a Trial. They would correct me, I am certain. "*It was not a trial,*" they would say, making careful distinctions. The British have a name for it, they have their own way of referring to it. They call it "assisting the police in their enquiries." When a prisoner is "detained" in an English jail, and the individual decides to talk rather than continue to endure what they do to him, the British papers always say, "The prisoner is being detained at Wormwood Scrubs, where he is *assisting the police with their enquiries*." It was a Trial, no matter what they called it.

It was thought wise to send the President of Mercyhurst College, Sister Carolyn Herman with her, to help her report to the Sacred Congregation. The two of them were brought into the session by the first female that women's influence had managed to get in there after centuries of years, a Vatican nun. "She was a flunky," Anne Francis says. "--There was much fuss about her being 'the first woman', but after she showed us in, the first woman retired back into the shadows and hovered around, waiting obsequiously to be of use".

But Carolyn and Anne Francis were real women; together they were two woman scholars with earned doctorates, facing a body made up of men who would be seminary people, with mostly churchly degrees. Carolyn was her friend, but under the circumstances felt that it was not appropriate to speak; instead she sat beside Sister Anne Francis and turned pages for her as she had to read 250 pages of material --which had now more or less been "subpoenaed." Anne Francis remembers sitting there all day long, until late in the hot Roman evening, reading and reading to the men, who had not seen fit to read any of it themselves.

She described it later. "--There was no provision for women at all. We were not permitted to leave, to go to the bathroom. And not even a glass of water was provided for us at our table." The Vatican had a thousand years to provide decent plumbing facilities for women, but they were never expected to come, and when women had arrived, even when two of them were present right in front of the men, it had not occurred to the men in their robes that any such facilities should be provided. The men up there peeked out from between high glass decanters filled with Acqua Vergine or Acqua Felice, and offered the two women not so much as even a glass of cold water; perhaps it was part of making things unbearable, like

358

keeping the windows closed in the Sistine Chapel. "It was a trial all right ---it was an Inquisition," she says.

What she describes has now become part of History; someone should pay attention to such chronicles of how the Vatican treated human beings. Yet it was not so long ago; when I recall the manner in which she was treated it makes me wonder why the two of us did not leave earlier. We were both educated; why in the name of God, did it take us so long?

There was of course pretense at work. The pretense was that, in spite of all the effort that she had made with her own Canon Lawyers that everything should be above reproach, the first election you see had been somehow "flawed" and "irregular": she was the elected representative of her community, but she was not to be trusted. Instead, the Sacred Congregation trusted the Informers. This is not too surprising, for in that traditional way of doing things, Informants are very precious, they are sources which must be protected.

In the stifling heat of the Roman summer, they would have been annoyed with her for coming there to confront them. Her case was a simple request for Justice, and they must have wondered: Why would anyone present themselves in a place like Rome in the name of nothing but Justice?

In the six or seven hours of her line-by-line analysis, she looked up often for where the windows were, which seemed shut so tight. She must have felt what Pope John did, when he was suffocating, when he said what this place needs is some fresh air.

The document she and her nuns had all labored over so lovingly had been created in the uplifting spirit of Good Pope John and the Vatican Council. But John was gone now, and his fresh healing air had been shut out with the closed windows. The men on the dais would have spent all day with the document; they had ample time to identify the scent of fresh air about it, and they knew that they must put a stop to such things for good; they had to make it clear that the windows were closed, now, and the days of fresh air were over.

A person like her needed God's fresh air to live, without it she would die. But they had locked her in with the pestilence of death. And it would soon begin to appear to some of us that she was at this time indeed starting to be headed for death. She should have slipped out, and packed her pockets full of posies.

Their constitutions had been duly voted on, in free elections. She had come to Rome only to defend what rightly should be defended. Now the Sacred Congregation was trying to attack what they had done, on the basis of complaints secretly made by an anonymous informer, and secretly forwarded to Rome. She was caught between two things that she loved and respected, and it was becoming impossible. One was her vow of Obedience to the Church which she loved; the other was the honest loyalty she owed her community. If she chose one, she destroyed the other. The men on the dais did not have to be concerned with such conflicts. The ones among them that I have known would not be caught in such a quandary; they amazed me with their knowledge of the escape routes from any such situation, each one paved with Canons from the Code of Canon Law. They always laughed, saying that any good Roman would always know where to find them.

"There was much scurrying around," she says, "over the next two days, the Head of all the Mercies speaking to the Jesuit advisors. Finally, in session with them I agreed that another, new election would be held. There would be yet another election, this time in the Bishop's office, with two members of the community present as each individual voted, as well as representatives from the Chancery. There would be a sheet of paper on which every sister would vote, with any comment they wanted to make about my administration. I agreed to this, and to everything demanded of me there in Rome, because then I could be comfortably voted out of office, and would feel no longer an obligation to the hard work of running that community. I would be out at last; I would be free. I agreed to this ---I only wanted out, anyway....." she says.

It seemed to be all over, she seemed on the way to being free, at last. It would seem that way to any normal person, for she had agreed to everything Rome had demanded.

"We were exhausted," she said . "On the way home, I thought we might stop off in Dublin, for some kind of respite from what we had been through. I went out to see old Mother Rosario; the tears streamed down her cheeks when she saw me"

And what was Mother Rosario crying for? For the death of Ciaran Ryan, I am sure, but also for what they were doing to her, I believe. Old Mother Rosario, Mother Rosario her dear friend, "Mother Ro" of the apple tree, of the branch over the wall, the one in charge of escape routes, who timed for them the patrol of the Night Watchman around the Convent, and told them when it was safe to go. Mother Rosario who cried with joy every time she saw her. She was Mother Rosario of the old things, of the life remembered from before this calamity, life led as a human being. For Anne Francis, the meeting must have been a blessed relief from the world of Inquisition she had just been through.

But it was not over yet. What happened next reminds me of something that Anne Francis wrote to me once; it reminds me of the question she had asked me, in that very first letter of hers to me, when I had just returned from Ireland: "Father, have you settled in?" she wrote, " How do you like the world of priests and men?"

"--When I got home, " she said, " There was something else from them waiting for me on my desk. It was one more thing that I would have to sign."

It was one more document from the diplomatic pouch. This time it was only a letter; they had not bothered to seal it with sealing wax. When she opened it she found something with the capacity to kill her. It had no red ribbons trailing after it, but it was a pretty piece of treachery, all the same.

38

LUCY IN THE SKY WITH DIAMONDS

I have never heard of anyone being sent to Rome because he had a great conscience. Persons known for conscience find themselves sent to rural areas, not to Rome, or they hear the Confessions of Novices. The men of the Sacred Congregation were not primarily concerned with the workings of conscience. It is Canon Law these men were good at, and they were at ease with their Canons. Sitting in Rome they sent out their decisions all over the world, by goose quill, into distant cultures they had never visited, with consequences which could not always be foreseen. Over the years I had personal knowledge of a number of them; they were not men of unlimited knowledge. They were truly learned in the ways of Church law, but many of them were also fools.

The men on the dais would not have been comfortable dealing with her, or with her presence among them. Rome has always had a fear of women, and by the time someone like Sister Anne Francis came to face them, the fear had become palpable.

But they knew how to do these things. They would send her a document that she could not sign.

After she had left them, after she had gotten home, and thought that the matter was finished and that her constitutions were safe, they would arrange to have something sent to her, concerning a matter that they had not been talked about while she was in their presence in Rome. It would be written up for them by Lawyers of the Sacred Congregation, and then copied by "some nuns" retained in Rome for such purposes. It would of course be written in goose quill. But what they finally sent her might just as well have been written in hieroglyphs, for in truth it was like something out of ancient Egypt, something from the age of the Pharaohs, or out of the land of Let My People Go.

"--- It stated that if I were on the slate to be elected in the Bishop's office," she said, "-- and if I were re-elected, I would have to sign a document saying that, in the name of every member of the community I represented, I would follow any directive that the Sacred Congregation sent. And in all future decisions, do whatever the Sacred Congregation instructed us to do."

She was to sign her name, on behalf of all the members of the community, and give her word that she would in the future bind them to do whatever the Sacred Congregation wished of her. "---They knew that I could not sign such a thing," she says. *"Those men had lied to me, --they lied!"*

" After all the work we had done together," she said, "making sure that each individual was participating through their informed assent and represented in the things that affected them, these men wanted me to sign a blank check, to commit others to things that had not even been thought of, things which Rome itself had not yet conceived. That was immoral, but they saw nothing wrong with it." It would mean that she would betray them all. For someone like Anne Francis, it amounted to a sentence of death. There is more than one way of killing a person.

"I was raised in the ancient Catholic tradition of the primacy of the individual conscience," she said, "-- We were always taught that though your conscience might be formed within the training you received, you were still responsible for forming your own conception of right and wrong, your own conscience, and that no one could make you violate that."

This is indeed the truth; it is one of the finer aspects of Catholic tradition that no one can be made to do something which they themselves according to their best efforts at forming a right conscience within them consider to be wrong. It is not an aspect which the Sacred Congregation would spend much time stressing, and there is no reason for your favorite Canon Lawyer to whisper it into your ear.

The Church is not a Democracy; it has always preferred the Monarchy with its Royal Court, which they say most resembles the Divine Rule. To Rome, Democracy is perhaps only a passing phenomenon. "--Maybe they were afraid of America" she said, "maybe they were afraid that we would bring all this freedom over there...."

She could not bring herself to sign it, not with her sense of right and wrong. Other people might talk lightly about it, but she doubted if she could ever do so, for no human being can say "Yes" to things as yet unseen and unknown. That was asking too much, even for Rome. Anne Francis had spent her life with words, and took words seriously. Scholars of her level know what words mean, they study what a sentence implies and all that may be contained in it. The men who composed such a document could scarcely have thought much about what their sentences might mean. They would simply say "What we have written, we have written." Moreover, such things cannot be drawn out forever, in the dreadful Roman heat.

When I spoke with her by phone she explained her anguish. "There were two things pulling at me," she said, "---One was my vows, the question of religious authority, what I had obligated myself to. The other was responsibility, all those people I was responsible for. They had entrusted me with everything, and I could not let them down"

"I went looking for help; I sought counsel from the Canon Lawyers we had used. One of the lawyers said, "Dealing with the Vatican is a game, and you can play the game and sign it. Then if something comes from them that you can't accept --you can deal with that then."

"-Another lawyer said 'Use Mental Reservation' --He suggested I say one thing and mean another, and allow them to come to their own conclusions..." She said that, but I doubted that she would hide behind a mental reservation.

"--I sought the counsel of the Vicar for Religious who had worked with me all during the dispute, Father Hastings. ---He was the Bishop's man, officially" she said,"--but really he was my man. He told me everything that was happening." He was a good man, too;

when he died, he left what money he had to various nuns who had taken care of him. ("-He died penniless" she told me, years later.)

He was the Competent Authority, which it was proper for her to consult. But the matter was a conundrum to him, too. "--He asked for some time to think, then came back. When he returned, he advised me to sign it, and then wait until the first thing came up which was something I could not go along with. Then she could resign. That would seem to solve things."

She asked me what I thought she should do. We both knew that I was not exactly an expert, but I laughed, for I knew what I thought. I said, "It is *words* that they are after, it is what they do for a career..." I had been raised by them, you see, I have always felt "raised" by Canon Lawyers. I would watch them; they behaved like mice before a piece of Swiss cheese --everything appeared to them as being full of holes. What looks like a stone wall to the rest of us looks like a Triumphal Arch to a Canon Lawyer, for them to pass through it and have a parade. All you had to do was throw them something to keep their books straight, and then go on about your life. That was how they conducted their own affairs, it was how they had taught us. "Throw them something" I said, "---They will have their Roman nuns copy it onto a roll of parchment, drip red wax all over it, they will keep a copy of it, for the Archives, and add it to the collection. It is what they do on either side of their siesta."

Finally I said, "--- <u>Sign</u> it! --It means *nothing!* " I was very sure that it was the right answer.

She went off by herself, to make a Retreat. She prayed over it, and thought. After it was all over she told me what had happened.

" In the end I signed it," she said. "-- I signed it, and got sick."

"I could not sleep for 3 nights." she said. That was the beginning of her illness.

She spoke with resignation. "So everyone went down to the Bishop's office, they voted again with the chancery witnesses present, --*to keep us honest, you see*--- as though we had all been trying to put something over on them, all along, and so that some *integrity* would be assured.... I understood: this time it would be done right, for the Panty Hose Bishop was present."

The result of the election under these stringent new circumstances was that the nuns overwhelmingly re-elected Sister Anne Francis all over again. It was announced that she had won by 89% of the vote. That was scarcely the outcome hoped for by those who had informed on her, and it was scarcely pleasing to the Bishop and to Rome itself.

And it was not good news for her. She was still Superior; she had escaped nothing. Above all there was still the document she had signed under great pressure from Rome, her blind promise binding the religious women who had freely elected her to represent their interests that they would all do in future times everything the Sacred Congregation should ever require of them in the name of spiritual authority.

That was the summer of "Lucy in the Sky with Diamonds," when Anne Francis was called to Rome. In South Africa, some graduate students were excavating for human fossils when they found one, the oldest yet discovered. It turned out to be a she. They did not know what to call her, but the camp radio was playing out in the field, it was playing the Beatle song, "Lucy in the Sky with Diamonds", so they called her "Lucy." She was 3.2 million years old.

You can imagine the young people out there in the heat, dusting the dust away from this girl who is gone, with the words of the song playing out on the field radio: Look for the one with the sun in her eyes. At one point in her long trail she stopped in her tracks, an eminently human movement, she turned on her heel to look back, to see what was behind her. No one knows what she turned for; there could have been anything behind them; but she looked back, to see what was back behind, to see what they had left, where they had been, if they were going in the right direction, if they were doing things right, no one knows. She seems to have been our predecessor. "The Footsteps of Eve", the magazines said; an African Eve had been found.

It was only the background music to life, but the summer of *Lucy in the Sky with Diamonds* was the summer Anne Francis was "interrogated", and that is how I remember it, for it was not only the summer of Lucy the girl who turned to look back, who turned in her path to see what was behind her, but it was also the terrible time for us, the time when Anne Francis was called to Rome.

It reminded me of what happens in places like Latin America, where the Church has often found itself too close to Dictators, where people sometimes disappear. They simply vanish, children, husbands, brothers, and sons. They disappear, but everyone knows where they go: they go to be finished off. Unless they are attractive young children, then they may stay alive, to be adopted by those who have killed their parents. Either way, they do not come back. People march in protest, but that does no good, they are gone. They are called *The Disparu*: The Disappeared Ones.

You could say that there was no good reason for me to think of such things in her case, to think of the Disparu, The Disappeared Ones, for she faced no Dictators; there were no police squads with smoke rising from their gun barrels, there were no killing fields.

But there are persons in this world who simply cannot lie, they cannot bring themselves to say they stand for something which they do not stand for, there are those who cannot with their own signature sign away the freedom of others who have placed their trust in them, the freedom that all have worked together to maintain. In her case, the simple act of signing her name to something she could not bring herself to believe was a torment to her, and amounted to a sentence of death. I think many people might find it hard to believe that the simple act of signing one's name would throw anyone into a deep wrenching illness, and actually push them in the direction of death. But I was watching it happen, and I knew quite well that she might not be able to survive the consequences.

My friend --that other I had shared everything with-- was now becoming deeply sick; and she would become worse and worse. There was not much I could do; I had no resources in this world except a vow of poverty and a vow of obedience; I would have to seek permission to do anything. I could not even think of a way in which I could ask permission to do something for her which would not at once have been refused. My superiors would want to know Who Is This Woman? They would ask it in that tone of voice which I knew so well, which I had spent my life with. Whatever I asked would of course have been completely out of the question, and they would have been surprised --*quite surprised*-- that I had thought to ask it. The two of us were entering a place of darkness; we were separated by that religious life which was supposed to save us, as well as by five hundred miles. I prayed, but my prayer consisted mostly of saying "*My God, My God--*" over and over, and it was as much a curse as it was a prayer. I went around asking discreetly about her condition from persons I hoped might know of such matters. I asked and asked, and approached many people, but no one was able to tell me anything. For there was only one thing I wanted to know; I wanted to know if this was the kind of sickness that could sometimes, be cured, or if this kind was always a sickness unto death? And I was able to do nothing.

39

FRANK SINATRA'S WARM-UP MAN

Then pain I me to stretch forth my neckke,
And east and west, to the people I beck
-Chaucer, The Pardoner's Tale

Things were not going well with Anne Francis, but they were not going well with me, either. I got warnings, little comeuppances, in the oddest places; a good pilot is always on the notice for strange sounds or an unusual feel to warn him ahead of time that if he is not careful something important is going to drop off the aircraft, and he will be going down.

One of these warning lights showed up on my usual weekend work at a parish near Stonehill, Saint Catherine's, in the little town of Norwood. I went there to help out, to say two masses and hear confessions. You were given the stipends for several "mass intentions" to be said for the repose of a departed soul, small monies which made your life easier. The parish was so full of people from Ireland that you could hear the Irish language being spoken outside the entrance after Sunday mass. I liked it; I would drive there through the back woods on roads that dated to the American Revolution, and brush up on my sermon idea as I bounced along.

One time at least, I changed my sermon topic, because of what I heard on the car radio while I was driving over: news came that the great English cellist Jacqueline du Pres had come down with Multiple Sclerosis. I drew in a breath. She was one of the best cellists on earth, yet now the hands she needed for her playing would be attacked.

I knew that she was married to Daniel Barenboim, another musician of great gifts, and it seemed tragic that God would strike down such a match, which everyone thought had been made in heaven.

I remember giving the sermon. Instead of speaking from the day's Gospel or the Epistle from the Sundays after Pentecost, I told the people of Norwood about Jacqueline du Pres, and Daniel Barenboim.

I sensed during my talk that Monsignor Sennott was very busy putting his head out of the sacristy door. He would be wondering why I was talking about these strange people, and I had the feeling he was going to come out and stop me, until finally---in some way which I do not remember---I was able to make the day's Gospel to be all about Jacqueline du Pres and her cello, explaining that what had happened to her was an instance of God's ways to Man. Although to tell the truth I do not know how I ended up, on that particular Sunday.

Monsignor Sennott let me go, that time. But one time he did not let me go. He was waiting for me in the sacristy right after mass. I had been much taken with a new film by Ingmar Bergman, for its spirituality. I don't know whether it was *Wild Strawberries* or *Through a Glass Darkly*, but I thought that it was better than anything I could tell them about from the pulpit. I urged them to go down town and see this new film, this great, new, religious film by the Swedish director Ingmar Bergman.

I was pleased with myself as I proceeded in from the altar and started to take off the green chasuble and slide it onto the vestment case, when Monsignor Sennott rushed up. "—there was a woman who just came in here who said, 'He's out there telling us to go to a movie downtown, but there is only one movie cinema in Norwood, _and it only shows X-rated films!_"

You see, I had made the mistake of saying "Downtown", by which I meant downtown Boston, where such films might be expected to be shown. But to the people of Saint Catherine's Parish, anyone would know that "downtown" meant Norwood. Father Sennott smiled at my ignorance, and he asked me to straighten the matter out the following Sunday. He was relieved I think that I had not been telling his congregation to go to dirty movies.

Most of my sermons were really stolen from class. I stole from Tolstoy and from Graham Greene, to give ideas to the people of Norwood. One sermon I wanted to give was The Pardoner's Tale, about a wandering preacher in the Middle Ages who told wonderful stories. His method was to first frighten the people with fear of hell, so that he could more easily sell them his indulgences: he went around with a bag full of knuckle-bones from sheep which he claimed were relics of the saints. After he had terrified them with his sermon, he explained that if they bought these wares, they would be saved from the fires of hell. He was a wonderful story- teller, but he was a scoundrel, too, who did not believe what he preached. *Treasure of the Sierra Madre* was made out of it, with Humphrey Bogart dying for his gold. Of course I did not give that sermon, about the Pardoner, because I could not think of any way to do it ---I could not tell about knuckle bones, with Monsignor Sennott listening from the sacristy.

One way or another, it began to be clear enough to me that I should stop bothering the people of Norwood with my sermons. They were better off just listening to the Epistle to the Corinthians, or the Epistle to the Romans, during those long, interminable, green-vestmented Sundays after Pentecost.

And so I gradually came to the end of things, at Saint Catherine's. One summer Sunday as I took off my chasuble I explained to Monsignor Sennott that I would no longer be able to come to supply help, that my life had become too busy. He asked if I would get them to send a replacement. And that was that. I knew they would not miss me. They were better off with Paul's letters to

Timothy, from the Sundays after Pentecost. Better off than listening

to my snippets from Tolstoy.

This is how it works. You take off your green Chasuble,
pulling it up over your head, and slide it away from you upon the
polished top of the vestment case, and do the same with the green
Stole, and you fold the green Maniple from your wrist. All these
things have other names: The Breastplate of Salvation, the Shield of
Truth, the Helmet of Faith. It has taken you years—all the way from
boyhood-- to work your way into them, now you are taking them off.
You unhitch the Cincture from your waist, so that you can pull off the
Alb, the white robe usually damp from sweat, meant to remind of the
seamless Robe of Christ. Then at last, the Amice comes, from around
your shoulders. It is called that because it is supposed to be a
"friend" because it straps you in, into the Mass, into the Gospels.
You fold that up neatly, for one is expected to keep track of one's
own Amice, but if you are not going to use it again -- if this is the last
time you will need one-- you toss it into the laundry hamper, and you
are gone. They are on their own, now, they will not hear from you
again. Thousands have done this; thousands of men have folded up
their last Amice and tossed it into the hamper, and walked out of the
sacristy, into the streets, and into ordinary life.

Of course that is only the factual version of how I left

Norwood, the simple facts, with me standing at the vestment cabinet

telling Father Sennott to get somebody else.

But there is another version --not one which ever really happened, but one which, still, in a strange way, is closer to the truth. You see, years later, long after I stopped teaching and stopped giving sermons, driving along by myself and with time to spare, I still find myself often giving great lectures to classes, about *The Death of Ivan Ilych,* or something called *The Laurel Trees Have been Cut Down,* or whatever strikes me. And I do the same with sermons, for every once in a while, though I am no longer a priest, I do come across ideas that would make great sermons, and I like to deliver them, in my mind.

One time I came across what I thought would be a fine idea for a sermon. I was watching someone being interviewed on television. He turned out to be the "Warm-up Man" for Frank Sinatra's show in Las Vegas. It was very interesting, his job was to go out there ahead of Sinatra, and keep thousands of fans happy while they waited, up to two hours, for their hero. The Warm-up Man must have been good pretty good himself; maybe, in his own way, he was almost as good as Sinatra.

But he was a very humble person. He explained to the interviewer what it was like, going out there to face the people. He said that before his first try at it, the manager of the Las Vegas hotel sat him down and said, "Now, we have heard that you are very good, and we are very glad to have you. Go out there and do a good job. But please just remember one thing: There are thirty thousand screaming people out there, *and not a single one of them came to listen to you!*"

The interviewer laughed, and so did I: the poor warm-up man --- no one had come to hear him. It sounded so much like life itself, no one wants to listen to us, they come to hear somebody else. I was struck by such honesty. I thought that a good little talk could be made out of it.

It was then I had my brilliant idea. For you see, while it may have been true enough for the poor Warm-up Man that no one had come to listen to him, it really ought not be true for the Believer, should it? The whole point of Christianity is that someone has come to listen to each and every last one, that there is someone who hears all prayers. The sermon could be very beautiful, you could conclude by saying to the people that they were indeed blessed, they were not like the poor little Warm-up Man, who had no one to listen to him.. It was a sermon I thought I would liked to have delivered, even at Norwood. (Except that Monsignor Sennott would never have let me get beyond the name of Frank Sinatra.)

But that is not truthful, I am dreaming. I could not have given such a sermon, not back in Norwood or anywhere else. I was coming to a difficult place. To give it, I in some way would have had to become The Pardoner, for I knew well enough that if I gave it I would be preaching things to others which I no longer fully believed myself.

Whether or not I would have explained matters in these exact words then, I do not know; but it is what I should have said, if any one was listening, for it is the closest I have ever come to saying why I left. He was a wise old buck. The Monsignor owned his own plane, and went out sailing with his buddies in Hyannis each Sunday afternoon, he would swish by us with his duffle-bag full of sails on the way to Nantucket Sound while we stayed at the rectory to count the collection. He would have his own thoughts, which he would not speak to me. (*So you are leaving us, is it? ---With your Frank Sinatra and your Swedish movie directors and your outlandish Tolstoy? I wonder if we are the only thing you will be leaving, now? I wonder if*

you will soon be leaving the priesthood, too?)

Too bad I could not have spoken the truth to Monsignor Senott, at the vestment case, but it was something I was only beginning to know, then: that it was not quite true that I was quitting because my life had gotten busier. I was quitting because I could not bring myself to play the Pardoner, and preach the Pardoner's Tale.

40

THE ICE-MAN AND HIS MONSTERS

"--I was vomiting my life away," Anne Francis says, when I ask her about this time. "I meditated a lot, I thought about things." She was thinking about how much she was obliged to remain in her position, she was beginning to think about resigning. But they had elected her, they had trusted her; to resign would be to abandon them to what was going to happen. Yet she had done all that she was capable of, it had begun to destroy her.

" --I remembered the words, ' I am come that you may have life'" she says, " but that place was death for me..."

What faced her seemed an insoluble problem. The advice of her counselors was that she sign the document, on behalf of her entire community. This might seem a matter of little consequence, to some. I doubt if the men who sent her such a command had spent much time thinking of what they might be demanding. But her word, her consent meant very much to her; she would not be able to live with it, if she thought she had given it wrongly.

"--The Good Sisters--" these men would say, "--Ah, the Holy Nuns!" and smile benignly. I used to have coffee with them as they spoke like that, it is not possible for me to forget how they sounded, I heard about "The Good Nuns" over years and years, it remains in my ears like a *recitative*, sung over and over, from an old opera. I used to talk that way, myself.

And it is too easy for someone living later to say that she simply should have refused, should have "left", that they were the last men on earth still ordering women around in such fashion and that she should have told them where to get off. But that would be to sell her short, and to have no respect for what she believed, herself. She was not primarily concerned with such things as the Sacred Congregation; her faith went back beyond them through the grand teachers of the Church, back through Teresa of Avila and John of the Cross, she had such things in her bones. She was deeply spiritual, and deeply Catholic, she loved the Church in which she had been raised. I don't know how Christian those men in red were. If you have been to Rome, and done a little more than look at the fountains in Saint Peter's Square, you understand easily enough that it would not be difficult for almost anyone to be more religious than some who forge careers at the Vatican.

The days went by, and she had to make her own mind up. If she said No to Rome, if she found that she could not do what was demanded of her, then she would have to leave, she would abandon all those who had placed their trust in her, who had fought alongside of her for a decent human life, the ones she had given her word to, who had counted upon her to lead them through their struggles. She would have to let the old nuns look after themselves, and it placed an intolerable burden of choice upon her.

"--I am Primly Propped," she said one day over the phone. It was a light touch, she was laughing, it meant that she had propped herself up on pillows, before calling me. But I did not like the way it sounded, it was a line from "*Bells for John Whiteside's Daughter*," which is about the little girl next door, who was once so full of life, and is now deceased. The poem walks up to her in her casket, and is vexed to see her, this little girl that was full of life, now so "primly propped" in death. And I worried, five hundred miles distant: *Alas for the heart that drove her*

But her struggle was not with men in gorgeous vestments. It was with her own sense of right and wrong. I witnessed the struggle, and every once in a while I try to express it for myself. I have a collection of these "Tries'" to share, for what they are worth. There are currently three of them.

Try One. There is an old Labor song about a man named Joe Hill, perhaps he was a miner, I don't know. Anyway, they finished him off, he was shot by a firing squad in Utah State Penitentiary. But the song refuses to believe this, he becomes like Christ, risen from the dead in the song the workingmen continued to sing: "I dreamt I saw Joe Hill, last night," the song says, "-- alive as he could be." The singer questions him, "Says I, 'But Joe--*You're ten years dead!'* Then the answer comes back, "'--I'm still alive' said he." And the song repeats it, over and over, "-*I'm still alive!*' said he".

Decades later, I thought I heard the song once again during the Anita Hill testimony before a committee of the United States Senate. Each day the suited-up males of the world of politics questioned this honest black woman in front of the TV cameras, and every day she answered honestly, confounding them, for it was clear that they did not know what to do with honesty, they were afraid that if she kept on telling the truth she would destroy the nation. They went home and got more suspenders, and wore new bow ties, but it did not stop her, Anita Hill still kept witnessing. She kept coming back and being truthful and they did not know what to do with her as she started to become part of the history of her country. I drove to school each day with the words of the song in my ears: "*I'm still alive,'* said she."

Try Two. When your conscience begins to speak to you up through the floorboards, when it begins to sound like Hamlet's ghost, you have to find out first whether it is a true conscience or a false one, for the devil can assume pleasing shapes. And with a soul steeped in literature, why, it will not be so surprising if you find yourself talking back to it: you may start calling it names as it follows you, for you know its names. "-- *Old Mole!*" you hear yourself saying, " *--Canst move in the ground so fast?*" And as you keep asking it questions, and it responds, you hear your voice say again, "--*Art thou there, True Penny?*"

It seems to me something like that happened to her, whether she thought of it herself or not. And sometimes, especially early in the troubles, she must have wondered about this voice, and whether it was saying "*Sign! Sign!*" up at her. And so she had first above all to ascertain whether it was a true voice, or a false one that was saying things to her, and not one that would tempt her to her doom, one which was tempting her over the cliff. And that took time.

But she could not get away from it, that was clear. Wherever she moved, it followed her, "Old Mole," moving in the ground and following her with its demands; sometimes it was a loud voice barking out that she *Sign! Sign!* and *Sign!* again, while at other times it seemed to be telling her to simply give up and lose her own Soul, for this ghost was not a good one, but a bad one, the one that would damn a soul for eternity.

For there are always two voices, I think, thumping up through the floorboards.

One with fearsome accents she had heard well enough, saying Submit, Gore your own thoughts, Sell cheap what is most dear. It is the departed voice of dead Kings and burners-at-the-stake and professional torturers, from the long line of those willing to turn the rack up another notch, and pull the victim apart some more, so as to save the tortured prisoner from themselves, from their own misguided intransigence. It is the Soul they are after, it is the victim's own welfare that they pursue. For what is this temporary torment, compared with that other, of burning in hell forever? The Sacred Congregation was pursuing her for the sake of her soul.

It is well within the tradition; this voice, it is an old voice that has spoken to us up from the floorboard and down from on high and out of pulpits and from the confessional. It is part and parcel of what we too easily call the Mainstream of Western Civilization Yet it is a bad voice, which leads us to our doom.

But then there is True Penny, the other one. It sounds rather simple-minded; saying things like To thine own self be true, which makes everyone want to smile. I don't know that it thumped for her as loud as the first; I think it was maybe quieter, like the one Teresa of Avila heard when she, too, found herself fighting with those men in Rome, or the one Saint John of the Cross heard in his cell, when the Holy Office of the Inquisition put him in jail.

Try Three. I have my own Meditation on Conscience. I found it in the Austrian Alps. That is a strange place to go, to find it.

You have heard of the little Ice Man they found up there, when the glaciers melted. He had straw in his shoes to keep the cold out, and was carrying a bronze axe, very early for that. And he had in his bag herbs and flowers against the plague, and best of all, he was actually carrying a burning coal with him, which was kept alive by being packed in leaves.

The burning coal was meant for him to blow on, so that it would burst into fire, giving him warmth, scaring the monsters off, and pushing the glaciers back in the night. When I try to think of conscience, I think of it that way. We are all making a journey, with our pilgrim's bag, trying to get through the pass before it gets dark, before the snows catch us and our fire goes out, with or without our fine bronze axe. And one of the things we count on is that thing we carry along with us, which if carefully nurtured will flame up, and warm us back into life.

But still, Fate must be kind. The ice-man did not make it; they found him 7500 years later, his straw shoes, his bag of posies, his coal long cold, and the surprising bronze axe. They examined him for years, trying to figure out what did him in, and then they noticed something, a finely polished stone arrow-head lodged in his ribs. You can have all the conscience you want, but it won't save you from an arrow through the back.

"In the end, I did it" she says, " --I signed it, but could not sleep that night."

" -I signed it," she says, "and could not sleep, because I believed that I had devastated my own conscience. I signed it, and that was when I began to get sick."

Sick, exploited, and feeling that she lacked strength to come back to health, she resigned. She was exhausted from trying get them all safely into their new constitutions, she was exhausted from dealing with Rome.

But these three tries are only mine. She had to respond herself to what she was being presented with, in the language of old Rome:

Here, sign this and you will be done. Sign it and we will be justified in terminating you. It is your death warrant. Sign it in good frame of mind, with full awareness, and we will have a document saying we are right and you are finished. And ordinary ink will be sufficient, don't bother to sign it in your own blood.

41

BRAZEN: MADE OF BRASS

Say the word "Blacksburg" to either of us and it means bleeding to death. Blacksburg is a college town in rural Virginia, where there was enough interest to invite the American Committee for Irish Studies to hold its annual meeting, the ACIS. Anne Francis was deathly sick there, and she was more and more all that mattered to me; yet the hope of survival for both of us required that I divide my attention between her and what was going on at the conference.

The ACIS is quite professional. Scholars from all over the world come to deliver papers; they are the leading scholars in James Joyce or in Middle Irish or in The Protestant Nation or in the prehistoric ruins at Newgrange, or Poyning's Law, any number of arcane topics, you expect to hear about disappearing vowel sounds. People attending speak German and Japanese, or a lot of other things, and you suspect that you are in the presence of some of the world's best and brightest.

And if you are the one designated to be Conference Director for the following year's conference, if your college has told you to go out and get it, get the conference for them, and put it on with verve and make a success out of it, why you had better pay attention, see how they are doing this year's conference, and find out who can help you. You do this whether you are a natural conference director or no, and if you are not one, you try to become one pretty quick. I was not one, but when Stonehill told me to "get next year's conference and put the college on the map", I found myself paying attention.

What happens is that, after all the learned papers have been given and the world- famous figures have had their say, after all the documentary films have been shown and the new art displayed in the campus art gallery, after performers have played on old instruments, and the harpists have played the music of Carolan and Purcell at the final grand dinner, why you go up into the smoke-filled rooms that have been reserved by the grand of figures of the movement, as though it is part of the fight for Irish freedom, and then they tell you what you are going to do, for next year's conference. Of course you listen to them; you listen to John Kelleher of Harvard and Emmet Larkin of M.I.T. and Alan Ward from William and Mary as well as people from Alberta in Canada and maybe from the red-brick schools of the British Midlands, for you have not yet done it yourself, you have never done anything like this before, and you take every piece of information from them, as to who can give you help.

My Department Chairman ordered me to do it, for Stonehill College. When that happened to me, I was frightened, anyone would be; but in my case I had a special reason to be terrified, for I was beginning to get the idea: that the future, if there was to be any future, depended in some way on how well my conference went. I cannot say that I grasped everything at once, but I knew well enough that I was fighting for Anne Francis, so that she would have a life, I was fighting for the two of us, that we would have a life together. It may seem strange, but it was a concept which unfolded gradually, and came to me over a period of time. Sometimes we do not recognize what is for you a new idea, and it can take a whole lot longer to comprehend its consequences.

It began to unfold in me while I was sitting there listening to how I should do things. My college was situated outside of Boston, not a bad place for the ACIS to meet. I listened in the night as they told me things, for what I intended was to go home and plan for Stonehill something better than had ever been done in that place. Everyone around the table there seemed to be thinking of just another learned conference, but I was not. I was thinking of a conference, of course, but of something far beyond that, something magnificent. I was thinking of something that made me wonder if I was not going a bit mad. I could feel coming into my eyes the look that I had seen on the face of Lenin, in those pictures of him, boarding what he called " the Great Train of History." Oh, I was not thinking of starting any World Revolution, of course, and toppling monarchies, all I was thinking of was turning my own little world quite upside down. But all the same, I tell you, we both had that same fierce gaze.

Anne Francis came to Blacksburg; for though she had had to give up poetry in order to deal with Rome, she still attended such meetings out of honor for her field, out of longing for what she had lost. She was becoming ill; alas for the tireless heart that drove her, she was going deeper into the suffering brought on by what she thought she had done to her order. She was not in good shape. My procedure was to leave her back in her room, then go to the Business Meeting; I whispered to her that I was planning our future for us. As I walked to the meeting I knew that I was marching toward something which had to work; those were desperate times.

With Maureen, I left her in her hotel room around midnight; the business meeting was being held in those small hours. Every once in a while, Maureen would dart in and out of the meeting to see how she was doing. Anne Francis was bleeding; she was in fact in danger of hemorrhaging herself to death. I knew little of such matters. I did not know how close she was to what danger.

Maureen would slip in to me and say, "--She is resting. --She is not so bad as she was".

I would turn back to what they were saying around the table. We went through the conditions for next year's meeting; they told me what had to be done. We talked about Themes for the conference, what needed to be covered. It was not something I was good at. From time to time I looked up, away from the details of scheduling and speaker panels, and thought of what might be going on back in that hotel room. If that failed, what was going on in front of me was useless.

The meeting concluded. I had won the next year's conference for Stonehill. I was not certain anyone would call that winning, but it was a start, it began to look like we might have a chance of pulling things off, of doing something great.

I returned to the room of Anne Francis, where Maureen was bent over her as over a patient in intensive care. It appeared that she was recovering.

Suddenly Maureen turned to me and said, "---*She can't take much more of this, you know!*"

I remember my response; it was pretty much, "--But what can *I* do about it?" I remember putting my hands out to either side of me and shrugging, in a kind of despair. A lot was going on. The business meeting was just over, it was not that easy.

Then Maureen said something else. "---This place you're at--this *Stone*hill of yours? --Couldn't you just-- _brazen it out--_ up there? Can't you just--- *brazen it out*?" I looked at her.

She was asking me to be a man. She was my friend, and the best friend Anne Francis had. She sought only our good. She was saying that I should just tell them to fuck off; that is what she was saying, though she did not use the words. I was not sure I had reached that point yet, of seeing myself telling them all to go jump in the lake, to stick my chin out and walk across the Stonehill campus defying anyone to challenge me. I thought of the meaning that the word "brazen" had; it meant: to be made of brass. It meant to have a brass rod stuck up your back, instead of mere flimsy human backbone. It meant to go around with your profile shining, as if it were made of metal. Oh, I knew what it meant---what it really

399

meant-- it meant to have the balls of a brass monkey, that's what it meant, and everyone knew it.

Yet, it was an apt phrase; Maureen is good at the apt phrase. It said in a few words what was required, what had to happen. I thought of things; I must say I thought of brass monkeys. I was beginning to know, now, incrementally at least, what was going on. I would wonder about my conference, who I should invite as speakers; but then I also wondered about how it would feel to slowly turn into something with a great deal of brass to it. It did not seem like me, you know, it did not seem like me at all; on some people, a lot of brass just doesn't look good. Everyone says, "It just isn't *you*..."

But Anne Francis would, if anything get worse, that summer. We were both about to be ruined; we had to do something.

My overall success at Stonehill had never been guaranteed. When I first went there, people had been told that I had replaced a beloved teacher of theirs, who had fallen ill. That was not at all the case, I had replaced another person who had simply not returned her contract. It gave me a lot of trouble before this was straightened out, and it took a long time to win the following with students I was used to. I worked to gain tenure, for I was determined not to be hit again by one of those arrows which go flying through the night. I walked down corridors there with an eye to what was behind me. Now, in addition to all this, Maureen was telling me to stick it to them. That would take some thinking.

I had been forming an idea on my own, anyway. It went something like this. I was beginning to see myself as one of those climbers, the kind who insert what are called "crampons" in the crevices of a mountain: they insert a crampon, and twist it, so that it expands between two surfaces, and becomes irremovable, and so secure that they can hang their hammock from it on the face of the cliff and even sleep through the night, knowing that they will still be there in the light of morning. But you need two surfaces for it to work: you have to have what is called "purchase", and you have to have leverage. My idea was this: I would force my crampons in between the great unmovable mass of American Academic Freedom on the one hand, and the obvious self-interest of Stonehill College, on the other. If I could lodge myself in between these two entities, why, I would have to be promoted, and they would have to keep me, even if I announced that I was leaving the order. (I pictured myself announcing that I was leaving the order.) The whole business would make them supremely uncomfortable --they did not want any former priests around-- but I would promise to behave myself, and not cause undue embarrassment to them; and anyway, my crampons would not

401

come out, no matter who shook them. I could do it, I thought; I could hang upside down in my hammock in the night, thousands of feet above the earth below. And still be there in the morning.

Of course it was only an idea; only a hope, really. It would be like climbing Mount Rushmore, pushing myself up into that cleft you can see if you look hard at it, that inviting space between the massive right temple of Thomas Jefferson and in behind the great left ear of George Washington: there was lodgment for me, I believed: up there with a decent respect for the opinions of mankind.

Maureen was only telling me to get a move on, to do what I was already thinking of doing, saying that there was not much time. And anyway, it was not as if I was robbing anybody; the conference, the thing I was going to do for them, was of real value; I was good for the place.

"Blacksburg, Virginia." The name reminds me of John Brown, man of the mountain hollows, with his streeling hair and wild gaze. *We are going to free the slaves!* He says. *We will seize federal arms!* He says. *We will take those arms and fight with them! Freedom for Mankind! Hosanna to the Highest!*

(N.B. Things have changed, with Jefferson's ear. There are fissures running up the faces on that monument, and the cracks go very deep. Perhaps counting on such a thing would not be such a good gamble, today)

42

WESTRUN WIND

Westrun Wind, when will thou blow,
and the small rain down can rain?
Christ, that my love were in my arms
And I in my bed agayne!

--Middle English Lyric

Back at Stonehill, I began turning into something of a madman: I was about to stage a production for them, which had elements of drama to it, and I had begun to grasp that it might be within my power, for the first time ever, to actually write the script for what was going to happen in my life. I profoundly changed; I became Hamlet, shouting *"The play's the thing! "* I went looking for Scene-shifters now, and for anything which might do as a stage; I saw things only as props for what I was doing, I sought lighting; I was in the market for make-up artists, I needed Duckey the Dresser, as well as prompters, to hiss out my lines, if the actors forgot what their parts instructed them to say.

I had not ever known someone like Hamlet to be my model, before; yet, except for that final scene where he pulls out the rapiers and leaves everyone running in their blood, my pattern seemed at every turn to echo, at a fair distance, his. I did not kill anybody, and I was a bit off-put by this new fellow of my name, hauling drops around, shoving actors out from the curtains on time, threatening to hit them with props if they did not produce. But you see, my idea was to pull off something excellent, on an academic level first, oh yes, but also with drama to it, altogether an outstanding thing, by which I hoped to catch success. If that happened, if the grand thing I was planning came about, why, see you, they would not be able to get rid of me, then; they would have to keep me, there would be a happy ending, after all.

But I well knew that if my courage slipped past a certain point, if that is to say, my blue eyes did not hold, against the darker ones trying to stare me down, --for example those who knew how large a bill I was running up-- why then I could forget all happy endings, the pair of us would be like those two figures from Dante, whose souls are blown about on the winds, this way and that, for all eternity. And you could be certain that there would be no Dante taking notes, to tell the world our sad tale.

Once I was convinced that my scheduled speakers were competent, and the very best available, I regarded them as players; they would come and strut their stuff. But I would be the one who controlled that which in the stage business goes by the name of "blocking," all blocking would be diligently arranged by me, for I was Prospero. Most of them in the end turned in a good job; but it was only the rare person among them, --like Samuel Beckett's good friend, Alec Reid-- who was ever aware of what a favor their performance on that stage was doing for me. (He pulled me aside and said, "--You know, when you do this, *Francis*--when you *leave*-- you are going to receive a few *stones*... Perhaps I can intercept a few of those---but that is the most I can do for you!") Alec Reid, from the bleak landscape of Samuel Beckett, somehow knew that I was leaving. Steeped in an old Protestant culture, he of all of them grasped my situation, and wished me well. For an office, the school gave us the old Aviary from the Ames Estate, a tiled room where birds had once been kept, and water still splashed down from fountains, as we invited the world onto what seemed to me that famous "Cloth of Gold" you read about.

It was my young students who kept me sane. They typed away, and they read the letters they wrote; they all knew who was coming. I began to worry for them; when the bright talents that we invited actually came, I knew they would fall in love with them. I knew what was going to happen, I warned them, all my yellow-haired girls, like Alice and the black-haired ones like Trish and Patrice, and the brown-haired ones like Mary Pat, about the bright-talking young Irish men, "the lads" -- and the older pub-crawling ones as well-- with their flutes and pipes, their paintings and films, their Guinness and their talk, all the Ginger Men with their goat-hooves soon to be let loose on our campus. I told them to watch themselves.

And they began to know everything; after a while it was clear that they knew about Anne Francis. I do not know how they knew, I never told them anything, or thought I did not, yet they knew, they knew in their bones and they would ask, secretly and individually, they wanted to know, "*Is she coming? Will Sister Anne Francis be coming, too?*" And sometimes it was as a little note to me, sticking up out of my typewriter

I surprised myself. I talked the Guinness people into giving free Guinness, I got Boston Logan airport to put our name up in lights on the exit road: so that "*Welcome Stonehill Irish Scholars*" was the first thing everyone would see that week as they arrived.

I told movie producers to go to hell, the ones with little home movies to show, and invited a young Irish Harpist to play authentic airs and dances, for cocktails the first evening.

We went after the Nobel Prize winners, first. We invited Sean MacBride, of The MacBride Principles, which stipulate how political prisoners are to be treated, the UN Councilor to Namibia, but he could only come much later, and we would have him long after the conference was over.

So we invited Conor Cruise O'Brien, another Laureate, and another UN personality. He accepted. I did not know then that the local chapter of the IRA would object to his presence at Stonehill, that they would phone in threats against the life of my main speaker and that I would end up having to pay police protection for him. I had to learn a lot. I remember dealing with Irish cut-glass, rare musical instruments, Saul Field's film on Leopold Bloom, Flora Mitchell's original line-drawing portraits of Vanishing Dublin, archaeological discoveries from the bogs, Samuel Beckett scholars, James Joyce scholars, collectors of monuments. And there would be those endless Conor Johnstons, the kind who stood up to challenge every speaker, " --Now what is your authority for saying that?"-- Where do you find documentation for this assertion of yours?"

Once upon a time, I followed the River Liffey with a camera, from where it starts, above Liffeyhead Bridge, in its "beautiful blue bedroom in the sky", all the way down through Dublin, and out to sea, to meet its "cold, mad, feary Father." It reminded me now,

408

somehow, of working with the young ones. Our fountain in the bird sanctuary tinkled and splashed like that river did, and filled the aviary with its sound around us. Parakeets and birds of paradise seemed to fill the echoing space, and it would have been nice to somehow hold the moment against Time, to catch it, and title it " Pretty Young Ones, with Birds of Paradise": a cascade of students, their heads bent in effort. Yet I was not happy, like they were; for all the excitement, I had no reason for asking time to stop, I wanted it to hurry, to sweep the two of us beyond what was so harmful, and to free us both. Then, much later, we could think about the river, flowing out to sea.

What I am trying to describe is the year of living dangerously, that whole year I was preparing for the conference, a year in which the two of us did not know where we were going to go.

Because, during all this time, Anne Francis was deteriorating. Every time I checked in with her, she was worse than before.

I was able to get time off, on a long weekend, to drive her from Erie to her sister Peggy's place in Washington DC. where she might get better help. I deliberately drove us along the Skyline Drive, so that it would lift up her heart when she saw the beauty, I thought it might help her to see High Nob and Big Cobbler. But she did not see them, could not look at anything.   And one time, perhaps the lowest point in all of this, when I took her for a walk down along the Potomac River, where Lady Bird Johnson had preserved the river habitat and there were flowers at our feet to look at, I would try to get her to look, I would pick a beautiful flower, and say to her, "Look at this. Look at this wonderful flower!" She would look down, to please me, for even in her worst times, she still loved me, and her attention would be on the flower only for an instant, before her mind upped and wandered away, flew away to other things, back with her conscience, to what was bothering her, and it was apparent that she had no hope.

I was walking with someone whose spirit was outside herself, was somewhere else, not walking with me on the river bank. Her soul kept fleeing, always being overwhelmed with her problem, the one which had no solution: the moral quandary she had been placed in of being ordered by religious authority to say Yes, against her own conscience, of being forced, on behalf of others, to agree to demands which had not even been thought up yet, demands which could make her future impossible, which would sell her religious community up the river and into slavery.

I wondered what was to become of us. I talked to myself, the way one does in tight spaces, I said to myself that I must be strong for the two of us, yet I was afraid that if one of us went down, the other would too, we would both disappear together. Yet, no matter what she was going through, I still remember the firm undoubting knowledge I had, that such a one as she was would bloom again, and that I would be there to watch it happen. And I thought of the name of that ship I once knew, the one that ran alongside for hours to keep us company on the wide ocean: it was called *The Rose Revived.*

One thing I remember vividly. We were in Washington together one evening; we were on M street in Georgetown, after eating at the little *Chez Francais.* When we came out, a large crowd had gathered across the street, in front of the *Rive Gauche* restaurant. They were excited, and cheering; one fellow was up on the shoulders of another, trying to get a look in. "It's Kissinger" Anne Francis said, "--That's Henry Kissinger; and Nancy, --he must be having dinner at *La Rive Gauche!*" Though she was going through a lot, she still knew what was going on, more than I did.

It was the evening of Richard Nixon's resignation from the Presidency. He had resigned earlier in the day; he had thrown his arms upward in an assertive "V" in back of the White House, and the green helicopter had flown away with him.

I was so preoccupied that I had not properly noticed much mightier events. And I still remember wondering, When the president you work for has been fired, do you go out on the town to eat with your girlfriend? And what was the crowd cheering about? That we had got rid of Nixon? Or that Kissinger had not let it bother him? The memory makes me feel guilty and foolish, I think it is because I seem sometimes to regard great world events as merely backdrops for what is going on in my own life, I seem to have got things backwards. But then, Kissinger was not letting events hold him back, either.

And it was during this period, in the absolute depth of everything, that I proposed marriage. I must remember this, that in a time when there was little hope, and no reason to expect anything, I wrote a letter suggesting a future for the two of us. I left her staying with Peggy, so that she could get help at the hospital, and I went home to Stonehill, and sat down and composed a letter setting out the future as I hoped it might happen. It was a first sketch, and not very convincing. It was long and involved, it must have sounded to her like the setting up of the United Nations Charter, and she was in no condition to respond. It seemed so unlikely and so ridiculous she told me that she laughed when she read it, and her sister Peggy heard her.

And Peggy said, about my offer, about my proposal of marriage, "--*I would not preclude it.*"

The two of us possessed nothing. That is the way things are set up. Sometimes Holy Mother the Church is a loving Mother, who creates a leprosarium for those no one else will touch, or sends Archbishop Lamy (Willa Cather's wonderful holy man) for miles on horseback to the lost ones of the Frontier, before death comes to him, and he dies, in grace. But it is also sometimes cruel and merciless, for often there is nothing more than what might be called The Economic Argument that keeps a lot of people in their convents and rectories that keeps them from leaving, for fear of starving. Old nuns, old priests, those who have given the best part of their lives to others. After the age of fifty, every one knows (the Church knows) there is not much chance, and we were turning fifty. We had no money. She would leave without Social Security, which ironically she had labored to arrange for the rest of them, for her old girls, for once being made Superior she had been moved out of teaching and a salaried position, and so she no longer qualified, herself. Thanks to her, the ones who remained gained an arrangement with the federal government, while she was left on her own. They say most of us are only one paycheck away from being homeless; where did that leave us?

I thought of those iron subway gratings that people freeze to death on. You see the homeless person, one day trying to keep warm in zero weather, and the next day they are gone. Such policies toward human beings are often called *Realpolitik,* and no one is better at it than the grand old institutions we give our lives to.

I went back to Stonehill. September came, and the school year got under way. She was seeking treatment, in Washington. I hoped it would all turn out.

Things moved on. During the day I was immersed in activity. But at night, when I would go to bed, I pulled the covers up, and tried to go to sleep. We were one, now, the two of us were one. It is not possible for one in this situation to simply fall asleep, without regard to the other.

I have heard of a man whose young wife wanted, more than anything else in this life, to row alone across the Atlantic Ocean in a small boat. She had her boat all specially adapted against taking on waves and capsizing, and besides, the thing had already been accomplished by men. So they had an agreement; he would do this thing for her, would help her get ready, and see her off, as she went rowing, rowing alone without him, into the dark deep sea.

He saw her off, went down to the dock and pushed her boat for her, and wished her well, and I suppose he went home and each night calculated how far she must be, how far against the currents and against the winds, and the waves.

I do not know how he went to sleep at night. How do you pull the covers up and feel the nice dry bed, when the one you love is rowing by herself across the ocean? What black waves are menacing her now? At this moment, is she still rowing, or is she, too, trying to sleep? Is she, even, still, alive?

Anne Francis was much in that position. It had not been her idea, it was not something we had planned, that she would go out there in the night, fighting against waves she could not see, we had not volunteered for that.

My dear young things, they looked at me and wanted to ask how far she was now? They left me notes, secretly typed in the typewriter, requests to be informed: Was she making it? Was she half-way yet?

But I could not tell them anything, I was far away from her, in my own bed again.

I did not know if it was raining where she was or was it dry, and I did not know how close her bravery was to capsizing, and if she would drown alone in the darkness. I had invited her to leave, with me; and it must have been true, at that moment, that I had finally decided to leave, myself.   Yet I did not honestly know if I would even see her again, or if I would only meet her on some opposite shore.

Safely back at Stonehill, I pulled the covers up, and finally went to sleep.

43

TO THE INNER STATION

*As long as men have illusions about themselves
and about life, as long as their values are
artificial, their conceptions fanciful and unreal
as long as they are not walking in truth, they must be
disillusioned in order to be true.*

-- *"Light and Darkness"*

When she was a young graduate student, Anne Francis wrote
a thesis, "Light and Darkness in Conrad's Heart of Darkness.'" in
which she tracked the struggle of "brooding gloom versus exquisite
light." Every high school student knows the story: young Marlow is
sent by The Company to find what their representative "Mister
Kurtz" is up to, in the jungle. We are led to expect evil. Marlow
follows Kurtz's leavings, traces his path up the slimy river, and
although the book was written long before there was a Doctor
Mengele for the world to bring to justice, before there was a Pol Pot
and The Killing Fields, it is hard not to think of such things when we
hear mention of the name of Kurtz. "I smelled the primeval mud in
my nostrils," Marlow says of going into the jungle, and as we go

deeper and deeper into savagery, we think we hear Freud talking, too, and we wonder if it is only a real jungle Marlow is talking about, or if we have not been invited on a journey up the rivers and rivulets of our own inner human psyche, a journey to the center of that wasteland which can lie in the hearts of humankind.

Why would a young nun choose such a subject? Perhaps it was because when you are told you are going to have to spend a long time laboring on something, you know you had better choose something worthwhile, better pick something that smacks to you of the way things really are. Why waste life on something unimportant? You can tell who people are by what they choose.

Her thesis says it is about " the darkness that every man may be forced to meet within himself." When she decided as a young person to go chasing after Light and Darkness in human endeavor, and was willing to go traipsing up that filthy river, she was making certain that her own life would not be about something unimportant. It also turned out that she was in effect writing a book about herself, the book of her own life. It always seems to me that she made some such journey herself, her own journey up river, that she tracked down, in the undergrowth of human fears, that clearing in the jungle, and discovered where fears hide, something very like what Conrad calls the heart of darkness. It is not surprising that one day she would find herself getting deeper and deeper into the hidden places of the human spirit, where so much courage is needed.

And so what she was called upon to go through now she must have felt was something she had seen before. The more she was in the presence of that authority which threatened her, the more she must have felt she was dealing with the same thing she had followed as a young girl, writing in the footsteps of Marlow.

I was like an outsider to all this, I was one of those members of The Company upon whom everything was lost. To me it seemed strange that anyone would be so bothered by a concern over such matters; I had been taught that there was always a way of dealing with difficult choices, for I had been taught by Canon Lawyers for years; I watched how they themselves got out of things, and always tried not to let them bother me, too much. But I well knew that I was in the neighborhood of one for whom it was not so: a person who simply could not bring herself to approve of something wrong, to say something was true which was not, to sign her name to documents binding others, binding people who were not herself.

I urged her to forget it, to let someone else worry about it, and have a drink. To me it was bad, yes, admittedly an unhealthy state of affairs indeed, but I supposed it was simply standard procedure, for Rome.

Yet it was a true horror which was killing her, for all I said. Some people are willing to go to jail for what they believe. She is of the breed of those Marlows who cannot walk the world without responding to the presence of evil in our midst. "They lied to me," she says, "--*They lied to me*." She could have nothing to do with the lie. No wonder she ended up where Conrad ended up; and no wonder she sounded so much like him.

He leaves us clues. There is the "dead hippo", that huge mass of corruption which fills the air with its stench; it blocks the path and penetrates everything; the story is really about those who could breathe in the air of corruption, as though they were not being poisoned themselves, workers for The Company. What does he mean by that? Does it not have much to do with the meaning of the whole journey?

At the end of the story the natives arrive, who bring their news at last, saying: "--Mistuh Kurtz, he dead." I used to hear her saying that, ---"Mistuh Kurtz, he dead" but did not know what she meant; she still says it, often, she says "Mistuh Kurts, he dead" about a lot of things. She had tramped up the river herself, the smell of primeval mud in the nostrils, looked at the stinking grave of Kurtz

She was following her own words, that as long as a person has illusions about themselves and about life, they must be disillusioned themselves, in order to be true. She was able finally to understand that she would no longer be part of the process, and it was after that she started to get better.

Maybe we are all on a jungle journey of good and evil, all the time, so that even an ordinary life is full of it, the stench of primeval mud filling our nostrils, and if we do not smell it, why, perhaps we should worry about ourselves.

I followed her from a distance. I telephoned a lot. We are lost, I said to myself, we are lost together, we are both lost, but I said it to nobody, for no one was listening. It was painful. I had no reason to believe that she would get better, or that either of us would ever be heard from again. Yet I knew I would be faithful. I was hardly certain of anything in life, but I did know that whatever happened I would be faithful to Anne Francis. I who have wavered in so many things in life never wavered a moment in that. I made many mistakes, my life has been an unending series of them, but I never failed her.

Then, she was cured. I got a call from her one day in October, after it had gone on for five months. She was her old self. Indeed, she seemed even more herself than she ever had been. *We were saved.* Life could begin again.

I think the burning coal must have come alive for her at last, that one we all carry in our baggage. She had cupped her hands on it and blown it back into life, it had flared up, lighting the dark for her and scaring the monsters off, pushing the ice of the glaciers back a little, enough to get through the pass and down to where safety lives. I think of the little Ice Man, the herbs in his pouch, and the pocketfuls of posies in the song we sing as children against the threat of infection and death, carried in the hopes of not falling down.

She did it, somehow, she pulled it off, and immediately began to know what else she must do. She must have first come to understand that no one really had such power over her, that she was in fact free to go by her own sense of what was right, she was free, and she was Lucy in the sky with diamonds.

And sometime soon after, she must have decided that if this was so, then there was one more thing she must do: leave. She would have to put her affairs in order, leave her people in as good stead as she could, and then walk out the front door, into whatever would befall her. Just outside of Avila, in Spain, there is an enormous statue to the great Teresa, and she is doing that, walking out of the Convent of the Incarnation, good old Teresa is walking off, for she too came to that point, to the point where she had to go get her walking slippers, and her walking stick, and just walk out the front door of her convent. You can look it up.

The people who work for The Company are somehow able to get on with their work, or they would not be there, they may not like some of the consequences of what it is they do, but they are the kind of persons who have learned to accept it, it is part of their way of life, they have somehow taught themselves to put up with it, they do not have to leave, they can remain.

What happened to Anne Francis is not difficult to grasp. She might not choose to couch it in certain terms, but it is clear enough. You can beat around the bush, you can employ such ornate language to describe it that people do not know what it is you are talking about, you can somehow manage to avoid coming out to actually express the whole point of the narrative, but she had run into something in the path of her little community.

Joseph Conrad, trying to describe things that go wrong, resorted to the odor of dead hippo.

I would not go that far to describe all that happened, I would not say that. It does not need that kind of talk; it was bad enough.

423

44

THE DOVE HAS BUILT HER NEST
IN THE ALTAR OF THE LORD

That was a strange time, a time of change not only everywhere but with the Church as well; everything was chaos, you did not know what was going to change next. There was a brief period, as they were turning the altars around to face the people, that you found yourself celebrating masses any place, not just in church. People were sitting on the floor and singing Spirituals and holy Rock Music, and we priests were offering up loves of bread --Wonder Bread or whatever, sliced or unsliced-- we were being Liberated From the Grip of the Past.

I had come down to Washington while Anne Francis was recuperating, and was a guest at Peggy's house in Georgetown. It was Sunday morning, and instead of going out to church, they wondered if we could have mass right there in the living room.

I felt that I was not good at that sort of thing. I was getting to be not so sure of what I was doing. Peggy got some bread and wine, and we sat around the coffee table, Peggy, and Anne Francis, and me.

When I opened up the book—the Roman Missal--- I suddenly recognized it as a most familiar mass. Some of those things are masterpieces; centuries of work have been done on the music that goes with them. It was "Turtur Nidum", it is the mass of the Turtle Dove. In it, a dove flaps her wings all the way through everything, you can hear the flapping of her wings, and the old Gregorian music is as good as one of Mozart's masses, for it is based on a little story.

I told them the simple tale. "In the time of David," I said, "the priests came running: " *A dove has made a nest in the altar of the temple!* The temple has been desecrated! What shall we do? Must it be consecrated all over again?"

"King David thought for a moment," I said, "--This poet and psalmist of the human spirit must have thought of all those laws, about Purification and the burden placed upon him. Then, to the astonishment of the chief priests of the temple, he came to his decision. He said, '*The dove has found herself a home in the altar of the Lord, and it shall not be taken from her!*'"

We went on, through the mass, through the *Orate Fratres* (Pray, Brethren) and to the *Sursum Corda* (Lift up your hearts)

425

sipping the wine from a glass, and with the breaking of the bread making a small community: myself, Anne Francis, and her sister Peggy; we heard the dove's wings fluttering with us to the end. Then we were silent awhile.

When it was finished, Peggy was very quiet; she is reserved in her words, and sparse with her judgments. But afterward, picking up the bread plates she said, "--That was *good* --what you did there. ---It was wonderful." She appeared lost in thought, perhaps about King David, and the Turtle Dove who had found a home. She must surely have known that it was about all of us, that the notes on the page and the music of the mass were really about the human soul, how it flies and flies, longing to find a home, to build its nest even in the courts of the Lord. Looking back, now, Peggy might have been thinking of what was to become of her sister, what was to become of all of us; it was a time of chaos; perhaps, she may have even been thinking of what might happen to herself. It was consoling to hear of the little bird that had found a home, which would not be taken away from her.

And as for me, though I did not know it that would be the last Mass I ever said, with a wine-glass for a chalice and store-bread on the coffee table. I did not know that this was true until much later.

But if is true that the soul is so like a bird---and many people think that it is --- then there is another one that I am very fond of.

Of all creatures in the world it is among the most astonishing. It is a sea-bird with enormous wings, of the Albatross family, which touches down to earth on a single island in the Pacific only one time a year, to launch the next generation. It flies for thousands upon thousands of miles, without ever touching land; scientists think that it circles the globe, on its wings, and they say that it even sleeps on them, that it can glide through the night, somehow keeping its balance, with its eyes closed. I find it amazing, that even at this moment, now, say, in some part of the world where there is darkness, there should be one of these Pelagic birds flying, flying in the night over the world's water. I cannot conceive of the storms they face, the pellets of rain and ice they seek to somehow avoid, but if you are human, and you hear of it, you cannot fail to feel, howsoever briefly, one with the bird, for you know that something of what it does is what your own soul has done, through all the nights and storms of your own lonely voyage.

45

OCTOPUS

Then something happened. On a Sunday morning in October, when I was back at Stonehill, I called her in Washington, and though I was no doctor, I knew immediately as soon as she spoke over the phone that she was well again, she had made it through everything, after all.

Things now happened quickly. She returned to Erie, and asked for a small apartment off to one side of the campus, the kind that students were being given.

She had to decide things. She resigned her position, she was getting well, but there were further matters for her to deal with. Anything I say amounts to the conjectures of a bystander, my account is exterior to what was going on, and it is based on my own memories of this time. But surely, she was deciding on such things as whether she should stay in that way of life, and remain among them.

428

She had to find out whether she could continue to pay obeisance to Rome, after what she had seen.

It was at this time that she found herself sitting across from Bishop Watson, at Erie's Holiday Inn. "He ate at the Holiday Inn a lot," she says, " it was actually rather upscale, and you might say he was a denizen. It was also a place where the nuns held our meetings. A group of us had been confidently discussing our legitimate common concerns, and how to handle them. But an alert was sounded; the other nuns who had been with me stood up, and scurried like a flock of geese, saying *'the Bishop is coming, the Bishop is coming!.'* They ran so as not to be seen when the Bishop arrived: 'Hurry! It is the Bishop, *he will not want to see us here!'* they said, and left."

Anne Francis did not see any reason to flee; she remained, left sitting at the table alone, except for the Panty Hose Bishop. She looked across at him, in the gloom of the dining room and said, to the empty space: "--I will not live this way." It was surely one of those moments that helped her decide things; only she knows when she decided, but I think it was in that gloom at the bottom of a deep dark sea. It makes me understand what happened next, that business about cutting legs off.

She was still attractive. She worked with Congressman Vigorito in Erie Pennsylvania, and found herself sitting next to him at conferences. By that time the nuns had gotten out of their habits, and dressed like other women. A gentleman was heard to remark, "—My, but that Congressman Vigorito *certainly has an attractive wife!"* It had to be explained to him that she was a nun, and nobody's wife.

But about the legs. She now turned her small apartment into a haven from what she had been through, a place of peace. She made a list of all the things that were tying her up in knots.

"I got a big piece of paper," she said, " and drew an octopus on it---" she made a gesture of drawing all those legs and tentacles. "---And I put it up on the wall over my bureau, and then over it I wrote the word 'EXTRICATE!" I determined that I would cut each leg off separately, and then when the legs were all gone, I would be free."

But she complained: "--Every time I cut off one, I found another would grow in!"

Indeed she was right about that. Octopuses are among that class of beings which grow new members in place of old ones cut off. Or they ought to be, anyway. It is a nightmare to fight them; they always live in the deep dark sea, I have read about that, darkness is their territory and they can see but you can't, and if you *can* see, why they have that black ink they squirt at you so that you are blinded again. It is a fight with tentacles which choke the living air out of you, a fight to the death with an undersea monster, each leg must be peeled back so you can breathe, you wonder if you will ever get up top, and breathe in God's fresh air again. The worried night becomes an octopus to us all.

[She likes the seafood dish of calamari. We talk of going to Barcelona, so she can try it there. She makes it herself, being sure to keep it from becoming rubbery. And each time we have it --while she cooks and I set table-- I think of "Extricate!" and the drawing up over her desk in the little room, when she was cutting tentacles off, and watching them grow back in. A life has many pieces to it; if you are fortunate to live long, things that made you miserable seem long ago, and have to be remembered with difficulty. And yet you should remember them, for they are what made you.]

If she was not yet certain herself, the rest of them must have known that she was going. She was visited by old friends, or by those who had supported her concern for the order. They kept her up with things. The order was heading for another election, and more response to the list of demands made upon them by the Sacred Congregation of Religious, still guarding the doors of Empire. But they could not help noticing: "--She has this picture up on her wall!" people said, "---Its this big *octopus*, with all those legs sticking out, and over it she has written the word 'Extricate!' We never saw anything like it! Now what do you suppose it means?"

One faithful friend was Helen Boyle; they had become close as members of the Board of Trustees for the college; they supported each other on the board, for the Bishop often annoyed them both.

Another friend, Sister Maria, one going all the way back to the Novitiate, came to her, and tried hard to understand. Maria wanted to think that it must all be simply a foolish romantic love affair that Anne Francis just wanted to run off with me, not that it could have been for reasons of conviction. That is a common reaction among your friends who stay behind: they think that anyone who "leaves" must be overcome by what is called "human weakness", that they are "misguided", they are misled by erroneous opinions, and are to be prayed for.

"Maria would tease me, " Anne Francis remembers, "One time she quoted Yeats: '---*But one man loved the Pilgrim Soul in you...*' she said, as though she knew all about everything. Later, after it had been decided, and matters determined, Maria came to lecture

432

me about it; she could not understand; she said, ' --But ---of anyone I ever knew, you had the truest conscience... *And now, this!---*' "

" I answered her; '--*Of all the decisions I have ever done, this is the most moral I have ever made'.*"

And Sister Maria could be quite catty. She said to Anne Francis, "Oh ---I see how it works. First you get the rest of us out of our habits, and then *you* wear black, because you look *stunning* in black!"

She is still friends with Maria, I think, who did not leave, who remained behind. For Maria there would be no need to extricate. She is one of what Scripture refers to as "The Remnant that is left". Maria always wants to save everybody, to go get the divine steam-shovel, and scoop them up, into the Everlasting Dumpster.

Anne Francis was going to make a Retreat. President Shane and Dorothy were to be traveling; and they invited her to spend a quiet time in their house in which to ponder what she would do

But I was going to have to wait to hear of her decision. There was a chance that I could secure speakers from troubled Northern Ireland. That is a very hostile place. If I could corral anyone from there for my conference it would make things pertinent to world affairs. After dealing with them up in the North, I would come down from Belfast to London, just as she was finishing up her retreat. A phone call would have to be made from London, before I boarded my flight home. We would time it precisely. I would hear her decision then, after coming down from the religious blood-hatred of Northern Ireland; I was not at all certain what she would decide, and would have to wait to hear about the future at that time, in London. But all the time, she was cutting off those legs.

46

THE RED HAND OF ULSTER

A few weeks later, I found myself sitting in the British Museum in London, surrounded by monuments of England's turbulent past. I had just come down from Northern Ireland, where my three hoped-for speakers had given me their answers: *"No"*, *"No"* and *"No!"* Each of them had given me their promise to cooperate earlier, but the religious climate up there had turned dangerous, it was not safe for either side to speak openly, and I could not get anyone from the middle.

Now all I was doing, essentially, was waiting to make my phone call to Anne Francis. I had several hours to wait for the proper time, to walk across Gower Street to the little Academy Hotel and ask the Pakistanis at the desk to put me on to the International Operator.

My mind kept straying back to that land of religious hatred in the North. My mind kept going back to the very first time I had ever gone there, years earlier. What I remembered most of all was the small town of Larne, a cute little postcard of a place, filled with hatred. I remembered how frightened I was, that first time. And yet, I did go, I packed my Roman collar and priestly things into a black suitcase, and I drove up through the British Army check-point, an olive-drab monster of military intelligence looking like the Cold War. They stopped me at the border, but eventually I came to Larne.

When you come into the Northern Ireland town of Larne there is a huge white-washed sign that greets you; it is painted all over the entire cement wall of the first Protestant Pub you meet, it says "NO POPERY HERE!" And it says "NO SUR-RENDER!" With the year "1688" alongside it, as well as a British Union Jack; and in the middle of all this there is a painting of what is known as the RED HAND OF ULSTER. It is red, it is blood red, and it means business. It sums up everything.

The Red Hand of Ulster is from an old myth. An ancient king had been promised by witches that he would be granted possession of the first province he touched. He got into his boat with his men, and headed for Ulster, the richest part of old Ireland. But just as he was about to step ashore and claim it for his own, the winds and the current changed against him, and began to push the boat out to sea: he was losing what had been promised. But being an old hero he knew what to do: he took his sword and hacked off his one hand, and with the other, sailed it like a Frisbee onto the shore, and when it landed there, he had touched Ulster you see, and so Ulster was his. It is the bloody beginning to a long bloody tale.

My first time, that was in "marching season", the weeks of July, coming up to Orangeman's Day, when the Protestants march and build huge pyres for burning on King Billy Day. The bands were out, and it made me very much afraid. I checked that my Roman collar and black rabbat was concealed and could not be seen. To do that was not to deny my faith, I told myself, and it was just plain common sense.

But I made every other mistake I could make. Instead of staying with "my own people," I checked into what turned out to be an abundantly Protestant rooming house, and later when I went out to eat I ended up in a fiercely Protestant Pub. I was not there long before we heard bands. Soon, in the alley behind us, five different bands came thumping along with their Orange marching songs. We went out to watch them. The last band was a full British Army Band, with leopard skins, and the names of battles printed on the hide of an enormous bass drum. The band director stopped them right in front of me, (they knew I was a Yank visitor) with the huge lambeg drum pounding away. The man next to me, who had been drinking with me inside, put his hand over his heart; it was a hymn to Orange loyalty. I looked at the drum; it had the words "Bullawayo" written on it, the name of a victory from the time of Kipling, in South Africa or someplace, a memory of the Boer War and the religious loyalty of the Orange North Unionists to what were left of Empire. I was almost swept away myself, at the emotion of it all. Then I looked at the drummer's wrists, they were wrapped in gauze, and from all that religious thumping, they were bleeding. The drummers' wrists are expected to bleed, it is a sign of the religious fervor of the pounding of the drum; it is as though the whole place bleeds, with religious fury.

It may be a bit shocking, if you have never heard it, but the Northern Protestants say they can smell you, if you are a Catholic. I believe them when they say this. I assume this holds especially true in a Protestant pub. I believe it because you have to use all five senses to stay alive in Northern Ireland. Maybe it is the faint smell of candle-sticks off you, or of incense and the Nine Fridays Devotion and fasting for Lent, or the blessings with Holy Water from the dried-up fonts of childhood. But I do not think it is only that; I believe that is you your own self that they recognize, it is the soul in

438

the body which they can identify, and can do even from far away, they can do your DNA count for you at a distance, so as to know whether to shoot or hold their fire. I thought I was reasonably safe; as an American I did not count. The strong soap of my morning shower would mask the reek of my Catholicism, which should be enough to throw them off. (But the truth is that most of this is true of "our" side, too: we are pretty good at it as well.)

It all made me think, sitting there, waiting there for my phone call. My mind wandered back to the story of a song called *The Oulde Orange Flute*. I have always thought that the *Oulde Orange Flute* sums up the North--- and what is wrong with a lot of the world--- better than anything I know.

In the song, *The Oulde Orange Flute* is owned by an Orange Protestant who commits the unpardonable sin, he marries a Catholic:

> *he forsook the old cause*
> *that gave us our freedom, religion and laws*

But though its owner is a back-slider, his instrument remains Loyalist and true-blue, and will only play Protestant songs. The priests want it to come to mass and play Catholic airs, but it will not, instead it bursts out with Protestant ones, for it is an Orange instrument. And so it is condemned to be burnt at the stake, in an attempt at exorcising its heretical tendencies. But as the flames rise up around it, as hot as the fires of Hell, it is heard still playing away; and it is not a Catholic hymn that it pipes out, it is playing *The Protestant Boys,* from the siege of Londonderry. They say you can still hear it, in Coleraine, when the wind is out of the South.

The story of the *Oulde Orange Flute* gives everyone a good laugh, but always after I am done laughing I find myself wondering if the story of that remarkable instrument is not a bit close to my own story. We are all asked, many times, to pipe songs we do not particularly wish to, and I have in my life not always paid sufficient attention to what I have been asked to play. I have more than once been in danger of becoming, myself, a kind of *Oulde Orange Flute.*

That first time, in Orange Week, I walked past the piles of boxes the children were building to burn as I returned to my boarding house, and said good night to my hostess; I looked at her, and the tiniest wisp of a thought crossed my mind: I told her I had seen the bands and found it all quite exciting, she smiled and said something, and I wondered suddenly how Catholic I looked? They said that they could smell us.

I wondered if --by the most outlandish of possibilities-- she might just possibly have felt it her duty to open my suitcase a crack, to see my collar and its *rabbat*, to make certain of things, while I was out? But then I rejected the possibility, I chided myself that I was really in what was only the most ordinary of situations, and I fell asleep, to the occasional creak of the old Protestant household. I longed to be gone, to be on the ferry to Stranraer in Scotland, and to be out of that hateful place.

Of course, all that had been many years before. Things were much more immediate, now. Now, sitting and waiting for my phone call, the questions raised back then were still present to me, and still made me wonder.

I asked myself, what was I doing, there in the British Museum ? Was I joining the Protestant Reformation, five hundred years late? I had drunk Protestant whiskey with them in their Protestant Pubs, while I was myself engaged in my own deliberate separation from Rome. There was blood on the gauze of the drummer's wrists, which showed his allegiance but what was I doing? Was I in the act of becoming a "protestant"? Was I becoming a "bloody Prod?" Was I, all by myself and five hundred years late, by declaring myself free of Rome, joining the persecutors of my own people? Was I about to turn a wash basin upside down over my head, and get one of those haircuts that the Roundheads were known for? -- And start beating the drums for No Popery Here?

Not bloody likely.

It was like Brendan Behan, and the BBC. British Broadcasting once left Brendan Behan alone with a bottle of whiskey before his scheduled interview. They waited, hoping to have another drunken Irish writer, and ensure themselves a lively program. Brendan came on rather soused. At some point, the interviewer asked him if --since he seemed to have given up his own religion-- he had ever considered becoming Protestant? At first, Brendan merely replied, " *Not bloody likely!"* But when the interviewer insisted, and asked it again, Brendan howled at him, "--I said I lost my faith, not my fuckin' mind!" The man persisted however; and finally Brendan shouted at the man and the whole BBC, "Well I might not be much of a Cath-o-lick, but I'd rather belong to a church founded on the rock of Peter than one founded on the balls of Henry the Eighth!" And so they got what they were asking for Good old Brendan.

I looked down at my watch. It was getting to be time. I went outside, and began crossing over Gower Street, first looking to the right, for British traffic, and then left, my head swiveling around in all directions, and still thinking of the British Museum. The place seemed full of bones. It reminded me of my Mother with the spoons, the bones of the past rattling away for me in the kitchen.

If I were not careful, everything would be the Bones of Aughrim all over again, tapping out their tune, playing what they wanted to play, and there would be no choice left for me. I finished crossing Gower Street, looking now to the left, to keep from getting killed from either side.

I knew what she would be reading. Anne Francis read the kind of books that allowed her to think. "Zen and the Art of Motorcycle Maintenance" had just come out, and she found solace in all that about the tappets and tightening the chain and checking tire pressure; though she had no motorcycle and had never driven one, the book gave her something about her own life. We had consulted schedules. I hoped we were right about our timing.

The Pakistanis helped me. I had to get the International Operator, and pray that it would work, that Anne Francis would be waiting, there at the Shane's house. I listened as the phone rang, and then heard it being picked up. We were both relieved to hear each other's voice, glad for this re-confirmation. She told me about the retreat she had made, told me about the struggle with what she believed. She told me that she had now firmly reached her decision: She must leave. She had pondered over and over the words, "I am come that you may have life" and understood that for her to stay in that place meant death.

I do not know what I would have done with my life if she had said that she could not go, that she must stay. I knew she had had to take this time to deal with her conscience, so that afterwards there would be no ambi-valence. Yet I expected her answer, and was not surprised. . She would leave, then. We both knew we each had to settle things for ourselves first, to decide to leave on our own; and after that we would feel free to face things together. After nothing but No's, I finally had a Yes to the thing that mattered. *Yes*, she had said, yes.

I sucked in my breath; when she said she was going to leave, I knew that we were in for something, now. But for the first time, for the first time ever, in my whole life, I think it was there after the phone call that I first began to think of the future as a thing which you had some say over, a future which was not already claimed for you by someone else who knew what was good for you, but something very other and quite different, a future which you might properly consider to be your own.

I remembered the Red Hand of Ulster, painted up on the wall, which tried to tell everyone what to think, Why, look you, would you play me as a pipe? These are my vents, these are my stops. It is as easy as lying. Well then what was I supposed to be, an old Orange flute, or a Papish one? One that piped Protestant jingles or Catholic ones? Or was I just to be one that piped anything, depending upon my owner, depending upon whose hands I fell into? *Not bloody likely.*

So it was going to happen, then. I knew that I would be leaving, too. But whatever happened, I resolved again not to turn into an old orange flute, either playing The Protestant Boys for one side or being played on by those bones up from the sodded fields of Aughrim rattling away on the other, those ancient fingers of the grave. And I had been growing a new understanding: that it was not just the North, it was not something confined to the Glens of Antrim or to the County Down, and it was not just the Old Orange Flute, either. It was a part of life. All sides could play you, if you were not careful, everything could play you as a pipe, and it was up to you to refuse to be played upon. If I had let that happen in the past, I would not do so now. I would be no one's instrument, I would never let myself be played upon again.

I went to my room, settled accounts with the Pakistani at the desk, and headed toward Heathrow Airport, to catch my future.

47

VANISHING DUBLIN

As soon as I returned to America, my conference was everything. Anne Francis phoned up from Washington: " What you need are Cambridge everything Ladies! I am going to bring you some Cambridge Ladies, you need them for your conference!" Anne Francis was clearly back among us.

I did not know what she was alluding to, over the phone from Washington. It turned out that she was quoting a poem that she expected me to know, one by ee cummings, about "the Cambridge ladies who live in furnished souls": They believe "in Christ and Longfellow, both dead" he said. They have comfortable minds, he said, and daughters who were shapeless but spirited. Anne Francis had to explain it to me, about the furnished souls.

But she knew what she was doing. She knew that for anything to succeed in Boston, you had to have a few New England

Brahmins behind it. She had found two of them, Dorothea and Abigail.

"They are not typical Cambridge Ladies," Anne Francis explained. "The other night, Dorothea --*who is 70 years old*-- showed up here at a ball wear-ing *decolletage* and deep cleavage, and she was able to pull it off! She looked gorgeous. I thought that was pretty good, for an event on 'Aging'..."

In Cambridge, I first found Craigie Street, then went looking for 26 Walker Terrace. I expected something from the world of Myles Standish. But I was surprised. An artist named Flora Mitchell had done a book called *Vanishing Dublin.* The old city was disappearing, they had been chipping away at it since before we left. The artist had most carefully drawn Dublin brick by brick --you could make out the outlines of each Georgian brick in her drawings. I had seen the book everywhere in bookstores, but Dorothea had the actual original drawings, hanging on her walls.

We talked, Dorothea and Abigail and I: Would it not be good for the conference to have this portrait of the vanishing city looking down on us? Would I like the loan of her collection?

I accepted the loving gesture. Our learned meeting would take place under this portrait of a disappearing past. Dorothea became a close and dear friend to us both, who always beamed on us like a Fairy Godmother, the kind who can support decolletage and cleavage, well into her seventies.

And something else had happened, too, which changed everything. I had gone to Dublin looking for treasures for the conference, but I did not have any real hopes. I was told to go see Conn Howard. Conn was with the Tourist Board, but had connections everywhere; "--Conn can help you if anyone can" I was told.

It was eleven o'clock in the morning, we were in the Arts Club, and were drinking whiskey. It amazed me that we were drinking that early in the morning, but, Conn liked to drink, while doing business.

Suddenly he slammed his hand down on the table "*I am going to do what we have to do!*" he shouted, "*--I'm going to send you Paddy Maloney and the Chieftains!*"

The Chieftains were just becoming world famous Rock Stars, known for rescuing ancient Celtic Music; soon it would cost millions of pounds to contract them, yet here the Irish Government was giving them to me, for free. They were an excellent back-drop to the conference, for they played on ancient instruments the music of Irish literature and history.

When Conn slammed his fist down on the table, I jumped. But it was one of those moments in life when you know that everything is going to be all right. Conn was with the government; he had the budget to do what he promised. The Arts Club, made famous by W.B. Yeats, was an astonishingly seedy place; it was not "genteel shabby", it was just shabby. (And maybe it was there that I began my drinking, at the Arts Club across from McDaid's Pub; I can blame it on having a few with Conn.)

A part of my job, which I was not paid for, was to acquire poets and other figures, introduce them to Stonehill, and then drive them back in my old Chevy Nova to their digs in Cambridge, at three am, if necessary, after which I would then bounce home to Weymouth. We hosted all of them, from Michael Yeats, the son of the poet, to Liam de Paor the archaeologist, to Roy Johnson the artist from the Protestant, Orange North, to little-known people such as another Northerner, like the young Seamus Heaney, before he was famous. I saw some of them, like the poet John Montague, with our whiskey sticking out of their pockets for the ride back. (He said Stonehill had "done nothing," that we had not done enough for him.)

I now learned to wile and wheedle people like a Child of Darkness. When Logan Airport treated my films like Contraband and threatened to refuse them entry, I told the officials that they were for "an Irish Con-ference" and they let them through. And when everyone suggested that I schedule John Kelleher of Harvard at the 8 am lecture spot, which otherwise no one would come to, I did so.

And I suppose I spent the school toward bankruptcy, too; that was what they claimed, afterwards, though I did not know I was doing it to them. I invited a "First Team" of experts-- everything from translators of the old Celtic *Annals of the Four Masters* to Canadian film makers doing Bloomsday, to Paddy Maloney and the Chieftains. I had friends of Samuel Becket like Alec Reid and there were even people who I had always imagined to be spies for the Crown of England, people out of the novels of John LeCarre, planted among the Irish Scholars to protect England's interests--for the field of Irish Studies has never been totally innocent. And when the First Team was superseded by new recruits who were more famous than they were, I moved those back to the Second Team. We had Nobel Laureates; the Nobel Laureate Conor Cruise O'Brien ended up as the main speaker. And for late night entertainment evoking some of the day's main themes, I had Celtic harpists and pipers playing authentic music, and then shooshed off hordes of stand-up Stage Irish comedians who would have turned my learned conference into a Pat and Mike show. And through it all, I knew that I was not only working for the noble cause of literature, science and culture, I was also thinking of that spot between Washington and Jefferson, from which I did not think I could ever be dislodged.

The campus began to fill with Laureates, established poets, United Nations Peacemakers, feuding playwrights who brought their feuds with them. Our young golden lads and golden lasses were astonished by such enormous talents, who stopped to talk with them on the paths and listened to them graciously.

There were some three-day love affairs. I had to push certain of our guests away from our girls and back toward where they came from. Yet the young ones survived, and I wonder if they remember it as I do, wherever they are. For though it was in truth only a learned conference, yet it prances on, that brief time in which we all walked on a field of our own devising, made from a cloth of gold.

The first night of the conference, as I prepared to produce our main speaker, Conor Cruise O'Brien, a message was passed to me--- a threat had been phoned in from the IRA: if Conor Cruise O'Brien spoke, an attempt would be made on his life.

" My God, " I said, " -- *They are going to kill my main speaker!* " Someone called the Police Department of Easton to arrange for Police protection. I went to the Administration and told them we needed more money. The town of Easton sent out a handsome young policeman, one of their finest, to patrol the hall while Conor Cruise O'Brien was speaking. But Easton was a town from the American Revolution; they had sent Minutemen to the battles of Lexington and Concord; they were not used to thinking of learned conferences on Irish culture. He walked up and down, without knowing what he was looking for; I doubted if he could spot an IRA man. The only person he stopped was me; and he nailed me at the door of my own conference, demanding identification.

Conor Cruise O'Brien needed a drink of water, and I saw that no one had provided him with one. I took a glass from the main table, and hurried out to a drinking fountain in the hallway. And there I ran into the North Easton Police protection we had hired. The handsome young officer reached for his gun: I fit his profile for the IRA. I told him that I was Conference Director, and that my main speaker needed water. He let me go through, but as I rushed back with the glass of water I thought: we are paying over-time to a handsome young officer who would not have recognized the IRA if they were tying a bomb to his police cruiser.

After his talk, Conor Cruise O'Brien was surrounded my reporters, he was assailed by all factions on Northern Ireland, and all the US newspapers. I fought my way into him and asked him if he wanted a drink of whiskey? *"--I like the way you think!"* he replied. That was the only time we spoke; I doubt if he ever knew who I was.

The first papers went off well, I was satisfied. But there was still the other side of things, that side which makes people remember a moment and a place as being remarkable. Until that was taken care of, things were not a success. Then late the first night, at an hour approaching two in the morning, after Paddy Moloney of the Chieftains had sat on a table and played ancient music which had long been lost and which even the musicologists had not heard, someone asked John Murphy of University College Cork to sing "Carrickfergus." I stood in the shadows as he threw his head back and began "-- *I would I were in Carrickfergus now...*" It is a sentimental song, among countless Irish sentimental songs, but it recalled for me the hulk of Carrickfergus Castle, that time when I passed through the County Down, the drums beating against me, and of that entire unending section of my life when I had no hope that we would survive, or that things would turn in our favor. People stopped and listened to him, for he seemed to be something out of Joyce, this voice singing of things gone by. I knew perfectly by watching others and knowing what I felt myself, that it had all been the gathering of learning and culture that I had hoped for, that it was already a success; I looked for her, and I saw her, listening across the other side of the room; she, too, was listening, and thinking that there must be hope for us.

At the conference were the two professor Messengers, a couple who were both anthropologists, Americans who had done work on the Aran Islands, Ireland's most primitive part, out in the Atlantic. Whatever is most genuine about Ireland still hangs on there last, until the end of land, and beyond the end; it is where the playwright Synge went to write about them. John Messenger wrote about his plays out there; chronicling the stone-age superstitions of my people, the simple Irish. And it was Maureen who saw him out there, sitting on a rock, thinking. She tells of an Aran Islander, whispering to her, and saying, "--Do you see that man over there sitting on a rock? ----Well that fellow---poor man, *he has lost his faith!"* [I cannot help it, I still think of John Messenger as a figure sitting on a rock with his head in his hands, the poor fellow who has lost his faith.]

By the last evening of the conference, word was out about Anne Francis and me, that after the last scheduled event was over we were leaving the religious life and getting married. The two of us had run across the street from the campus to catch a quick supper. In the restaurant were the Messengers, --the fellow who had lost his faith, and his wife--the two anthropologists, at another table. Soon a gift of two cocktails arrived for us; they had inquired of the waiter what we were having, and had paid for congratulatory drinks. I don't know what the two of them thought at such a moment. They saw in us friends to be congratulated, surely; but perhaps as Anthropologists they saw in us the dying out of one more human way of behaving, the end of something that had flourished unbroken through the Dark Ages, or for as long as scholars like them had been recording it, out on the Aran Islands or in the bogs of Ireland or in the starving hedge-rows or within the ruined churches and abbeys, with their roofs gone, and open to the sky. That the whole thing had run its course, that the two of us were now items to be catalogued by scientists, that soon there would be no such things as nuns and priests.

I thought I understood. I had always felt like the inheritor of the Round Towers and the mud monasteries and the dying prisoners giving their splendid speeches from the gallows, and that, now, in me it was going. Or maybe it was only going in me. 'Take a good look--" I might well have said to them, and to anyone who cared, "--We will soon be gone. Our like will not be seen again."

Finally it was all over, and closing down; a few members were still at the Business Meeting, dumping next year's conference on some other poor soul. I found Anne Francis; we were to attend a function at the Irish Consul's house, Mossbawn, in Chestnut Hill. We had our bags ready, for we would be staying ourselves at a place out on Route One. It was the first night in our lives that we spent with one another together, and it was at that moment that we truly left. After all the learned papers and the learned speakers, after the Messengers' parting drink, after "Carrickfergus", and the IRA, and the Chieftains and everything else, it was at last finished. We walked out under Flora Mitchell's Vanishing Dublin, the city perfectly outlined in its bricks, then the two of us were gone.

Anne Francis Cavanaugh and Frank Phelan on the deck

When we got married, Maureen handed us something; it was a quotation, copied in her own felt-tipped pen, framed, and ready to be hung up at once. It read as follows:

THERE IS NOTHING NOBLER

THAN WHEN TWO PEOPLE

WHO SEE EYE TO EYE

KEEP HOUSE AS MAN AND WIFE,

CONFOUNDING THEIR ENEMIES

AND DELIGHTING THEIR FRIENDS

---Homer, Sixth Book of The *Odyssey*

V

48

BACK WHERE YOU BELONG

We heard that there were grand houses for sale cheap in Charlestown, the oldest part of Boston. With start-up help from her sister Peggy and my sister Babe, we were able to buy one, to start "rehabbing" it. From there, we liked to walk over to Boston's Italian district, the North End. It reminded us I think of our times in Europe.

One time, on a summer Sunday, in the midst of one of the parish religious feasts which the North End celebrates, we came across the statue of the Virgin Mary, the Madonna, parked outside an Italian restaurant. The crew had left her there on her mobile, hand-carried throne: the men were inside eating lunch. We looked at the statue: it had dollar bills attached with safety pins all over it, as well as bills of higher denominations. We smiled at one another: "That money is going to be safe----" Anne Francis said, " --No one is going to touch it...." We waited, for a band was gathering, a kind of John Phillip Sousa band from one of the parishes, and they were picking up their instruments. The statue's Swiss Guard came out of the restaurant, all six of them; together they hoisted the statue up on their shoulders, and the band started in, playing *"Hello, Dolly! Well, Hello Dolly! --It's so nice to see you back where you belong!"*

Anne Francis had given up everything when she came East; she had been on the Governor's Task Force on Aging back in Pennsylvania, and was used to seeing her picture in every newspaper, where everyone would want her for every job

But she had to get up off the floor, literally, to find work. She paid a lot of money to a "Headhunter" group called Jameson Associates. They helped her with her letters and resumes. The living room floor at Number 22 Trenton Street became filled with pages from their program. We went around stepping over them, looking for page eighteen to put after seventeen

But it worked. She got job offers from all over the place. The first one was from a Torpedo Factory, down in Rhode Island. The CEO there wrote, "There is always a need for good communicators." and wanted her to come down -- I believe he was an Admiral. AF thought about that, working for a Torpedo Factory down in Rhode Island. But I think she knew that such things had gone nuclear by this time, and killing people was far from all she had dedicated her life to.

But then GTE---General Telephone and Electronics—hired her. They had started up a program to help the frail elderly continue to live safely in their own homes.

She would jump up in the morning. "---*I have to put on my rags"* she would say, " --I have to get out and *pow* the universe!" Before, in the old Mercy habit, she had been Chairman of the Board for college, school and hospital; now she had to "put on her rags" and "paw the universe", to help keep us afloat.

"--Getting you off to work," I told her once, "is like launching an Intercontinental Ballistic Missile every day--- after you leave, it takes two hours to cool down the pad!"

She found herself suddenly in the company of men. It was all engineers around her, and lawyers and rabid Boston Celtic basketball fans. These engineers and accountants played life as a game of hockey, they were men in groups, and they reminded me of a hockey team, themselves.

But they liked her. They knew her background; word seeped out to these men that they had in their midst a former nun, who might be expected not to know certain things, and they made a game of trying to slip double entendres past her to see if she would catch on. Once they were using the word "mooning", fully confident that she would be innocent of its meaning. Charlie Doherty called over to her, "--Anne Francis, I bet you don't know what "*mooning*" is!"

"---Let's see now-- " she answered Charlie, "----Does it have anything to do with something _big_ and _round_?" and they laughed some more with her.

Yet she learned business and its politics quickly. One boss was a salesman who had little formal education; and had to have everything she said explained to him. He drove an Oldsmobile 98, because he said a Cadillac was a "Jew Canoe" and he would not drive one. She must have found herself far removed from that world described by Great Teresa, and *The Interior Castle,* the soul surrounded with solitude.

No one was speaking of "Aging" then; Anne Francis was one of the few persons in Boston talking that way. A Congregationalist minister named Reverend David Works heard of her. He had two friends, Caleb Loring had been Treasurer for Fidelity Mutual Funds, an honest good man. Ezra Merrill had retired from the Agri-Business and wanted to help experienced retired executives with the opportunity to do good after their careers were finished. With her experience in Aging she was a natural for the job, and they all worked well with the Boston Chamber of Commerce to launch Operation ABLE. And in words which seemed to come out of the Old Testament Reverend Works said to her, *"--Walk between Caleb and Ezra, Anne Francis, and you will come to no harm!"*

Ezra Merrill was the first Boston Brahmin I met. As soon as I saw him I knew he was a Yankee because he wore a black hat, and although it was possibly of ordinary size, he managed to wear it in such a way that it became the kind of stove-pipe hat that Abraham Lincoln wore.

But he was a good and generous man. He had just retired from AgriBusiness--- running the huge Hood Dairy--- and wanted to do something for retired, experienced executives like himself in the way of a second useful career. The one thing he was interested in was something called Executive Service Corps. Every day Anne Francis had to pummel him into doing something for the vast number of persons in the same plight who were not executives, for something she wanted to get going in the Boston area, Operation ABLE --- Ability Based on Long Experience. Each day she would come home to complain of how hard it was to get Ezra interested in ABLE, how he would listen to nothing about it, but she eventually managed to get him interested. Finally he relented, and became enthusiastic. Few people know it, but ABLE was founded largely through her efforts; an Executive Director, seeing AF's name everywhere, said "Without Anne Francis Cavanaugh, there would not have *been* an Operation ABLE in Boston!" It was a triumph: thousands of talented persons have gotten jobs through both of them and have led happy lives.

All of these men were distinguished and with and remarkable personalities, but by far the most pronounced of them was General George Patton III --the son of "Old Blood and Guts " the famous World War II General, and a distinct personality in himself.

He was flamboyant and pronounced, in his response to things. He came on board to help ABLE, and worked with Anne Francis. He was very Right Wing, of the John Birch kind, and the two of them went to war constantly about their political opinions. I am sure that Anne Francis did not get the worst of it. One day George stuck his head into her office and asked if he could use her phone?

"Yes, " she replied, "--*But not if you're calling the John Birch Society!"*

"Anne Francis," he shouted. " *That is exactly who I was going to call!"* and he roared laughing.

After being with her for a while, and getting to know her, he took her with him and his wife Joanne to visit a Veterans Hospital, still filled with casualties from Viet Nam.

" --It was very sad," she told me, " but it was clear that the men loved him very much... I asked him about all the black soldiers among the veterans, and he said, '--Anne Francis, didn't you know that Viet Nam was a poor man's war?"

But the most touching thing she tells has to do with the young George Patton, whose mother, Joanne, mentions in the family history as "intellectually challenged," which was how we used to speak, in those days. Anne Francis remembers: "I sat with that boy at breakfast, and he was quite fine..."

Young George was to be in the Special Olympics, which in his case had an Equestrian component to it. Joanne invited Anne Francis to be with her one day. She selected a table for lunch where they would be able to look down, and see the performances. Anne Francis knew that Joanne was much concerned: I think they both knew that young George was to appear, on horseback, somewhere in the activities. But as the time grew longer, and he did not appear, Anne Francis could see Joanne become more and more concerned, that he would appear at all. As AF describes it, it was a time of unbearable suspense. Then, suddenly, a military band which had been playing let out a flourish of brass, and out came young George. "He rode very fast, on a very fine horse; he made it twirl around in a wonderful maneuver, and then went prancing off, to join the parade. His performance was magnificent! I looked over at Joanne, and she was crying. We both had tears in our eyes."

As she tells the story, I think of the young son, so much within the tradition, galloping off on horseback, to join the long string of cavalrymen who go before him.

I have found over time that Anne Francis has her own way of saying things. We were getting dressed to go out to something over in Boston. Anne Francis wanted to know what to wear. She said, "Is that rain out there, or is it just-- *scowl?*" I looked out, and said, "Well there are no drops, so I suppose it is just _scowl_." She complained that her hair was "streeling", and would say that she was "scuntered" on something when she was disappointed with it. [*Streeling, scunter, scowl*-- I found myself looking up things in the Oxford English Dictionary] When we drove down to Sullivan's Square, which is a dreaded New England "roundabout", full of ruts and trucks, and I headed into it, she said, "Look out, or they'll knock us for loop-holes!" Once I asked her if she was going to need a hat. She said, "No, my head feels full of hair!" And as we got up to leave a restaurant, I noticed that she was not carrying her purse. I asked her where it was. She thought a moment, and then arched far over to the opposite side of her chair to pick up something.. "---Its *au floor!*" she said, and we left.

But of all the things that happened to her after she left everything and fought to find her way in the world, there is one incident that says the most.

At GTE , they were very proud of Anne Francis. Mister Lynch, her boss, took her down to the company's new Corporate Headquarters along the Connecticut Turnpike in Stamford, for a meeting with "Corporate". After the meeting, as they walked out into the lobby, Mister Lynch proudly gestured toward the enormous amount of tinted glass and the polished marble which surrounded them. I think he could not wait to see how this former nun would be astonished, to find herself surrounded by one of the latest structures raised by the world of corporate America.

She looked at it; but as she did so thought of another, far different world, one filled by the Carrara marbles of Michelangelo, and the bronzes of Bernini and Bramante; or perhaps her mind even touched quickly on her great ideal, Saint Catherine of Siena, the visits which that courageous woman had made to Rome, to face up to the Pope himself, to confront him in his seat of power, surrounded by the grandeur which filled the Vatican.

Mister Lynch allowed her time to be suitably impressed. Then he asked her, "Well, Anne Francis, ---How do you like our new World Headquarters?"

She smiled at him, and said, " ---Very impressive, Mister Lynch, ---*But not as impressive as my last World Headquarters!*" He laughed and laughed, General Telephone and Electronics could achieve marvels, but they could not match Saint Peter's Basilica and the Sistine Chapel.

Where did her sprightly answer come from? If I were to answer for her, I might guess that her mind would have gone back to the great façade of Saint Peter's and its square, with the columns of Bernini's colonnade, with Michelangelo all over the place, and the obelisk from Egypt, erected for Pope Sixtus V.

I am sure that the question from Mr. Lynch took her memory back to her days before the inquisition she went through, back in her days with all that marble.

Her answer to Mister Lynch carried her whole life with it; she was speaking not just to him but speaking, out loud, to herself: Yes, she found the office building along the Connecticut Turnpike impressive enough, but it was not as impressive as her last World Headquarters. The things she found in the world since leaving were often full of pretense, but few things could possibly be as glorious as what was left behind. We all remember what we remember.

49

A VIEW OF THE MYSTIC BRIDGE

Now it is time to confess something painful. I have always been better at handling hard times than good times. After we had gotten what we wanted, my response was to celebrate our victory. I started drinking. In Charlestown, I had my own Battle of Bunker Hill, it was with the liquor store around the corner. Each day I traversed the same cobble-stones that the British redcoats had, bringing up the whites of their eyes to where the colonists could shoot at them. After all we had been through, I failed Anne Francis in this respect. I don't know why I drank. People do it for different reasons. I did it, I believe, because the struggle seemed to be over, and at last we could celebrate. But the battle is never over. I did succeed in stopping, however, and have not drunk for twenty six years.

Soon after we got to Charlestown, Anne Francis asked me if I could build us a deck, on top of the Ell to the house, something we could walk out on, and sit on. I do not know exactly how it connects with the end of my drinking, but it must have been part of the solution.

Zen and the Art of Building a Deck. I spent an entire summer at it, my famous, remarkable deck, from when school was closing in the middle of May until late September after it had started again, up there hammering in the sun, and when I finished with it I was simply not the man who started it. I was up there with the electric saw, and wood clamps and huge lag bolts, and what are called in hardware stores Bright Shiny Nails, trying to make things "plumb". There would be a fountain, and a grape arbor; maybe even some fruit trees, in tubs. I had made drawings, and clipped pictures out of magazines for it, and as I clamped and drilled, I knew what I was doing. I was nailing up my own Hanging Gardens, a kind of Holy Place for us, at the top of things. As I breathed in the smell of newly cut lumber, on top of our Ell, it seemed to me that I was half way to heaven, fastening things and tightening them to the blue sky itself.

Anne Francis had come to me and said, "Build us a deck. And don't make it one of those slanty little things, make it something we can invite people to, and eat on!"

I looked at her. I wondered if she really knew who she had married. I had never done anything like that. I had never been allowed to.

Well, if it wasn't going to slant, and just slope down along the roof, why then it was going to have to rest on the outside walls, it would have to "cantilever", like something by Frank Lloyd Wright. For that, I needed the blueprints that Sergio the architect had left behind. They had not been used, but we had paid for them. I never would have tried a thing like that without professional help. I asked him if he thought I could do it; he said he did not see why not.

The day the lumber truck arrived, two Townies in a jeep were held up by it. "You aren't going to unload that _now_, are you?" one of them asked angrily. When I said yes, we had to, they furiously backed up the whole of Trenton Street; and one of them shouted as they were backing up, "--I'm going to *burn* that lumber, tonight!" Welcome, Strangers in the Street.

It didn't happen; but I had enough to worry about. I found myself doing dangerous things, like looking down over the gutters on the roof of the ell, bracing myself, and pulling up hand over hand three boards at a time with the kind of slip-knot John Mac-Donald had taught me. That was a day's work. Each day I could only hammer in a few boards, five was a lot.

It is humiliating to tell what follows, but I will do so. The first day up on the roof, so that I would not fall down, I put in a safety rope, from the chimney to the corner of the house. Then I actually placed a rope around my middle, the way a toddler sometimes has. When I did this, a great guffaw of laughter came from the second floor of the house behind us, on Green Street. A Townie there was watching every move I made: *Look at the professor, building a deck!* He knew that if I fell with that rope around me, I would cut myself in half.

After a few hours, I got rid of it, and later, even the one tied to the chimney. But the Townie was still there, watching; he either had a lot of time off, or was out of work. I never heard him laugh again, but once I heard him say, " I'd like to see the whole thing falls down on him." Another time, he was no longer concerned with me; he was having trouble with his wife. He was drinking, and shouting about somebody, saying "---I'll whack him---- I'll *whack* him!" He was going to put out a contract on somebody, and have the fellow bumped off. His wife interrupted: *"---You've been drinking now for four days! When are you going to stop?"* Decades later, I have finally figured out that it was me he was talking about: he was going to "whack" me, for making so much noise with my hammering that he could not sleep-- a long time to realize you are going to be shot.

I was not just afraid of heights, to be quite honest I was afraid of my own tools. When I ran over to Somerville Lumber, I felt appalled by the great size of it, and by my own ignorance. The workers there knew all the things that I did not; when I attempted to order anything they had to try to keep from sniggering at the way I pronounced things, and sometimes they were reluctant to sell something to a person like me, saying that I would only kill myself. I finally found my own Wood-Meister, a wizened up troll of a man from Austria who became my Father Confessor. I took things to him upside down and he would turn them upside right and show me how they worked, and then send me back, as if we both knew I could do it. It was from him that I heard there actually was something called Bright Shiny Nails. I still remember it as the Summer of the Bright Shiny Nails, though in fact I really never used them, I used galvanized ones, for wear.

As I worked, Caitlin the Cat watched me, and the bells from the steeple at the top of Bunker Hill Street rang out the hymns of my childhood. Charlestown is a Catholic place, and the hymns the bells knew were 60 years out of date, from my own time, so that I was able supply the words. The Angelus rang out, three times a day, but

476

my favorite was one to Mary: "She the Queen Who Decks her subjects, In the light of God's own grace." It always seemed to arrive when I was having trouble with the drill and was cursing: it always sounded like Heaven was ready to deck me, make me hit the deck, and floor me with my own project. I knew all the words; I was probably the only one in Charlestown who could sing with the bells.

I am a Parochial School product; Anne Francis went to Public School. It always upset her to hear me singing out such things, like " 'twas never heard or known," and "made to Thee his moan." I told her that I was more Catholic than she was.

And so one day, after weeks of beams and joists, the first five boards of the deck floor itself were tacked in, forming a surface. There was just enough room for a person to stand. I was now battle-hardened, like a Roman Centurion who had fought Hannibal at Cannae. I lifted up my tool-box from the gravel roof, and placed it on this bit of deck. I got two chairs and a small table. And Anne Francis and I had supper, on the first five boards of deck. Every day after that, the surface expanded out farther, five boards at a time in the hot sun, 26 1/2 feet, to the end.

I wanted a Pergola, a free-standing grape-vine trellis, which would rise up over the further end of the deck and shelter it, so that when you came out of the house, you were in the sunshine for a moment, and then stepped into the shaded cool under the grapes. Which would be hanging down in bunches, so that you had to dodge your head to keep from hitting them. In other words, I wanted Paradise. The people of Charlestown thought I was mad. They did not waste money putting a deck on top of the house. I ended up with most of what I had planned, except for the grapes, they never dangled far enough.

When it was finished, with the grape vines starting to grow on the pergola, we had our friends up there. We had so many friends I worried it might collapse. We were like those ancient Persians who invented the first gardens, we were eating fine cuisine under the shade of the grapes, to the sound of our little French fountain, water spurting out of the mouth of a neoclassical lion. One time I counted 35 persons up there, and hurried around to the ones I knew suggesting that they return to the house. But it never collapsed; nothing ever happened. I returned to Boston a while ago, and the chief thing I wanted to see was my deck, if it was still there. It was, 22 years after it was built.

I comprehend now that I would never have started something like that if Anne Francis had not said I could do it. I would not have done a lot of things if she had not said that I could; I would not have lived my life.

That answer of hers, "---We grew up together--" is not literally true, for we both set eyes on one another for the first time when we were each forty years old, and the great wheel of life was beginning to slow down, but in the deepest, real way, it is still the best answer.

Raise high the roof-beam, carpenter. The day it was finished, that late afternoon when the ship's ladder I had gotten off a tug-boat was snugged in against the high roof, leading up to our Crows Nest, I climbed up to look out: Caitlin was the first to try it, she passed me on the steps, she was there ahead of me, looking to see if she could jump over to John MacDonald's roof, too. I took a deep breath of the fresh air. You could see everything; I looked out at Boston Harbor, and at the planes coming in to Logan. It had only been a piece of carpentry, of course, but I knew that it stood for other things. "Follow your bliss", we are told. My hands felt different now, they felt very strong, a bit tired from the work. I would now have to start putting my tools back, which I was never good at.

But before I headed back down I took a long look at things. Looking out reminded me of Vermeer's painting, *A View of Delft,* with its famous patch of little yellow wall; they say that in doing it he was telling the story of his life, of what his art stood for, and Proust used it for his Past Lost, and Past Regained, how we make sense out of our lives by recollecting what we have been. For sometimes it seems that we only walk about on our own little legs, and that is as much as we amount to, but in truth there is more to it, for each of us really moves about on tall stilts, on very long thin ones, that reach far down, into many levels of our past and deep into the history of all of us. If I were to recall the meaning of life, it would have to include the sight of Mary, her back turned away from us and walking off for good, after telling the two of us that we would never see her again, walking along Lansdowne Road toward Sandymount, taking much of everything with her, into Eternity.

From where I stood on the roof-tree I could see the Mystic Bridge, looping in a huge graceful curve toward us from the North Shore, along the same route that brought the First Comers down from Salem, walking with their belongings in the winter snow to found Charlestown, and ultimately, to start Boston. I could see the docks, the stumps of the piers where the famine ships had emptied us out, my people, "the mere Irish", dumped onto the sidewalks paved with gold. It was really quite like Rivera's great branch bending over the chasm ---and like another branch, too, old Mother Ro's, the one she took persons to, to help them escape, showing them where it arched over the wall--- out upon which they could clamber, if they wanted to, badly enough, so as to hang their two feet down until they sensed the safety of the ground below and with an act of faith let themselves drop into the darkness, through the empty air, onto the pavement, and to a life they had not known for certain was even there.

It was six o'clock, the steeple bell at the top of Bunker Hill was ringing out the Angelus, *My Soul doth magnify the Lord,* but I climbed down to help Anne Francis up, so she would be able to have a look, I wanted to show her how far it was that we could see now. But more, it was to share with her what I had been thinking all summer long, about how far the two of us had come, from that moment starting at Bewley's in Grafton Street among the Round Brown Rolls and Sultana Buns, with Warren and me looking at her thesis, telling her that she could not do it, that no one could ever do it from a convent out in Donnybrook, that time long ago, when I stood up to be counted.

It was true; we had grown up together.

50

THE POISON TREE

There is a poem by William Blake:

I was angry with my friend:

I told my wrath, my wrath did end.

It goes on:

I was angry with my foe:

I told it not, my wrath did grow.

He nourishes his wrath, he treats it like a potted plant:

And I watered it in fears,

Night and morning with my tears. . .

Its fruit is bright, but deadly; one morning he wakes up:

In the morning glad I see

My foe outstretched beneath the tree.

He sees his neighbor dead, underneath his poison tree.

I was now with her, living a new life. In among the good memories of my old life, there were a few painful ones, of persons who had done things to me, but I determined not to carry them with me. I did not paste any faces up on my medicine cabinet to hate. I did not want to resemble the famous Vito Corleone, who plunged the butcher knife into his enemy as he said, "My Father's name was Antonio Andolini......*and this is for you!*"

But I did remember; I tried to remember what I hoped was sufficient, in case I ever wanted to speak of things to anybody, so that I could tell things honestly, with truth enough to be believable. And so I must admit that for a long time I nourished my wrath, I saw that it kept healthy. I began to forget, and to live a normal life; but still, I was careful not to let go of it entirely. I chided it when it grew faint: "There, there, my dear Little Grievance," I said, "--Hold your hcad up, and march on." I don't know what should be said about such behavior, but it seemed something I was entitled to.

One day I opened my mail and saw that someone had mailed a clipping to me. It was a Xerox from the National Catholic Reporter: "NOTRE DAME'S BURTCHAELL TO RESIGN, SOURCES SAY." It went on to tell that Father Burtchaell had "agreed to resign following an investigation into charges he had engaged in sexual misconduct while counseling male students." And in accompanying material a young man went on and on into humiliating, intimate detail.

"--So they have nailed the bastard at last..." I said out loud, and some part of me wanted to ask, *"---What took them so long?"* I have to be honest; that sounds like me, it is an accurate expression of what I felt. But after a few moments, which lasted not very long, of a kind of satisfaction that a person who had harmed me had now had something dreadful happen to him, I began to stop wanting to feel that way, and I curtailed what we all like to consider behavior that is beneath us. The Black Prince, clothed in armor, and thought to be impervious, had fallen. And I wondered about other people, all those who had done things which would not be found out.

He was said to have been exiled from Notre Dame; a friend there told me "He will never be allowed back. They will *never* let him return". The Provincial of the Order was quoted as saying "Father Burtchaell brought this on himself." For a while the case was infamous, and his name became bracketed with those of pederasts, in that horrible time when priests were being hauled into courtrooms all across the country, and you wondered how those who had remained, those who had not left but had continued on, trying to be good priests, were able to do their work.

But there was also a copy of a letter included with the article; a letter of apology or of explanation. It was his letter to the Congregation, and it was what affected me most; he had written a letter to the order--to what for him would now inevitably be his Absent Brethren. "--*Oh the pain...*" it said, "--*O the pain...*" and that is all I remember. I had had enough of my own pain, yet I could not begin to conceive of the pain a man like that must have suffered. Poor human nature; we are here for a short while in a kind of darkness, and we look for love. Those of us are blessed who find it.

I looked up from the clipping. I was finished with old scores. "Enough, Burtchaell," I said, "--I am done with my poison tree."

* * * * *

NOTE: Long after writing about James Burtchaell, I heard from Christopher Lehmann-Haupt, a respected writer for the *New York Times*. He called my attention to something he knew, but that I did not. He was surprised that I had not known that Father Burtchaell had contracted Alzheimer's disease. He corrected me, saying that this certainly put a different complexion on anything I had written about him, and that it was something I might easily have known.

I was surprised to hear this. I had been very angry with Father Burtchaell, but the news affected me as it must have everybody else: I was astonished, and very sad for a fellow human being struck down on this journey we all make together. I know nothing about what it is to lose all memory of what you have been.

But it is wrong to say I might have known easily. People need to understand that when you leave a religious order, one which you have spent your whole life with, you become very much a non-person. Your name disappears from lists. The operative phrase is "they no longer walked with us." (Anne Francis, who amounted to more in her community than I did in mine, even had her picture taken down; we hear that it is now back up.) A few people keep in contact; they are not the ones you might expect.

So it was a surprise. I thought about it. And I came to the conclusion that I should simply leave things the way I had remembered them, and beg mercy upon all of us.

51

VISIT TO THE CEMETERY

I thought I would never go back to see them, back to Notre Dame. Of course we are all tempted, and sometimes often, to go back to an old place where we have been, where we have been nurtured as well as perhaps injured.

Yet if it is permissible to narrate the story of one day in the life of a potato, as James Joyce did, why then the rest of us should be allowed to have our say. I am even grateful at times, grateful for all that has sent me on this chattering goose-chase of mine.

And so for a long time I did not go back. I remembered Newman, not returning, only seeing the spires of his beloved Oxford from the train. Someone could say "--But you are not John Henry Newman..." Eventually, I had to go to South Bend to see my Brother's wife, then up in her nineties. Anne Francis and I stayed in a motel built for football games and graduations. I expected that Notre Dame would by this time have influenced its surrounding with bookstores and music houses, the way other universities do, but there appeared to be nothing, except chain-restaurants and motels.

I almost did not try to get on campus. I knew what it would mean, I would have to drive to Visitors Parking, and be told by a young car-park what Notre Dame was all about. But coming down the Dixie Highway, I was surprised by a traffic light where none had been before; it turned out to be my old escape route, the one I had used so often to slip out ahead of the football crowds. I knew that if I tried to get in by telling them that I had grown up there and had spent my life among them, they would have thrown me out, and sent me two miles away to Stadium Parking. But God had fixed it: I was entering through the golf-club entrance, I would park among the golfers; if I appeared as one of those, I knew I would be acceptable; the place had not changed much.

It had a strange effect; by making that decision I was projected, not onto the campus, but to the old community area, where I had grown up. It was a hot August evening; I led Anne Francis around the end of St Mary's Lake. I took pictures, for I was a tourist in my own childhood. The trees were much bigger; they were fifty years older; they were enormous, I did not remember them so overwhelming.

Dujarie Hall, named for the Brothers' Founder, was now called Carroll Hall; that meant the Brothers were gone; they had always been considered more or less in the way.

The Little Seminary of course no longer existed, I had expected that. But its actual site was hard to find. I thought I saw the outlines of the old potato house, over the steam room, where I had scuffed potatoes with Tom Roemer. The lawns did not seem so sweeping. I looked up, to an empty spot about thirty feet above our heads,. "-- I studied Greek --right there--" I said, pointing to the circumambient, empty air, and to the death of Hector. The slate stairways were gone too, where Father Fiedler had waited with his railroad watch: "*Return to the locker room for Second Retiring, get dressed again, and retire on time!*" The Locker Room was gone, as well, there was not even a hole in the ground, a declivity, to mark where we took showers to get warm. I thought of Rockne's saying about the place, "It all comes from there." I tried to get a picture of the tree where Fiedler's sign had hung; but there was no hint of it, or the sign. Young women now filled the paths; athletic-looking women. They were not sitting or lying on the grass, they were running, in sweat-suits.

Then there was the visit to the cemetery. I had walked that walk after every meal, to pray for the Community Dead, yet nothing seemed familiar. I now had to go exploring even to find the right entrance in the iron fencing. See the crosses, row on row. My Absent Brethren. Traveler, go ask the long-haired barbarian what we did here.

They were all there, somewhere. The Brothers first: Linus, Cletus, Clement, Xystus and Cornelius. I went running around, yelling to Anne Francis as I found someone: "Here's Felix Duffy! My old Novice Master!" I saw Jim O'Halloran, Christopher J. O'Toole, William T. Craddick, also known as "Crads", and Brother Seraphim, the German machine-gunner It was as though each departed soul stood standing over his grave, like in that painting of Judgment Day, where every person stands as they were in life, the lid of their tomb pushed aside. They stand in the painting as they were: a young girl, looking the way she must have on the day of her marriage, an old man looking as though he would never die. Their voices echoed down hallways; I heard some of them singing in chapel, or shouting to be thrown the ball on the field next to the cemetery.

Some spoke to me directly things they had spoken in life. The Confessor, Mathias Oswald gave his usual penance: "--Say t'ree Hail Marys!" Old Doc Kenna boomed in his foghorn voice: "*You took vows! I presume you intend to accomplish them!*" Father Molner called out "Punch and Judy! Punch and Judy!" as though he were having a nightmare. Assorted Superiors smiled up at me; a man can smile and smile and be a Superior. Absent thyself from Eternity awhile.

But Anne Francis was doing it her way. She was looking for Shilts. She had known Jim Shilts, who had stayed in contact with us after we had left. He had had a beautiful nun friend, who wanted to leave with him and get married, but Shilts had said, "I am happy in my priesthood." She went off to Marshall, Texas and married someone else; Jim died unexpectedly on the operating table in one of those routine operations that went awry. Suddenly she called out "-- 'James Shilts!' -- *Here is Shilts!"*

I kept looking, taking many pictures which would reveal, when I got home, things I was not able to see in the declining evening light. Then I saw, in one row, Tom Engleton, (who had asked me, "*What kind of life do you have?*") and in the other, old Father Tom Brennan. I thought of the day young Engleton had planted beans in the same place Brennan had earlier planted corn, and old Brennan, when he found out, saying "Hell, We're not going to have *corn* at all --we're going to have *succotash!*"

And then there was that fine old Brother, hardy-handsome, the one everybody loved, a saint among them, who in his last years had whispered privately to me: "We were sold a bill of goods..." I asked him what he meant, he said "*The Religious Life*---they sold us a bill of goods!"

And there were Casimir Czaplicki, and Stanislaus Mykytinsky.

I knew them well, better than most, for I had had to read their names out countless times, at the noon meal, between the Rule and the Roman Martyrology, having practiced them beforehand. Stanislaus Mykytinsky, his name was wont to set the tables on a roar, for we thought other people's names were funnier than our mostly Irish-American ones.

I had my own thoughts, standing there; but whatever I thought, it was the end of a long procession stretching back to Chrysostom and to Benedict, to the monks who copied down civilization in their scriptoria, and planted Chartreuse in their vineyards, along with Benedictine Brandy, making possible the coming of the connoisseur. "Brewed God" someone called it, who had arrived with bicycle clips around his ankles, to visit an empty church, robed destinies. "--Here endeth" he said, reading from an opened book of Scriptures.

What was before me seemed a last windrow of accomplishment. I wondered what would become of it; I had not the mind to foretell the future. Perhaps there would always be Mykytynskies and O'Brien's, as well as the odd genius, some William Byrd or other, composing great music for men in groups, walking in long lines of prayer. People might still some day want to be buried there; serious earth it is, certainly; there is grass from the place in many lawns. And do not forget William of Sens, who built houses for God.

The world would not long remember what they did here. It had already forgotten.

I wanted to protest, that these unremembered dead should not have died in vain. Perhaps it could all be turned into a tourist attraction that might preserve it: THIS WAY TO THE CEMETERY, THIS WAY TO THE DUSTY GRAVES. GIANTS UNDER THE HEADSTONES,

I had always sung for them as they were lowered into the ground. (Except for one day, in January, when the ground was frozen too solid for Brother Cemetery to dig the grave, for it was in the Time between the Chairs.) I sang for them the "In Paradiso, " that

493

lovely thing echoed in Hamlet: *May a chorus of angels conduct thee, and lift thee up on high.*

I had sung them all into Paradise, at least most of them, holding up my chant-book and preserving them from the Gates of Hell, over half a century, calling down a chorus of angels to conduct them, along with Lazarus --that one-time poor and holy man-- and with Job himself, into Paradise, that they might find eternal rest. I meant them no harm.

We passed Moreau Seminary, a lawn party before Labor Day was being held there, presumably for the new young men wanting to join and live that life; and I thought I recognized Father Monk Malloy, the university President, talking to a circle of them, telling them what it was going be like.

Then past the place where Brother Boathouse used to chase kids off the dock. Then Ave Maria press, where I had written editorials condemning Elvis Presley and Birth Control and praising I suppose Joe McCarthy, enlightening the century with my views. I wanted to visit the Grotto, but it was hot and we were getting tired; I waved towards it instead. Past Corby Hall, past the fake log cabin, to the car. And then we were gone.

It was only beginning to strike me that I had not come to see the living, I had apparently only come to see the dead. There was silence as we drove away. Anne Francis waited a while. Finally she asked me, as we were driving out past the clutter of motels and fast food-restaurants along the Dixie Highway, what I thought?

I was quiet for a long time, as I drove, trying to think, to say honestly how it made me feel. Then I said, *"--How small it's all..."* She nodded, and smiled back at me, knowing everything as well as I did. We had to cross into Michigan to find a place to eat.

52

VIA CAELI

Suddenly I saw the cold and rook-delighting heaven
That seemed as though ice burned and was but the more ice.

-The Cold Heaven, WB. Yeats

There is a prison in Rome for hardened criminals, you see it in the news every year when the Pope visits it; the prisoners wear what looks like striped pajamas and you may recall a poignant picture of John Paul embracing the young Muslim who tried to assassinate him. It is called "Via Caeli," which is the Latin name for Gate of Heaven, so you have a prison in Rome named for the very Gates of Heaven, through which it is hoped the criminals will pass, when they have changed their ways and become good persons worthy to be saved, and who knows, in some cases Saints, even.

So when a saintly man named Father Gerald Fitzgerald years ago decided to dedicate his life to saving fallen priests, and got some money somehow to build a haven of recuperation for them in the mountains of New Mexico, it seemed a good idea for him to call the place "Via Caeli" with the idea that, whatever their failings and misbehavior had been, they might be saved, they might pray and do penance and one day perhaps pass through the very doors of heaven and be saved for all eternity, with the Blessed.

I knew something about this. When I was a young novice appointed to stand at the lectern and read during meals, the first book I had to read was called "Juxta Crucem." It had been written by Gerald Fitzgerald as his own novitiate project, years earlier, for he had studied with our order, on the way to found his own, the Servants of the Paraclete. "Juxta Crucem" means "Next to the Cross" and the idea is that on this earth the only hope any of us have is the Holy Cross itself, with its suffering. I also met him once, he looked a fine man, standing in his gray habit.

Later on as a young priest I was a prefect in a student dormitory on the campus of Notre Dame, and one of my assistants was a young brother named Bill Tobin, who himself wore the appealing gray habit of that order, who wanted to help save wandering priests. He seemed a good chap, very dedicated to what seemed to me a rather rarified apostolate.

There were not many fallen priests, in those days, or at least you never heard of them. They were almost always alcoholics, fathers who had hit the bottle, who had a drinking problem, and who went away, and usually came back, after their treatment, to work again, and sometimes to fail again. But you never heard of any of them being guilty of any sexual offenses, least of all, offenses with children. Once I heard someone say, "His problem is with little boys---he likes _altar boys!_" , but I only once heard the name of a priest who had offended in this way. He was a priest more or less known as a Boy-Scout Director, who came to town with a bag of tricks and entertained the young children. Eventually it was reported that he had fled the country, had gone to Cuba. I knew of one priest who " had a woman". I heard of another who went to a house of prostitution, and then afterwards asked for absolution from the priest who had driven him there. Those cases were the most I ever heard, although there were books written with titles like "Shepherds in the Mist."

For a long time, Whiskey Priests were a dime a dozen in each diocese that was no big deal, someone else could take care of that, they would disappear, and come back.

But then you began to hear something different. The focus moved to something horribly and unspeakably different: Pederastic

Priests, priests who bothered children, priests involved with altar boys, priests defended in lawsuits. And as far as Via Caeli went, you heard of priests being sent by their bishops from every diocese in the country to that peaceful place in the Jemez Mountains which Father Fitzgerald had founded decades ago, in another era, where they could find peace and meditate and maybe be repaired from what they had done. But it was not so much alcohol any more, I think each diocese began to have its own alcoholic facilities, so that Via Caeli began to be reserved for this other matter.

That may have been the problem: it was considered a spiritual failing that the sacraments and Spiritual Direction would fix the man, and all would be saved. They did not know that it was not fixable, at that time, by any means available to them, and so the offenders were sent back out, to do it again.

Anne Francis and I left our orders at the age of fifty. We lived for many years working in Boston. The Catholic Church faded in our memory, along with the years of our lives spent within it. *What to make of a diminished thing.* The small crunch of dust on the forehead on Ash Wednesday, the kneecap's recall of countless genuflections before entering one's pew, and the familiar sound of wooden kneelers, and the sweet anointings from above, all that receded. We decided on the deserts of New Mexico when we finished our work and wanted a meditative place to retire. And soon the peaceful beauty of the Jemez Mountains and Jemez Springs was a favorite place of ours, with its stunning Red Rocks, and falling water. We would drive out there to explore, and saw various centers of meditation in the valley, such as Yoga practitioners enjoy, and there was a hot springs, where you could get a massage and dunk your body in the heat and be wrapped up in sheets of rice-cloth, with balsam and aromatic herbs.

And of course there was Via Caeli. I told her about it, about the men in gray habits who had tried to help fallen priests. She told me of visiting Saint Anselm's Priory in Washington, with another young nun named Regina."--She wrote a poem about it," Anne Francis remembered: '--*This is the House of God and Gate of Heaven.*'" After that, whenever we visited Jemez Canyon, entering into the long beautiful valley with its always blue skies and tumbling fresh water, one of us would repeat it, would say the line: "This is the House of God and Gate of Heaven...."

By this time it was known that the emphasis of the place was no longer on alcohol. But it was still early in the crisis of the American church, back when the number of cases acknowledged in the courts was relatively limited; yet you thought you knew when you saw them, you thought you could recognize inmates of the establishment.

I used to see them, my brothers, walking the wild roads, in twos, sometimes in threes: "--There go some of them, that look like them," I would say to Anne Francis. And I would see the black shiny shoes, maybe, below the rough outdoors jacket. The girl in the barber shop in the town said they came there, sure she knew them, and they came to get their haircuts. It made me think of that question of Yeats, asked between poems like "He Remembers Forgotten Beauty" and "The Folly of Being Comforted," about what happens, after death: *Is the soul sent out naked upon the roads, as the books say?*

I remembered Community walks, in the old bleak novitiate, a cold, mandatory two hours on a Sunday, out and back. Walking together we occupied ourselves. We spoke of what we wanted to be, and of sanctity, we all wanted to be saints. Now I wondered, what did these men talk of on their walks? Their "disease," if that is what they called it? The bitterness of how they had come to that place? Of court hearings and enraged parents? Of going out and doing it again? Of the victims themselves?

I gather that the Fitzgerald Center is still there, I am not certain. The place has gone through permutations; there were huge lawsuits. I think it is a Retreat Center now, although I don't know how Catholic it is. In the village, up on the wall of the mountain cafe where you can get pie and coffee, there are notices for plays and concerts to be held in its conference rooms. I sometimes wonder how much the "Servants of the Paraclete" knew about what they were dealing with. I always got the impression that the place took the fall for the rest of the church in America, that those dedicated people, servants of the Holy Spirit, that the poor saintly men who tried to help their fallen brothers were socked with lawsuits, which perhaps by rights had better been absorbed by bishops back where the troubled priest came from, not by that little haven in the valley. I wonder what became of them, the men in gray, and if they were destroyed in the calamity, along with so many other victims?

Indeed, when we drive past it, when we decide to go up there to the plunging water falls in the Jemez, to the scent of pine and rare air, into that red-rock country, we go to see other things, not thinking of that, but the road passes by what is left of Via Caeli and what was tried to be done there. I think of the Pope in Rome with those prisoners of his dressed in their striped pajamas, and if there really is a gate that opens out onto something, somewhere, an exit out of this that we find ourselves in now and into what is to come. But at other times, it only seems to me a piled-up detritus, the frightening remains of a whole way of life gone wrong, a remembrance of things past, I think of the human soul, stripped naked under heaven, sent out naked upon the roads, for punishment.

We knew a person named Dorothy Shane, renowned for her uniqueness, who kept repeating a line from Robert Frost: *What to make of a diminished thing.* In her mouth, it sounded like it came from some great opera, for to her, it somehow managed to be the question which is asked of us, over and over by life. Dorothy died, and as we grow older, we hear her line again in our own ears, as though she might be a singer, singing it to us. When we drive past a place like Via Caeli, or come up against anything which reminds us of our old lives, and all that is gone, we find ourselves repeating it, sometimes together: *What to make of a diminished thing.* We think of Dorothy.

53

MUD IS CLAY

O Lord, Let something remain.

--A Vision, W.B. Yeats

I would have missed it, except for Anne Francis. I would have missed everything.

In a film called *The Last Picture Show*, a woman speaks; she talks about a man, someone she refers to as " Old Sam".

"--Old Sam the Lion " she calls him, "--Sam the Lion." She speaks of first meeting him. She pauses for a moment, thinking back on him, and says, " ---I guess if it wasn't for Sam, I'd just about have missed it---whatever it is."

So we have "Good Old Sam", and we have "Sam the Lion", but what I value most is her "---whatever it is."

"Whatever it is." What does that refer to? We know what she is talking about, though she does not bother to explain. It is something we all know. It is the something which must not be missed. It is that "whatever" which, if it is missed, takes life, too, along with it, as well as meaning, and anything worth remembering. But does it mean "identity" also: who a person is, or was? Surely it does mean that, if it means anything at all. Sam the Lion had it, whoever he was. He passed a part of it to others, at least to her, an "it" which must have been something of life itself.

"Whatever it is," indeed. What is "it"? Is it a certain nothing, a "nada", or emptiness as Hemingway says, and all it needs is a clean, well- lighted place? He has an old waiter tell us about it, a person who cannot sleep. You push back the darkness, the man says. You do not want music, certainly you do not want music. And the place must be clean. So what is Hemingway's "it", then? In the end he says that, after all, it is only insomnia, and that many people must have it.

My thought is that he sees life itself as insomnia, the inability to sleep. What is life? Life is that time during which we remain awake, between our two eternal sleeps.

That is hard; I do not want to follow him. This old waiter who cannot sleep.

I know New Mexico through her, through Anne Francis. "Mud is clay" her pottery teacher told her, and said that clay was where you found it. The teacher took us to five places where it was: red clay off the Interstate turnoff to Cochiti Pueblo, yellow clay near the Volunteer Firehouse above Placitas, green clay on the banks of the Rio Puerco, and two other clays, one up above 7000 feet beyond the Sandia Crest, and one in Tijeras.

I went with her, and it was as though we were pulling pots out of the ground. We smoked them, too, we had salt firings; you see, I know some of it, I know about "slips", and I have also extruded long coils for her, pulling down the big overhead arm of the extruder.

All pottery is not done on the wheel; in the Southwest it is hand-building. It was hand-building she chose, and to be covered all over with the clay; she returns home, her spirit caked with the clay, from hand-building and coiling and pinching it into shape. I quote Yeats: *"It is myself I must remake",* I say to her, that she is her own product.

One thing she works with is Terra Sigilatta. The "terra" there stands for the earth, the clay itself that is used---terra being the same "dry earth" that is used in Genesis, to separate the dry land, the Firmament, from everything else, and the "Sigilatta" means "inscribed" or "written upon".

So it can also be translated as "signed earth" and it always gets me to thinking whether this earth is in fact a signed piece of work or an unsigned one, whether we live in a sponsored universe, or an unsponsored one.

Someone should write a play called "The Pottery". For a pottery is as much like life itself as anything could be. First there are the individuals, hard at work on something that comes out of them. Then there is the politics of it all, fierce politics. Everything depends on who runs the firing, for they are the ones who do the placing of the pots within the kiln, and decide whose work gets into which firing. This person understands their own pots, but cannot know much about everybody else's. The firing is long and hot, sometimes too hot or not hot enough, often someone has to stay up with it through the night. There are flagrant potters and reserved ones, gifted potters and hopeless ones, and they take their turns. There is the roar of the flue, occasionally there is a loud noise: something has broken, inside there, someone's piece has cracked or exploded, has been destroyed, and with it ---almost, maybe-- the person who made it. Finally there is the opening up of the kiln, to yelps of happiness and relief, and almost always, to cries of despair. It is what the Almighty does, for all of us: first He makes us out of clay, and watches us in the heats and stresses of the try-works, then judges us as we are lifted out, to cries of grief or happiness. Either way, there is nothing more lasting than the shards, which now refuse to turn back into the earth. *Shall the pot say to the potter, Why hast thou made me thus?* It all sounds like the Bible; I think the Old Testament is mostly about clay pots.

And I saw the old *Leonardo*, too, one more time, in Boston Harbor, docked as a charter vessel across from the Pier Four restaurant; it was very late in its career, it was painted a sickly green and they were chipping rust off her. "Most things break" the poem says. And then, later, it was gone. It was being towed to the ship-breakers in the Bay of Spezia when it caught fire, it burned and then sank into the mud: first fire and then water.

I found myself thinking about the little room I had, six levels down, under the "d" in da Vinci, and the escape path I found up from Tourist Class, climbing to that grand self-por- trait of his at the top of the stairs. I wondered if they had bothered to save that, to preserve his view of himself, half frowning and half smiling: *Sfumato.* "Italian liner sinks and burns" the report said; and I thought of the wandering hero Jason, in his old age, sitting on the beach under the prow of the old *Argosy*, to seek shade from the Greek sun, and being killed by a rotting piece of it. He was finished off by a great falling chunk of his own life.

One day long ago, when Anne Francis was struggling with *The Meadow of the Dead* and Seumas O'Kelly in the Kildare Street library, trying to keep warm at her desk, a note was passed to her from Maureen. It was something that young Maureen had found, a quote she had discovered in her own rootings in among the Folklore she studied, and had scribbled upon a library take-out slip: it described a custom intended to ease the crushing presence of death:

> *"In Ireland, in the country places, it is customary, when a person is borne down by unassailable grief, for someone to take them by the arm, and to step with them, across the mouth of the open grave."*

That was a help, for it was what Anne Francis had been studying, and it surely was at the center of what *The Weaver's Grave* was about.

When I first saw her that morning at Bewley's in Grafton Street, and first heard about *The Weaver's Grave*, I wanted to go away from her at once, because she was so bright and beautiful, but was a Nun, and so was not to be approached by someone like me. I decided to flee from her, and I commended her to her Maker, as the Holy Rule required. I did not know then how our own two lives would weave themselves into the story, and entwine themselves into that long sonata of the dead, the tale of Cloon na Morav, where the shriveled old men do not win the girl, but she is allowed to flee its place of death, and to live her own life. Everything was hidden from the two of us, who were concerned with other things, and I do not know whether we first lived the life and then told the tale, or if the tale was told, as we lived our life.

But now I am grateful, and see how I was fortunate beyond all telling to have been on this journey with such a one, so that the two of us were able to find one another, in that Land of Loneliness, and that I should have been there, to take her by the arm, and to step with her, across the mouth of the open grave.

We live in the desert of New Mexico, now, looking up at the Sangre de Cristo Mountains; they were called that by the early Spaniards because on certain evenings in winter, the sun suddenly turns them blood red a few moments just before it sets. We find ourselves looking up together to see it happen, calling out to one another, for fear one of us will not be there to see it, to watch the

Sangre de Cristos turn into the blood of Christ, as the sun sets, in the winter of the year.

THE END

ABOUT THE AUTHOR

I was born in 1925, the very middle of the Roaring Twenties, but there is not much of those years left in me. I remember a lot; our family was very religious, and some young nuns visited us on the way to entering the convent. One of them gave me my first water-pistol, and I went around shooting Sisters of Saint Joseph all afternoon. I am able to date this event as August of 1929, two

months before the Crash. I remember the great Dirigibles. They were longer than a city block, and sounded like a vacuum cleaner. The Akron, the Macon, even
the mighty Hindenburg, passed low over our house, each on the way to its destruction.

I ran away from First Grade, out of fear. I must have gone back, because at age 41 I was still going to school, after getting a Master's in
Russian Studies, a Master's in British Literature, and a Ph. D in Irish Literature.

I entered the seminary at Notre Dame during Frank Phelan the Battle of Stalingrad, and never heard how that ended. I conceive of my life sometimes as one long effort to learn how the Battle of Stalingrad turned out. I was taught by remarkable men, but it was strange being awakened at 5 am, to translate Cicero's *De Senectute* from Latin: old men teaching little boys what Cicero said about how to be old. I was the Eternal Little Seminarian. Anne Francis says that I am still a Little Seminarian, and will never get over it. I wrote something and sent it to *The New Yorker*, the first priest to ever appear in its pages. "Xavier Rynne" came later.

When I was very little, a streetcar man friend of my Father tossed in at our front door a market-basket full of old National Geographic magazines. I saw that there was a world outside Pittsburgh. I determined to go see it, not an easy thing to do if you sign up for the Vow of Poverty. But they sent me on to study, and I went around Europe on Five Dollars a Day. I rode a little moped that got 173 miles to the gallon. I was a fool, for I took it on the Autobahn, a moped in among the Mercedes. When they passed me they first pushed me one way, toward the breakdown lane, and then sucked me back again, into traffic. I went to the US Army camp in Grafenwoehr, Germany as a substitute Chaplain.

I left the priesthood. At first I wondered if I left because of the Beatles. But no, it was not the Beatles. I left because though I loved the Old Things I had been raised on, I no longer was able to believe in them. I married Anne Francis, the best thing I ever did in my life.

Frank Phelan and Anne Francis Cavanaugh

Boston Herald – June 27, 1982

"Frank Phelan's '**LEAVING: A MEMOIR**' tells the story of two individuals who are badly used by the institution to which they have in good faith dedicated their lives, the Roman Catholic Church.

It is often a harrowing story but one illuminated with moments of grace and goodness and redeemed in the end by the triumph of love. Yes, this is a love story, beautifully written, and a must-read." ---Chet Raymo

Chet Raymo, a widely-read contributor to The Boston Globe, has been Professor of Science for many years at Stonehill College, where he shared with students his passion for both Science and the Humanities. He is known for many books, including "365 Starry Nights", a book on Vincent van Gogh, and has seen his work produced as film.

12441899R00274

Made in the USA
Charleston, SC
05 May 2012